Please return this book to:
DWP Library - Steel City
Upper Ground Floor, Steel City House
12-18 West Street
Sheffield S1 2GQ
Renewals: 0114 294 3598

618.406 GAR

This book is due for return on or before the last date shown below.

2 7 JUN 2008

- 1 OCT 2008

10/11/09

Reading the Mind of the Organization

This book is dedicated in memory of my father

For now I see the true old times are dead,
When every morning brought a noble chance,
And every chance brought out a noble knight.

Morte D'Arthur
Alfred Lord Tennyson

Reading the Mind of the Organization

Connecting the strategy with the psychology of the business

Annamaria Garden

Gower

© Annamaria Garden 2000

All rights reserved. No part of this publication may be reproduced, stored in a retrieval system, or transmitted in any form or by any means, electronic, mechanical, photocopying, recording or otherwise, without the permission of the publisher.

Published by
Gower Publishing Limited
Gower House
Croft Road
Aldershot
Hampshire GU11 3HR
England

Gower
Old Post Road
Brookfield
Vermont 05036
USA

Annamaria Garden has asserted her right under the Copyright, Designs and Patents Act 1988 to be identified as the author of this work.

British Library Cataloguing in Publication Data
Garden, Annamaria
 Reading the mind of the organization
 1. Organization – Psychological aspects 2. Organizational change
 I. Title
 158.7

ISBN 0 566 07998 4

Library of Congress Cataloging-in-Publication Data
Garden, Annamaria,
 Reading the mind of the organization / Annamaria Garden.
 p. cm.
 ISBN 0-566-07998-4
 1. Corporate culture. 2. Organizational behavior. 3. Psychology, Industrial. I. Title.
 HD58.7.G37 1999
 302.3'5–dc21   98–53697
                                                                  CIP

Phototypeset in 10 point Sabon by Intype London Ltd
and printed in Great Britain at the University Press, Cambridge

Contents

	List of figures, tables and questionnaires	xiii
	Introduction	xix
CHAPTER 1	Reading the mind of an organization	1
	Figuring out the organization for its own good	1
	Some components of being able to 'read' an organization	3
	The first component: using our innate perception far more than we do	4
	The second component: using a psychological perspective as a key aspect of running an organization	4
	The third component: taking account of the subtle connections within organizations	6
	Illustrating the approach: figuring out what happened in the financial insurance company	8
	The key events that arose that shouldn't have	10
	Illustrating the first component: the need to use your own eyes and ears	10
	Illustrating the second component: the need for a psychological perspective to have been applied	13
	Illustrating the third component: paying attention to the subtle connections within the company	16
	Learning from the financial insurance company	19
	Needing a framework to work constructively with organizations, not against them	20
CHAPTER 2	A framework to help you see the organization in a new way	23
	Seeing if the image matches the reality	23
	A conceptual framework to help us interpret the meaning of what we perceived	27
	Using psychological ideas to understand the whole organization	28

Three core areas of experience for an organization: inclusion, control, affection	29
Different organizations will vary in their success at meeting these three aims	34
Describing 'who' the organization is	35
Identifying the way the organization projects itself to establish that it exists and has presence	36
Some key features of the Connoisseur and Populist approach in an organization	38
Identifying the way the organization expresses its power and effectiveness	42
Some key features of the Juggler and Boss approach in an organization	45
Identifying the way the organization establishes a sense of purpose and genuine engagement with what it does	49
Some key features of the Professional and Attractor approach in an organization	52
Using the conceptual framework	55

CHAPTER 3 Understanding the emotional change required in the organization 59

Making the deeper change required to accompany the strategic response	59
Seeing the connection between the strategic events and their deeper meaning	60
A brave new world for the pharmaceutical company	61
A challenge to the way the company fulfilled its inclusion purpose: being known	62
Feeling forced to do things instead of willing to do them	63
Understanding why the company found it so hard to make the transition	65
Being able to ignore incorrect and damaging advice	67
Figuring out the degree of change a company needs to make	68
Receiving the support they needed in order to make the transition	69
Figuring out the meaning of the situation the organization is faced with	71
A reference point to help you see if the organization is really in tune	72
A process you can use to help the organization understand what is happening	76
Understanding the organization as if it were an individual person	76
The meaning in the strategy	80

CONTENTS vii

CHAPTER 4	Deciphering the meaning in a strategy statement	83
	Understanding the meaning in the strategy itself	83
	Reading between the lines of any statement of business aims	83
	A statement by the chairman of Daimler-Benz	85
	'Five things' to be globally successful	86
	Getting an overall impression	86
	Interpreting the aims by reading between the lines	87
	The first thing: being in the growth markets around the world	88
	The second thing: a leader in innovation	90
	The third thing: 'exciting and rewarding for our people', 'creating jobs', 'exceptional executives' and 'the right corporate culture'	92
	The fourth thing: being a good corporate citizen	95
	The fifth thing: access to global capital	95
	People have been given 'something to go on'	98
	Development in the organization	98
	Seeing the connection in various debates	102
	Comparing this statement with that made by other companies	102
CHAPTER 5	Some questions to help you work with the organization	105
	Taking stock of the organization	105
	Using the three components: seeing through, the psychological perspective and taking account of subtle connections	105
	The purpose of the questions	106
	Uses to put the questions to	106
	The first stage: assessing how well the organization is fulfilling the aims of the three areas of experience	108
	The second stage: describing 'who' the organization is	109
	Remembering the purpose	109
	The first series of questions: evaluating how well the organization is fulfilling the three purposes	111
	Five golden rules	111
	The second series of questions: describing 'who' the organization is	113

CHAPTER 6	Understanding the feelings and atmosphere in the organization	123
	Coming to land	123
	The importance of knowing what people are feeling	124
	A set of terms to link the business world and the emotional world	125
	Facing up to the feelings that may be present rather than avoiding them	126
	Understanding the feelings that would have been present with the flying boats	128
	Figuring out the sensitive area in the organization	130
	Taking an organization's particular sensitive area into account	132
	Applying your knowledge of feelings to the business world	134
	Understanding the emotional explosion in the communications company	134
	Making sense of the 'data' I had gathered even though it seems that I had no data	136
	Understanding why these particular feelings had exploded	139
	Working out the emotional context of the company	140
	Figuring out the long-term sensitive area of the communications company	140
	Using this emotional analysis to understand what 'set their people off'	142
	Taking into account any past emotional history	143
	Being precise in knowing which feelings to address or you will escalate the problem	144
	General signs you can use to 'read' the feelings	145
	The sum total of the way people feel creates that organization's atmosphere	147
	Figuring out that all is well from the atmosphere that exists	148
	Identifying the atmosphere or tone of the organization by the effect it has on you	148
	Starting with a knowledge of the feelings of the organization	151
CHAPTER 7	Designing work so that it fulfils feelings and business aims at the same time	153
	Creating the effects you want rather than just working practices that 'look' right	153
	Creating virtuous cycles in the organization	153
	Same job title but a different world	154

CONTENTS ix

Having my own territory, or having a job	156
The concept of immediacy	157
Taking responsibility for your effects, not just what you do	160
Putting the organization chart in its place	161
Understanding why the three design features make psychological sense	164
Understanding the psychological purposes of the individual	165
Territory creates an experience of intactness and identity: the inclusion purpose	165
Immediacy in responsibility creates a sense of capability: the control purpose	168
Taking into account the wider effects of what you do: the affection purpose	172
Meeting the needs of the individual as well as the organization	174
The general principle holds for any system or practice in the organization	175
Understanding the emotional impact different performance criteria have	176
Different performance criteria will fulfil very different feelings	177
Seeing how the behaviours relate to the business aims	180
Moving on	182

CHAPTER 8 **Helping the organization move forward in its own way** 183

Figuring out which area of experience is the most 'real' to the organization	183
Creating forward movement in the consumer retail company	184
Working with one company in South Africa and another in Nigeria	184
A different scenario in Nigeria	186
Taking stock of the organization	189
The same business analysis but a million miles apart psychologically	190
Using the conceptual framework to help you decipher the meaning of the events	191
Deciphering the South African company	191
Deciphering what the underlying purpose is	192
Seeing beyond the obvious in the South African company	193
What people will most want to find out	195
Deciphering the Nigerian company, in contrast	196

x CONTENTS

	Detecting the language and voice of the organization	198
	Helping the organization move forward in its own way	199
CHAPTER 9	Understanding the perceptual realities of customers and the organization	201
	Setting a new tone	201
	Being able to anticipate how others perceive and receive any communication	201
	Being able to identify what the different perceptual filters are actually like	202
	Seeing what different customers see and what they ignore in an advertisement	203
	An ad from the Union Bank of Switzerland Private Banking	204
	Getting an overview of the advertisement	206
	This ad actually 'reaches' all six psychological natures at once	207
	Seeing if the message gives us the emotional information we need as human beings	207
	Being seen through the eyes of both Connoisseur and Populist customers	208
	The Connoisseur customer: going to the opera with a company with manners	209
	The Populist customer: talking a lot with a company that is 'everywhere'	212
	Being seen through the eyes of both Juggler and Boss customers	215
	The Juggler customer notices that work is like play and they won't be bossed around	219
	The Boss customer notices that they will be provided with a reasssuring sense of order and 'management'	220
	Being seen through the eyes of both Professional and Attractor customers	222
	The Professional customer: 'getting on with it' seriously, even at the opera	226
	The Attractor customer: living life to the full and having a personal love of something	227
	Conveying a complete set of emotional meanings to customers simultaneously	229
	The general principles of the different perceptual filters, aided by some music	230
CHAPTER 10	Taking care of the special essence of the company	233
	Identifying the essence of the organization	233
	A visual approach and an emotional approach	234

A conceptual context for thinking about changing a company	235
The essence of a company	235
What do we mean by 'changing' a company, then?	236
Using a metaphor of the organization to put it in perspective	236
Seeing the essence of a company through an advertisement	237
Merrill Lynch	238
Looking at the ad to see what makes this company 'who it is'	240
Taking a short cut using your intuition	243
Thinking about what you are doing with the company	243
Bringing out the essence of the company rather than just identifying it	244
Aiming for some emotional stability for the chemical company	244
Discovering the company	245
Helping the juggernaut ease up	246
Drawing the sting of a past event	248
Letting them be	249
Taking the right overall stance: you can help organizations live inside or die inside	250

Index 251

List of figures, tables and questionnaires

Figures

2.1	The images of the Connoisseur and Populist	36
2.2	The images of the Juggler and Boss	43
2.3	The images of the Professional and Attractor	50
3.1	The areas of experience of the pharmaceutical company	65
3.2	Bringing out the Connoisseur more	69
3.3	The psychological change in the pharmaceutical company	70
4.1	The psychological natures apparent in the statement	99
9.1	Union Bank of Switzerland Private Banking	205
9.2	Noticing what a Connoisseur customer notices	210
9.3	Noticing what a Populist customer notices	211
9.4	Noticing what a Juggler customer notices	217
9.5	Noticing what a Boss customer notices	218
9.6	Noticing what a Professional customer notices	223
9.7	Noticing what an Attractor customer notices	224
10.1	Merrill Lynch	239

Tables

1.1	Three key components to reading the mind of an organization	8
2.1	Three areas of experience for the organization	30
2.2	Key features of the Connoisseur and Populist approaches	39
2.3	Companies that reflect the Connoisseur or Populist	42
2.4	Key features of the Juggler and Boss approaches	46
2.5	Companies that reflect the Juggler or Boss	49
2.6	Key features of the Professional and Attractor approaches	53
2.7	Companies that reflect the Professional or Attractor	55
2.8	The meaning of the details on the medical–bionutrition company	57
2.9	Advantages of using the framework	58

xiv LIST OF FIGURES, TABLES AND QUESTIONNAIRES

3.1	The meaning of changes that reflect the inclusion area of experience	73
3.2	The meaning of changes that reflect the control area of experience	74
3.3	The meaning of changes that reflect the affection area of experience	75
3.4	A process to use to think through the implications	77
3.5	Applying the process to the pharmaceutical company	78
4.1	Key ideas in deciphering the strategy	85
4.2	'Five things' for Daimler-Benz	87
4.3	Understanding the 'first thing'	90
4.4	Understanding the 'second thing'	91
4.5	Understanding the 'third thing'	94
4.6	Understanding the 'fourth thing'	95
4.7	Understanding the 'fifth thing'	97
5.1	Five golden rules	111
5.2	Summary	122
6.1	The feelings in the organization	127
6.2	Characteristics of the most sensitive area of the organization	133
6.3	Detecting what was going on in the company	139
6.4	Signs to pay attention to to understand the feelings in the organization	146
6.5	Signs that all is well	150
7.1	Key design features	164
7.2	Job territory as the first design feature	168
7.3	Immediate responsibility as the second design feature	171
7.4	Taking into account the effects of what you do: the third design feature	175
7.5	Feelings associated with different talents, qualities and performance	179
7.6	Meeting the individual's purpose as well as the organization's	181
8.1	Different priorities assumed by different organizations	197
9.1	Identifying the perceptual filters with the help of some music	231
10.1	Some questions to remind you why you are doing what you are doing	243

Questionnaires

5.1	Looking at how well the organization meets its inclusion aims	116

5.2	Looking at how well the organization meets its control aims	117
5.3	Looking at how well the organization meets its affection aims	118
5.4	Connoisseur or Populist	119
5.5	Juggler or Boss	120
5.6	Professional or Attractor	121

Disclaimer

Many of the companies described in this book have been or are clients of mine. It has been a fundamental principle of mine in my consulting work never to divulge who my clients are, or what the nature of any assignment is, even if asked to do so by future clients. Because of the particular kind of work I do, which typically includes a psychological and emotional component, it is quite important that the privacy and sensitivities of these clients are respected. Because I am privy not only to strategic information but also to more confidential and personal information, I have to disguise the client companies I refer to in this book. As a result, I have usually changed some detail about the company concerned that will ensure that its real identity will not be discerned, except perhaps by those within the companies themselves. Other companies described in the book which are publicly known and referred to with their standard company names will, of course, not have been disguised in any way or had any detail about them altered to protect them and ensure their anonymity.

AG

Introduction

Years ago, when I was studying at university in Boston, an imaginative professor set an exam question that caused a minor rebellion amongst the students. The question, and the reaction, captured one of the key problems that this book addresses, and it is one that applies beyond a university setting to most organizations in the world of work today. The class was an economics one, and the question he posed was something like this: 'You have to write a report comparing the Industrial Relations systems in three different countries in the world. You have only one day in each country to do this. What information would you collect in that day that would enable you to make that report? How could you collect this information?'

The reaction from the students was one of anger and resentment. The course consisted primarily of MBA students in the second year of their course, as well as some PhD students like myself doing the required syllabus. The students made an official complaint, hoping to rescind the exam results, irrespective of what those results might be. They argued that they should have been given a 'proper' economics question. They made it clear that, since they were at the esteemed Massachusetts Institute of Technology, not just 'any' university, they expected a question more in keeping with this. They insisted that they had had no preparation for such a question, and were given no information with which to answer it. In any case, they said, there was no standard answer to the question, so how could they be fairly marked?

Yet the question the students were faced with was wonderful. It was challenging, it required them to think for themselves, to be resourceful, to make their own rules, to take a risk – talents which are needed in organizations anywhere in the world. What was at the heart of their problem, though, was that they were being asked to use their own experience of life and the real world. The question required them to figure things out for themselves without the usual sources of information being available or already prepared for them. It required them to think in a truly original way, rather than to just be 'clever'. They had, literally, to 'make something up' from nowhere. It was these elements that made them feel it was 'unfair'. This was outside the rules.

It is easy to see this episode as merely confirming the idea that MBA courses are too analytical rather than practical. I mention the Massachusetts Institute of Technology because that name conjures up an image of a cerebral group of nerds who can use computers better than they can talk to each other. However, since my time at MIT I have worked as a business school teacher and run my own consultancy for ten years, and what I have learned in those roles is that the dilemmas highlighted by that event have come to affect all of us who work in organizations, not just analytical MBA students, IT or computer department people or those with Economics degrees from famous universities.

It is increasingly the case that being able to operate in a truly original way rather than just being clever at using prepared information is every bit as unusual for managers in organizations today as it was for the MBA students. Doing so requires people to act, decide and figure things out with none of the back-up from the systems that exist in every organization and which are so taken for granted that most of us fail to recognize how much we use them or even need them.

In my work as a consultant, to take one example, I sometimes ask managers to visit another organization and work out what its key strategic and organizational issues are simply by wandering around for a few hours, watching and listening, sensing and feeling what is happening in front of them and around them. I am told, often, that this is impossible and I am told also that such key issues should be determined in a more 'systematic' way. On the contrary, it is certainly possible to understand what is going on in an organization in this direct way and, what is more, you should be able to do so. You should, in fact, be able to figure these things out without relying on so many reports, so many pieces of paper, so many surveys and projects, and so many meetings poring over even more pieces of paper to do so. The interesting thing in my consultancy work is that, when I insist that these same managers go off and try out this approach anyway, they come back beaming, full of energy and life and enthusiasm. Why? Because in the process they have come to realize just how much more they are capable of figuring out by themselves, directly, than they had ever thought was possible.

One of the purposes of this book is to illustrate how to do such things. I call it 'reading the mind' of an organization. I use this term with some reluctance since it can sound as if the method is analytical, like reading a book, when, on the contrary, it is akin to the way we use the word when we talk of 'reading' a person. It is a perceptual skill and, by this, I mean emotional perception more than intuition. Part of this approach involves using your own eyes and ears. The other part is to use emotional awareness and a psychological perspective to help you run organizations effectively.

Reading the organization, figuring it out, is what I do as a consultant. Writing this book is my way of trying to explain what the process entails. In doing so, I have created a set of terms and tools that are somewhat unconventional. The ideas and methods I explain are based on the perceptual and emotional awareness I have referred to. In practice, these need to be housed within a framework of ideas and methods or they become only 'instinct' and there is, in fact, an art to the process that makes it more than instinct.

The framework which I use and explain in this book was inspired, initially, by the field of psychology. My use of such a perspective, however, is very different from the way psychology is usually applied in organizations. One difference is that I use it to understand the organization as a whole rather than, say, the individuals, teams or groups within it. It is thinking of the organization at this level – as a single unit rather than as an aggregate of its smaller parts – that is often missing when we try to run organizations, so this is the level that I 'talk' in. However, you can also 'read the mind' of any individual department or area within an organization, or even a small group within it. It is simple to translate the ideas to whatever unit in the organization makes sense to you.

Another difference with the psychological perspective which I use in practice is that it is applied to every aspect of the organization, including strategy, systems, advertisements and customers, as well as to the feelings and morale. Different chapters of this book focus on one or other of these themes so that you can see the organization from a completely new angle. Everything an organization produces, whether a speech, a strategy or a promotional campaign, can be read, seen through and interpreted in a way that allows us to go straight through the 'covers', the superficial appearance, to figure out things about the organization that are fundamental to it. This can be done through such seemingly unconnected and diverse things as wandering round the buildings with your eyes and ears open and your mouth shut, sensing if there is life in the organization or if it has gone 'dead', or through looking at a strategic statement and figuring out, by reading between its lines, why the intent to expand overseas might be slow to take off because of subtle factors in the whole psyche of the organization that fail to match the explicit goals. We have simply never been taught how to do these things, how to read the organization in this way. Yet, by doing so, we have a way of seeing the connection that exists between apparently dissimilar parts and functions within the organization.

It is these three aspects – making use of your own perception, applying a framework based on psychology to business decisions and strategy as well as emotion, and understanding the way seemingly disparate aspects of the organization are subtly connected together – that define what is distinctive about this book. It attempts to make a contribution that is additional to our present interpretive frameworks and tools. Many of these existing approaches are profoundly useful and the ideas in this book are intended to add to these, to provide a completely new angle, rather than to say that the existing methods are wrong. The fact that the framework and tools explained here will work in practice I have no doubt. I also have no doubt that they can work for others, since I have trained clients to apply them for themselves in order both to understand their organization and to move it forward smoothly. I have written about them here because I believe in them and because they are helpful and practical, but they are different and unconventional and depend on your readiness to see the organization in a way that you probably never have before.

The ideas and methods described in this book work only so long as they are truly understood. They require a bit of thought, and the book is challenging and far from being a 'quick fix'. Its advantage, however, is that it gives you answers and ideas in a fresh way. And, by encouraging you to acknowledge that you have innate talents that you have probably forgotten you have it will enable you to feel much more confident that, when you walk into an organization, you already have everything you need within you to figure it out.

Annamaria Garden

Reading the mind of an organization

CHAPTER 1

Figuring out the organization for its own good

This book shows you how to 'read the mind' of an organization. It shows you how to 'figure out' what is going on in that organization and what to do, directly, yourself, without needing an MBA, a training course, a task force report or an e-mail system to enable you to do so. Reading the mind of an organization relies on skills and abilities which we have come to think of as being too unsophisticated to apply to business in the face of all the computer printouts, presentations and analyses that people are provided with. It requires, instead, skills such as 'figuring things out' and making use of your own eyes and ears, as well as basic human assets and abilities such as your common sense, your own knowledge of life and your own psychological understanding of what makes human beings and organizations function. The approach described in this book emphasizes and uses these more neglected aspects of ourselves in order that we can understand and work with organizations in a way that not only helps them be successful but also enables them to achieve that success with grace and ease. My aim, then, is to illustrate how you can read the mind of an organization for its own good as well as your own.

We are dependent on sophisticated systems for information and deny our own innate 'knowing'

One reason that we need to learn the art of reading the mind of the organization is that we have become too clever for our own good. We are using methods and systems that are undeniably sophisticated but we have, in the process, left behind some of the capacities we possess as human beings that are more valuable. We analyse problems better than we solve them. We determine decisions from reams of quantitative data and competitive analysis, by wading through pages of financial and customer reports. These are certainly relevant in their own way, but they have become 'the truth' in organizations. If our own observations or innate sense of knowing suggest differently, then we ignore or suppress what that tells us.

Reading the mind of competitors and customers as well as your own organization

One thing that has always stood out in the companies I have worked for, whether as a manager or as a consultant, is the necessity of being able to work out what is *really* going on, beyond what the formal reports or information systems are saying. You need to do so in order both to understand what is happening within your own organization as well as to figure out what competitors are up to and the dynamics of the marketplace. Being able to read the mind of a competitor, a strategic partner or a set of customers is just as vital as being able to analyse their business results or their overt actions. It is only by reading their minds that you can figure out *why* they are doing what they are doing – the data by itself can tell you only *what* they are doing. If you know why they are behaving in the way they are, you are in a position of being able to predict a competitor's next move, or why customers are responding to one promotion or product in a way that is quite different from how they have responded previously. As you would expect, there is a skill and an art involved in being able to do these things well.

Being able to read the mind of your own organization is equally vital. However, instead of silently walking around their organization noticing the subtlety of what is going on and sensing what is happening, most people tend to walk around thinking in terms of resources, deadlines and plans. Or they walk around talking all the time, 'communicating', 'networking' or 'influencing', instead of taking in, registering and seeing beyond the obvious. It is only by taking the latter approach that you will know what an organization is really like, and what is actually going on in it. If you can figure that out, you can also predict what is likely to happen in the future, even though it is yet to become evident. There is a skill and an art involved in knowing these things, too. Being able to operate in these ways requires that we learn, or relearn, the art of 'reading' the organization.

Being able to figure out what is really going on is a key factor in promoting people

I have never come across any formal appraisal or reward system that has included such a skill explicitly. It is hard to even know what to call it. I have, however, come across many organizations where the ability to figure things out in this way is one of the primary factors in deciding who should get the really top or key jobs. There is a very good reason for this – the success of both the individuals within the organization and the business performance of the organization as a whole depends on this facility of 'reading', of 'figuring things out'. Yet what is this facility and what does it involve?

Some components of being able to 'read' an organization

It involves knowing what is *really* going on, and why, in the organizational dynamic, as well as knowing what is *really* going on, and why, in a more strategic sense. I emphasize the word 'really' to signify that it means 'seeing through' the obvious, going beyond what is presented, knowing when something else is happening other than what is apparent and being able to interpret any information or fact in terms of its real meaning. It means figuring out what will truly work rather than just what will work superficially for a while and being able to anticipate the effects of certain actions and decisions even where this is counter-intuitive. It means also knowing what creates invisible but palpable things like esprit de corps.

The key activities are very different from those we typically focus on in managing an organization

The contribution I make as a consultant that seems to be most valued by clients is in providing precisely that type of interpretation of the organization. Reading its mind: *interpreting* and *translating* the dynamic in an organization and reading the flux and flow of the events, *letting them know* what is really going on, *predicting* what will happen if they take this decision rather than that decision, *explaining* why people are doing this rather than that, and *deciphering* why the promotional campaign is having this effect rather than that effect. This is what I actually do, even when I am formally hired to do something else. And these components can be put into practice by managers in just the same way that I use them as a consultant.

The first component: using our innate perception far more than we do

So far, my description of the art of reading the mind of the organization has focused only on the first of three components that are required. The first component can be summarized as the need to make more use of people's observational and 'seeing-through' skills as I have described above. For simplicity, we can think of this as the need to apply people's powers of **perception**, but it also includes an acute awareness and common sense, and is far more than simply applying intuition or vision. It means 'seeing through', rather than just seeing. Once we have perceived or 'seen through', however, we need to understand and interpret what we have seen. This brings us to the second key component of the approach needed to 'read' an organization, which is to apply a psychological perspective to organizations, and I explain what this means below. The third component can be summarized as the need to allow for the subtle and emotional connections that exist across an organization, rather than only the structural or technical connections. Together, these three components provide the general orientation to my approach, and each one builds on and links with the other two. First, let me explain what the second component entails.

The second component: using a psychological perspective as a key aspect of running an organization

We need a framework that can help us make sense of what we perceive and 'see through'

Using our common sense and perception can give us more relevant and accurate information, but we have to make sense of what we perceive in a way that goes beyond using our 'instinct' or having a hunch about what it means. This requires the second key component, which is a **psychological perspective**. It is this that gives us the conceptual means to interpret what we 'see through' when we work with organizations. Unfortunately, we have tended to make a psychological approach secondary to a strategic, marketing or financial one in the way we run organizations. When I am working at the most senior levels, for example, I often have to disguise the knowledge I am really using and position it instead within a strategic framework. Consequently, clients are sometimes unaware of the fact that the interpretations I give them come, very often, from a psychological perspective, yet the latter can none the less be very useful in helping them run their business.

We need a way to understand the organization as a whole, not just understand individuals

In my consultancy work, as well as in this book, this process of interpretation is derived from one of several frameworks I have developed that originated from the field of psychology. I use these frameworks in a rather unconventional way, however. We tend to assume that psychology is something to apply in order to understand what motivates people, or to understand leaders, but these are, in fact, only some of the ways of using it. We can make far more use of it than this, and apply it to other levels than simply individuals or groups. The framework set out in this book looks at the organization as a whole, although you can apply the ideas yourself to smaller units within an organization. The focus I take is of the organization as a single unit, because that is often a missing piece in the perspective people have when they are working within their own organization or trying to understand another.

We can understand both the strategy of the organization and the feelings within it at the same time

The framework is unusual also in taking account of strategic and business decisions as well as feelings. When we use the word 'psychology', we assume it refers only to emotional things or as a way of understanding rather mysterious events in people's lives, yet it applies also to normal everyday events and decisions in the organization itself. The way I use the term is not in its usual sense of a demanding academic discipline which enables us to unravel mysterious things – instead it means making use of our natural everyday psychological understanding of organizations, in order to help them function better. And in this book I show you how you can use this perspective to work with the issues that are important to the business and its strategic aims at the same time that you can use it to unravel and understand the feelings that exist in the organization.

For some reason, the priority we give to such a perspective when we are outside work, such as when we are running sports, educational or political organizations, is discarded when we are 'in business' or 'at work'. Yet, psychological factors are implicit in any situation where an organization keeps changing its structure but fails to get the results it hopes for by doing this. They affect the success of the organization in promoting itself or in relating in a straightforward way to its customers. These are key aspects of running a business and are the kinds of decision areas that we explore in this book, where you can see the insights that are added to our usual analysis if we have a simple way of making psychology a central part of our thinking.

To achieve these aims we need a vocabulary of terms and concepts to name and identify these intangible factors

However, in order to achieve this, we need to be able to talk about such things, as well as legitimize them. The psychological factors that exist in companies are never considered as being as real as the structures, systems and procedures, but this is only because we have no way to describe them. We have conventional agreed words with which to label systems and structures, for example, so we talk about them, write about them and make decisions about them. Strategy is intangible, but it can be written on a piece of paper and spoken of in accepted terms so that people can communicate about it. The organizational structure of a company is equally intangible, yet we have no difficulty thinking of it and making decisions about it, as if it were a real thing. In much the same way, the psychological factors and forces in an organization can also be named, labelled and formalized. We can put words to them too, and the framework of ideas in this book provides one way of doing so, so that they also become real, visible and straightforward.

For example, as I shall show you, we can discern the psychological features of an organization through a wide range of things, such as its strategy, advertisements, job structures and systems. All these things have a psychological meaning and an impact on the dynamic of the organization of which we are usually blissfully unaware, and the psychological framework provides a way of deciphering them. When we take account of them, events and business decisions can often proceed in a more straightforward manner, as many of the organizations described in the various chapters illustrate. We can do more than use psychology as a device to figure out other people's psyches, therefore. It becomes, instead, something that is practical for the business as a whole.

The third component: taking account of the subtle connections within organizations

We need a new way to understand the connections that exist across an organization

The third and final component to the approach which is implicit throughout this book is that of providing a way for different parts of the organization to think and manage in a connected way. This third component builds on the two already described. By using the perceptual skills I have talked of, and by making sense of the organization by using a psychological perspective, we have a way of **connecting the organization together** in a subtle but important way. At present, we tend to apply different conceptual frameworks to different areas of the business. There is one set of terms to understand what is going on and what decisions to make in the finance area, another in marketing, and yet another in human resources. As a result, each of these areas tends to develop its own way of doing things. This is one reason why an individual department or business area can spend a lot of time trying to figure out what some other department in the same organization is up to, rather than both departments or business areas getting on with creating a secure place and a winning strategy for the organization as a whole. We need ways of connecting an organization together so that each part acts in step with others and they feel connected to each other.

We need to go beyond procedures, culture and financial measures as ways to connect the organization

One way we try to get some kind of connection across the separate parts of the organization is through procedures and rules. This used to be called bureaucracy. The intention is to provide a way for different parts of the organization to make decisions that fit in with those that need to be made for the organization as a whole, and to create some coordination. Having common procedures does nothing, however, to get the different parts of the business to figure out what each other is up to and why. It gives them a common rule book rather than a common understanding. This has been replaced in recent years by attempts to provide a common culture but, in practice, this too has provided another set of rules, based on norms and values. Adherence to this common set of cultural rules also does little to facilitate mutual understanding across the organization or mutual adjustment.

There is another way in which the separate parts of the organization are connected together at present. This is through the organization's financial framework. We use financial terms and procedures – budgets, plans and results, for example – so that separate parts of the business are understood. This is the main way in which we put the organization on a common footing, and it is a way of measuring different areas of the business with the same kind of ruler. This is fine, but it only goes so far. The approach in this book puts the separate parts of the organization on a common psychological footing instead. In this way, different parts of the business have some way of speaking the same language, of making sense of each other and the decisions they take. This provides a subtle psychological connection that is more fluid and mutually accepting of different parts of the organization than a common set of procedures, a rule book of cultural norms and values or a financial ruler can ever provide.

Bringing all three components together so an organization takes account of the subtle connections that exist

Connecting the organization together in this subtle and emotional way thus forms the third key component of this book. By applying all three components of figuring out and reading the organization – namely making more use of our perception, adopting a psychological framework to understand all areas of the business and accepting the importance of the subtle, emotional connections that exist across the organization – we have a way for different parts of the organization to understand each other with the same set of terms, and to take into account, within that set of terms, things that are important both emotionally and strategically for the organization.

Table 1.1 summarizes the three components to reading the mind of the organization.

Table 1.1 Three key components to reading the mind of an organization

brings to the forefront the need for **perception**, 'reading the mind', as skills to run an organization

applies a **psychological perspective** to all aspects of an organization, strategy as well as feelings

focuses on the **subtle connections** that exist within an organization, its intangible and invisible aspects

Illustrating the approach: figuring out what happened in the financial insurance company

Using the three components to make sense of a series of events that occurred in a client

These three components lead to an approach to working with organizations that is rather unusual. The way I use psychology, in particular, is very much my own creation. One way to illustrate the approach in more depth is by describing a series of events that unfolded in a company that

READING THE MIND OF AN ORGANIZATION

was a client of mine. These events can be clarified by using the three key components to reading an organization's mind, and we can see how they help to make sense of what happened in this company. In later chapters of the book, you will see how these ideas can be applied in a more detailed way – the following description is aimed simply at providing an overall perspective.

A bird's-eye view of a process re-engineering project which somehow went strangely wrong

This particular company was in the financial insurance industry. During the time I worked for them, I had a bird's-eye view of the series of events that unfolded during a period of about a year when they hired one of the large consulting companies to conduct a large-scale business process re-engineering project for them. In what follows, I set out some of the key incidents and themes, and try to illustrate why the strategic changes the company was engaged in became derailed, and why the consulting team was eventually unceremoniously fired.

The background to the project and the client company

The team's mission had been to create large-scale change in the client organization, focused principally on the core processes since the consulting company was itself oriented towards information and computer technology, although it was intended that the client's strategy, structure, systems, skills, culture and management style should also be included. The overall objective that had led the company to express a desire for the process re-engineering project in the first place was to acquire greater flexibility, in order to be able to respond to opportunities in the marketplace. The company was medium-sized, and had been very successful for many years. There was great loyalty and an esprit de corps in the company, even though it was rather unsophisticated (the managers were poor at setting strategy, and the company had inadequate and incompatible information systems). The company was original and idiosyncratic in its ways, which was part of the reason for its success, and its products had a very good reputation and brand name in the market. In the past, they had ignored the 'group' trends and management fads in the industry and had taken their own independent stance on many issues. However, they could also be rigid and certainly needed greater flexibility in many areas of the organization. They were faced with increasing competition and could anticipate a more difficult trading environment.

The re-engineering project had a sponsoring committee of three senior managers, who had formal responsibility for the project, reporting to the company's main board. The team doing the work were a mix of both internal managers from the company itself as well as the team of external consultants, who led the project. The sponsoring committee met once every one or two months with the leaders of the project and had frequent interaction with them in their other management roles.

The key events that arose that shouldn't have

The project starts 'taking over the company' and the consultants amass a 'virtual' power base

During the year the consulting team were present, the financial insurance company was effectively taken over by the project. In terms of structure and decisions, as well as ongoing business activity, the project effectively became another 'organization' inside the client organization. The consulting team had decisive roles within the company, with little accountability to match their actual power. This kind of occurrence, in which a consulting team embarked on a large-scale project is basically 'running' the company that hired them, is relatively frequent in organizations. Certainly it was a major feature of this company during the time of the project, yet this fact was neither discussed nor noticed at board level nor by most of the senior management committee. This is not to suggest that it was a case of their knowing about the situation and sanctioning it. On the contrary, they were aghast when they finally realized the extent to which the consulting team had power within their own organization. The implications are described in more detail below, but consider first why this very important fact went unnoticed.

Illustrating the first component: the need to use your own eyes and ears

The fact that the project team were virtually running the company itself only went unnoticed or failed to be registered as such because the re-engineering project itself had never been formally allocated such authority. However, the signs that they were actually doing so were highly visible, and the evidence was unmistakable, in front of everyone's eyes and ears. Decisions would be referred to the project team, or delayed until they had made their reports. Members of the team were present on all major committees. Their work dictated what other work proceeded, and so on. Yet people failed to register these signs because they were composed of so many minutiae, of things that happened bit by bit every day, as well as because the team's actual power and scope had never been formalized by being sanctioned on a piece of paper. This is our first clue that the perceptual scanners in this company seem to have been put out of action. Let's look at some more clues that this might be the case.

An innocent child would have easily noticed what was going on

Most people in the financial insurance company were very cynical and even hostile towards the project itself as well as towards the consulting team. This was in spite of the fact that the general mood in the company towards change was quite positive. This negative reaction was palpable as you walked around any of the company's buildings. It was reflected in the carefully blanked out faces when any discussion of the project occurred with the consulting team present. It was revealed by the lack of enthusiasm in the company as a general rule during this time, and in a myriad of other signs that would have taken an innocent child less than an hour to figure out. Yet the sponsoring group, plus the project team, were oblivious to all of this.

'Communication exercises' evoked no real questions or dialogue but this fact went unnoticed too

'Communication exercises' were specified as part of their action plan. The aim of such exercises was to explain what the project was about, but they did so in very broad outline only, and conveyed primarily the timings of the phases of the project. These exercises were meant to serve as a way for questions to be raised and subjects to be aired, but those that were brought into the open in this manner were trivial and different from the ones people discussed in other, less public places. The fact that serious discussion never took place and that no challenging questions arose was accepted by the sponsoring committee and project team. This was because they weren't aware of the lack of such dialogue and because they never registered the significance of its absence. Yet it was obvious that questions and real debate should have occurred merely because it was such an important project. Their absence was a red warning. The team, however, heard only what was actually spoken instead of what was unspoken. But why? If, for example, they had been suggesting a radical new programme of events at a sports club, involving changes in its structure and processes, and no questions were raised, they would think something was up. They would know they had to probe and find out what was really going on. In this company, however, as occurs in many other organizations, the team saw and heard only the superficial things, the polite behaviour, the 'innocent' questions, the formal presentation, without applying their normal everyday common sense. What was absent also, though, was an emotional awareness, a psychological comprehension of what the thoughts within the company must have been. Had the team possessed this, they would have 'heard' the fact that something that should have been said had failed to be said, and they would have known what that meant.

A dynamic of 'having' to fire people emerges which is peculiar but is also unremarked

Let me illustrate this another way. The general tenor in the company during the time of the process re-engineering project became that of 'having' to fire people. In the project team, working out who should be dismissed or 'let go' was an unceasing aspect of their activities and deliberations from the beginning. A new human resources manager actively sought evidence that people were unable to keep up with the changes implied by the project and gave that information to those who would fire that person themselves, or who enabled this to happen. Needing to make people redundant in a project like this is hardly unexpected. Such a preoccupation with it, however, is peculiar. It tells you that there is 'something going on here', or it should do. People started to collude with the team in charge as a way of saving their own jobs, a process called 'collusion with the aggressor'. That this was occurring was the main reason why there was so little open debate in the company, and why so much had become hidden, even in what was a rather independent company.

Cult-like behaviour and management-speak emerges: why don't people start to ask 'what is really going on here'?

One of the other indications that something abnormal or disturbed was occurring was the cult-like behaviour that emerged. The company representatives on the project became visibly glazed-eyed and leaden-voiced, speaking as if from a prepared script about the benefits of their project and reciting some of the mantras of management-speak. The closest comparison was with the Moonies. This served to make these people on the team an object of ridicule. The fact that this was occurring was widely known and was obvious to anyone still using their eyes and ears. It said there was something going on here that was strange. Such cult-like behaviour in a large-scale project like this is unhealthy for the organization as a whole. How could it be otherwise? It tells you to start looking at how and why it is happening. It tells you, if you are wide awake, that something else is going on here than simply a project operating in the best interests of the company as a whole and making decisions for good business reasons.

Each of these events illustrates the need to take into account the evidence of your own eyes and ears

Each of the events and themes described so far illustrates the first key component of the approach adopted in this book, namely the need to make more use of your perception, to use your own eyes and ears, common sense and intuitive and emotional antennae to see what is actually going on instead of relying on what is superficially presented or on information that is formal and explicit. We can also begin to see the need for a psychological comprehension, an emotional interpretation of events. This forms the second component of the approach in the book, and we can see the need for this more clearly in the events described in the following section.

Illustrating the second component: the need for a psychological perspective to have been applied

Using one of the terms from the vocabulary: organizations have a 'psychological nature'

There was another set of factors of which the project team and managers were unaware. At this point I am going to start to introduce some of the terms and labels I use in the psychological framework described in the next chapter, to help explain what happened at the company. The full description of these terms needs to be set out in some depth, but we can use them for now in a general way to make sense of the events. One of these ideas is that organizations have a 'psychological nature'. This is quite different from an organization's culture, which focuses on norms and values. Instead it describes many aspects of the way in which the organization as a whole functions. While the detail of what this 'psychological nature' is will become clear in the next chapter, we can think of it for the moment as simply describing 'who' the organization is, its identity.

There was a profound misfit between the nature of the client and that of the consulting team that went beyond 'culture'

One of the most important factors that affected every aspect of the events that unfolded in the project at the financial insurance company was that the consulting team was at odds with the client in terms of this underlying psychological nature. The focus of everyone's attention was, instead, on the decisions that needed to be made, on the reporting structures and on what was to be delivered and by when. Everyone focused on the 'what' of the organization or the 'how' of the procedures, but nobody focused on the 'who' of the company or the project team. Yet it was the profound misfit between the nature of the two that underlay a lot of what went wrong and which eventually railroaded the project. Note that the consulting team did think about the 'culture' of the company. They defined this as most organizations do, as the predominant norms and values that existed at that time in that particular company. They set out lists of what the culture of the company was, and what it 'should' be. But this has little to do with a psychological understanding, or the actual psychological nature, of the company.

The consulting team saw the client as 'wrong' rather than as merely different and unique in its way

The project team's approach to trying to assess the 'who' of the company ignored two key things. First, the approach looked only at the company and avoided defining the nature of the consulting team or the sponsoring group in the same way. Yet taking the latter course would have revealed a true psychological awareness on the part of the project team. This requires taking into account who you yourself are as a consultant or change agent and the impact of that in relation to the company. Secondly, instead of seeing the nature of the company as 'different', the consulting team saw it as 'wrong'. The team made no allowance for the possibility that their own assumptions about themselves and the client, or their implicitly held belief that their 'way' or nature was better, might affect their view of what needed to be done with the company. On the contrary, they attached no importance whatsoever to such considerations. Yet it was undoubtedly the case that their assumptions influenced their analysis, their definitions, every item on their seemingly objective questionnaires, and every recommendation. This lack of psychological insight pervaded everything they thought, did and decided, yet was unseen and unaccounted for. An analysis of 'cultural norms' adds very little of the psychological and emotional understanding actually needed in such projects.

This led the consulting team to their most profound mistake: they focused only on removing people, not on building up the business

Because the project team ignored such factors, their actions had effects that went way beyond what they anticipated. For example, one of the ramifications was that the team assumed incorrect objectives. The explicit objectives of the project included the aim that they should recommend something 'radical'. This became the project team's main

READING THE MIND OF AN ORGANIZATION

reference point or criterion, the one they worked with on a day-to-day basis. However, this was interpreted by them as meaning an aim of 30–50 per cent redundancies. They could see no other way of improving the organization since, to them, it was so clear that the company was 'wrong'. They were so clear about this that no other interpretation of the word 'radical', other than removing people and outsourcing as many activities from the organization as possible, had been made by them. This was how the consulting team would measure their own achievement and success. They talked disparagingly about the financial insurance company and its people almost as a matter of course, yet the company had been very successful, and still was at the time of the project. The consulting team had never even thought in terms of finding new revenue sources for the business to explore, for example.

The board belatedly discover what the team is up to and how negatively they view this successful company

In fact, neither the board nor the senior management of the company had any assumptions about a target level of redundancies or about outsourcing, and had assumed that the project would, in fact, investigate new sources of revenue. While most had assumed that there would be redundancies, they were stunned when they finally discovered just what the project team had taken upon themselves to 'achieve', and were dismayed by the implicit negative bias that existed in the consulting team which had prevented them from thinking that this successful company, and its people, might be capable of generating other sources of revenue. To the consultants, the client company was simply 'wrong', instead of having a quite distinctive style that had, in fact, been the very source of its success. The only 'problem' was that this particular uniqueness, the company's 'way', was different from the implicit style and assumptions of the consulting team.

The consultants are oblivious to the fact that they are attempting to alter the psychological foundation of the company

This process of aiming to alter the identity of the client had nothing to do with the objective of installing new business processes. In reality, the consultants were trying to install a new psychological foundation for the company but, because they were oblivious to such things, failed to recognize that this, in fact, was what they were doing. For example, the practices which they advocated the company should adopt were those that followed the trends in the finance industry generally. Since 'doing what everybody else did' was the consulting team's own style, they automatically assumed that the company's image and natural style should likewise be in keeping with others in the industry. To them, this meant 'keeping up to date', being 'modern'. The company certainly needed to be more up to date in its information and computer processing, but it needed nothing less than to be the same in identity, style and image as everyone else in that particular line of business. The fact that the company was distinctive and went its own way was seen by the consultants as being out of step or even 'backward', yet it was precisely the company's individualistic approach and image, its having a mind of its own and a panache, that was the primary appeal to customers in the first place. Customers may have wanted faster administrative processing of their orders, but they also wanted 'who' the organization already was.

It is possible to update the systems and technical processes and still retain the unique nature of a company

It is perfectly possible to have an organization modernize its systems yet still retain its own unique spirit, its special sense of self, 'who' it is. Unfortunately, however, we have few ways of figuring out how to achieve these things. The approach in this book is aimed at providing one way of helping you do so. The basic stance I take is that it is possible to enhance the characteristics that make an organization 'who it is', its own essential self, and at the same time alter the business tasks, systems and processes as needed. Achieving both of these objectives together requires an approach of looking for, and valuing, those aspects of the organization's psychological nature that really work well for it, and which need to be preserved rather than removed or changed.

Illustrating the third component: paying attention to the subtle connections within the company

The project unintentionally damages the connections that existed within the company

One of the other main consequences of the fact that the project team failed to fully account for the effects of what they were doing was that the invisible connections that had previously existed across the company were broken, yet the purpose of the re-engineering project should have been exactly the opposite. This brings us to the third key component of the approach of this book.

The impetus behind the project was to link the company's administrative and information processes from one end of the organization to the other. The project team were aware of the need for these aspects of the organization to be technically compatible, but there are other kinds of compatibility to consider as well. One is whether the processes will enhance the emotional connections that exist within the organization or whether they will have the opposite effect. This other kind of interdependence was never considered by the project team, who thought that any damage to the cohesion of the company could be 'fixed' after the project had been carried out, by the internal managers still there. In that sense they saw the need to maintain cohesion and a subtle interdependence across the company as outside their brief, rather than as an intrinsic aspect of the project which they were responsible for from the beginning.

The project team is oblivious to the fact that an organization is more than a series of lines on a chart

The project team had no idea that they needed to take responsibility for the fact that the company needed to be connected in these other, more subtle ways. They thought about the organization as a whole only in terms of its overall structure, the reporting lines, who was responsible for what, and as lines across the organization chart to work out what business processes should go where. However, this is to think of the organization as merely a series of lines. The idea of the company as a single *connected* thing at a more invisible and emotional level was something to which the project team were oblivious. That is why they thought they could break it into pieces and put it back together again as if it were some kind of jigsaw. Consequently, by the end of the project, valuable aspects of the organization that had served to connect different parts together had been damaged.

Evoking a holy war between certain divisions within the company

One disconnection that resulted was a split between certain parts of the company. Two divisions in the company withdrew increasingly from the project throughout the time the consultants were present, partly because of the kinds of incidents I have described. Mainly they objected to the change in nature that the project implied and its effect upon 'who' they were. They also thought that the project was damaging the trust and commitment within the company, which they saw as a key ingredient in their success. They saw their strength as a company being violated by the assumptions implicit in the project that affected their psychological nature, and they resisted fiercely the attempts by the project team to break the emotional foundations linking people, and the connections that served to coordinate and smooth their day-to-day actions.

There is less understanding and mutual adjustment after the project than had existed before it

As a result, one of the divisions explicitly banned the project from having any impact on them at all, and the other delayed the project from having any impact on them for a year. While it is true that, prior to the start of the project, the first division had functioned as a separate department within the company, with its own laws and style, there had never been the kind of ugly, holy war, nor barricades erected to ward off the project team and the sponsoring group, that existed during and after the project. There was less common understanding and interdependence in the company after the project had been in existence for a while than had been the case before the project began, and less of a common footing for the organization to move forward with. Both of these divisions knew that the business changes the project team recommended could have been made quite successfully without any loss to their own identity or sense of well-being or to the emotional viability of the company as a whole. And what is more, they could have been.

We need to take into account the subtle emotional connections at the start, not fix them after the project has finished

This kind of connection and compatibility is vital to the functioning of any organization. It is one of those things that we all know about yet have few words with which to refer to it. As a result, it is treated as a kind of residual factor, something to be 'fixed' after the organization has done what is considered to be the 'real' work, like getting the business processes changed. But this connectedness can and should be included as an explicit part of the 'real' business at the same time as everything else, at the beginning. In addition, it should be treated as coming within the area of responsibility of the project itself.

The end result: the company is damaged in many ways, although great progress has been made to get a new computer system

By the end of the project, then, the company was damaged in several ways, even though great progress had been made towards installing a new computer and information system. No strategy had been determined, as this part of the project had been banned along the way. Many activities had been withdrawn because of the existence of the project, or because the project team were deciding something related to one area of the business and no decision could be taken on that area until they had made their report. Most long-term decisions had been put on hold, and work suffered generally because people were in a rather shell-shocked state much of the time.

The effects took a while to become apparent externally, but the company's reputation eventually began to suffer. They began to be seen as 'just another company', as they had failed to retain that clear spirit of uniqueness that had made them stand out in their own way. Their sales were worse even though the market had improved, and some third-party sellers of their products were refusing to recommend them as a company to potential customers. Their actual performance had been seriously affected by the kind of events I have described, and because the project team's actions and decisions had been fundamentally wrong for this particular company and insensitively implemented.

Yet the project team consider they have met all of their 'deliverables' specified on the required pieces of paper

Yet the project was considered a success by the team and the sponsoring committee up until the moment when the board belatedly put two and two together and fired them with great aplomb. In terms of the project's required reports and deadlines, the team proceeded at a rapid pace and, by and large, met all its 'deliverables' and deadlines. The project team members themselves considered that they had met their objectives and, in terms of those specified explicitly on the required pieces of paper, so they had.

Learning from the financial insurance company

There are many lessons we could take from this tale, for there are many ways in which the events surrounding the project at the financial insurance company could have been better handled. But the important lesson to me is that none of it need have occurred if they had applied a more perceptive, psychological and connected perspective, the three key components that underlie the approach in this book. This was a company that had been successful and which functioned reasonably well both in terms of business and in terms of morale. If we looked at these events from a strategic point of view, we might say that the problem was that there was no defined strategy to put everything into context and guide the right decisions. We could say that here was a problem of culture change that was managed incompetently. Both these assessments would be correct. But they would be beside the point.

The project failed because people didn't use their own eyes and ears, didn't apply a psychological awareness and had no appreciation for the subtleties in organizations

Having a clear strategy was a result of the events that occurred rather than the cause, and even if the company had had such a strategy it would hardly have altered the kinds of events and effects I have described. The issue of culture change also ignores the full reality of what happened. This is an example where the focus was on the formal specifications, reports and deadlines, on what was going on on the surface. It was the absence of seeing what was *really* going on, the absence of any emotional or psychological perspective or of the idea that the organization needs to be connected together at more than a structural or technical level, that caused the real lack of success of the project.

Needing a framework to work constructively with organizations, not against them

The financial insurance company is but one example, and in this book we explore many other instances where we can apply the three key components to reading the mind of an organization and see how they can give us insights into what is going on, and how to manage it. By doing so, we can make sense of organizations and change them in a way that is positive and which keeps them in a well-functioning state. The three components serve as a general orientation, and as we progress through the book the more complex and detailed are the concerns of the organization that the ideas can be applied to.

Moving on to the next chapter to learn a new way of seeing an organization and understanding it

The next step is to set out some of the specific terms and ideas that enable us to achieve these aims. Chapter 2 is the primary reference point for this and sets out the basic psychological vocabulary used throughout the book. This gives us the formal means to apply the three components in any organization. However, the approach requires not just the set of psychological terms described in the next chapter, but also the orientation of seeing through the surface appearance and using our own eyes and ears, and the perspective of seeing the subtle connections that exist in organizations and respecting them.

READING THE MIND OF AN ORGANIZATION

The aim is to create healthy organizations that are successful and stay in one piece

The framework does more than just give us a set of terms and tools, therefore. It provides a way to legitimize those aspects of the business, and its strategy, that create healthy as well as successful organizations. It gives value to factors like the subtle connections that exist in an organization which we ignore, with consequences like those we have just seen in the financial insurance company. By giving them some time, attention and space, we will be able to build up a picture of the business from several angles and to see it in a fresh new way. This is the purpose of the ideas set out in the next chapter, and it is to this that we now turn.

A framework to help you see the organization in a new way

CHAPTER 2

Seeing if the image matches the reality

One client company of mine, whose primary business was medical technology and 'bionutrition', considered its success to be due to the fact that it had a personal rather than an impersonal style, and because its stance towards customers emphasized trust. The company's promotional strategy was consistent with this: the adoption of a logo, and a picture of a single face alongside a name whom you could ring and speak to 'personally'. It is rare for an organization to emphasize things like trust in a way that works, or for a company's assertion of its integrity to be anything more than something manufactured solely for external presentation purposes. However, in the case of this particular client, there was such a match between the image and the reality. The real nature of the organization fitted with the way it projected itself. This means that its marketing message would have been received as it was meant to be, rather than being a mixed message. The organization was believable, whereas few companies that convey a similar message are.

Customers react in a very perceptive and subliminal way to their sense of the overall organization behind any promotion or product, and use this judgement to decide whether the organization is 'for real' in the message it sells. This is one of the reasons why it is helpful to have a clear assessment of 'who' your organization is, because any message the organization sends needs to be consistent with its own internal reality in order for it to be believable. Determining whether this kind of fit exists is one of the reasons we need to 'read the mind' of the organization and also why we need to be more skilful at assessing the subtle aspects of organizations as well as the more apparent businesslike aspects.

In this chapter, the means to do these things is explained and you will become familiar with some of the words and names that you can use in practice to make the more intangible aspects of organizations explicit and visible. These words will give you a means to describe 'who' the organization is, but they are useful only if you know what to perceive about that organization in the first place. So in this chapter I try to introduce you to a new way of seeing the organization as well as a new way of describing what you see.

Knowing what to pay attention to: the apparent trivia as well as the usual strategic facts

In what follows, we use the medical–bionutrition company, which will be described more fully in the next few pages, as an example of how to figure these things out. The process which is used to gather the information we need on this company is almost certainly different from that which you are accustomed to using. In keeping with the idea that we need to make more use of our own eyes and ears, I describe the kind of details I noticed myself just by visiting the client and observing, listening and registering a wide range of things. As you will see, the kind of features I draw your attention to are often mundane, the sort of things you would probably ignore or else assume would tell you little of significance. However, you can use these both to figure out an organization's nature and to determine what issues should be of importance to it at that time. After I have set out some of these details, I present some of the more usual 'facts' that we typically use to figure out an organization, such as its strategic stance. These also are crucial to know, and the interesting thing is that they lead you to exactly the same diagnosis that you gain just from looking at the equivalent of the flower pots, so long as you know what to pay attention to and have the conceptual means to make sense of it. I do not use the organization's financial results to describe the organization, but that is because my focus is on the relationship between strategy and psychology, rather than a financial analysis of a company.

While, in practice, I wait until I have registered many pieces of information before figuring out what an organization is about, let me illustrate in a simple way how you can get an idea of its nature quite quickly. In the medical–bionutrition company, these are the sort of things you could have taken notice of.

Shedding light on the ordinary everyday things you typically ignore in an organization

The company's main headquarters building was, at first, hard to find, as there were few external signs, and no name or street number. Clearly you were supposed to already know where it was in order to find it. It was a tall building, very distinctive, and stood out from others in the city street. When checking in at reception, there was a face-to-face

A FRAMEWORK TO HELP YOU SEE THE ORGANIZATION 25

personal approach rather than an impersonal or electronic approach. Although security arrangements were present, they were discreetly in the background and claimed little attention. In reception, visitors were seated apart instead of being grouped together. I was always guided around personally rather than being given verbal instructions about how to reach certain offices.

There were always abundant flowers in the building. The displays were different each week and had a flair to them, something expressive. There was unusual art work and unexpected sculpture dotted over the front entrance and reception area. These were present in an almost affectionate way, as part of the furniture, just as they would be in a home rather than a more impersonal building.

Spaces were set aside in central areas in the building for individual use, meetings and informal discussion. Companies with a different psychological nature would have considered these unnecessary and have turned the spaces into additional offices, for example. These areas were filled with comfortable, brightly coloured furniture, in contrast to the functional furniture and blue or brown colours usually found in other companies. In these central spaces were bright pink chairs, magenta colours or splashes of yellow. There were often unused offices at the top of the building, which could always be relied on for more private meetings.

There were clear territories or boundaries between different departments on the same floor, and partitions separating groups. There was individual ownership of space, with people having their own desks. There were personal objects decorating work space in addition to the more conventional photographs of families. Work areas were designed so that people could talk to each other. There were larger offices for managers within each work area, and a separate floor for the most senior managers. These were grand and elaborately furnished and instantly conveyed the impression that you were amongst the senior people in the company. Each of the offices in the executive suite had a personal secretary, with a separate office that you had to go through to get to the executive. The secretaries monitored who went in and out, and for how long, very carefully.

I usually passed some people laughing at some stage in a visit. This was true throughout the building, including in the executive suite. It seemed legitimate to laugh, instead of people seeming to need to be deadly serious all the time. The atmosphere in the company was always sedate. I never saw anyone run in the building or heard them make a lot of noise. Few people were distracted by others talking as they walked past.

In general they preferred one-to-one meetings in the company rather than big group meetings. It was usually easy to develop rapport with different people. The general style was for everything to be planned. They would always have my next appointment arranged while I was already there, rather than doing it by phone after I had left. They needed to know in advance what would happen, and what they needed to do to prepare. They rarely cancelled appointments or changed meeting times, and they were uncomfortable if I altered prior arrangements.

All of these observable features can be used to characterize this company and we shall do so to determine the particular psychological nature it had. Each of them has an implicit meaning. They are consistent also with the strategic and business details that we look at next.

Strategy and business strengths

The company had few strategic partnerships. They relied primarily on their own sales force or on agents directly tied in with their business, rather than having third parties in general sell their products. They were careful in recruitment. They were well known as a company, but mainly because of their financial status. 'Who' they were as a company was less well defined. They had a dominant 'voice' in their different industries and they participated in external networks and conferences, but only when there was a very direct connection with their business. They believed in having a clear strategy and invested a lot of resources to ensure that one existed. They had extensive budgeting systems and retained an extensive set of central functions and funding, an approach which was at variance with industry trends in general. They had a clear aim of investing in their human asset base. They had a 'name' brand, and their products had a certain cachet to them, which means they could, and did, price slightly above average. Their customer base was long term, and they received a high proportion of repeat business. In the past, this had led them to be quite complacent at times, although they were also capable of being highly innovative, and their products were often leading edge.

Being able to assess whether the organization is focused on the key issues

In general, the company's competitive strengths derived from a sense of trust which the market had in them. They were well established and knew the industry. They had a good track record and a name associated with quality, but were seen as being a little arrogant. They aimed to be a global company, but structured themselves with a home base in Europe and an offshoot division in the US. This was one of the main objectives they had set themselves. The other primary focus of management attention was to lessen the amount of management control and overt hierarchy in the company. Whether this was the correct focus of their management time and attention is something you can gauge even from a brief description, such as that given here. In fact, their attention should have been elsewhere. The conceptual framework we look at next provides some of the means to figure out things like this. First, however, as we have just done here, you need to gather the data, register all the minutiae, even if you are unsure exactly what it means. What you need to bear in mind is that the initial process needs to be one of pure observation and not a description of your personal likes and dislikes about the company.

Both the ordinary trivia and the strategy tell you about the organization

Throughout this chapter, I use the medical–bionutrition company to illustrate the conceptual framework that helps us figure out both what any organization is like, what its psychological nature is, and to decide how well it is performing. Most people would assume that it was only the bits at the end of my description of the company, focused on its business and strategy, that were really important. In fact, both the ordinary everyday things and the business stance will inform you of issues of importance to that organization.

A conceptual framework to help us interpret the meaning of what we perceived

All the details itemized earlier can reveal a great deal about an organization, if we have some concepts that help us interpret their significance. The conceptual framework that I use and outline in this chapter can help you determine how well such an organization is meeting certain aims. Because the ideas I describe here were originally derived from a psychological discipline, the aims which you will assess the organization against are called psychological aims or purposes but, as you will see, these nevertheless correspond with the usual business aims of an organization. The conceptual framework simply gives you a way of understanding an organization like the medical–bionutrition company through a particular perceptual lens in order that you can work out the deeper or more hidden significance of what that organization is doing. The framework will enable you to work out the particular psychological nature of any organization as well, and these natures are a way of summarizing key features about 'who' an organization is. In the following sections, both these different psychological aims and the various psychological natures are explained so that you can evaluate for yourself any organization you have contact with.

The ease with which you can apply existing psychological knowledge to a new arena

First, though, I need to put my own framework into context and explain the basis for using psychology as a means to understand the whole organization. My own conceptual framework was inspired by an early theory of interpersonal behaviour, and it is this link that I need to explain in order for you to appreciate how easy it is to use our existing psychological knowledge within a quite different arena, namely to understand organizations.

Using psychological ideas to understand the whole organization

There are a number of theories that can be applied to help us understand organizations in a psychological way. The main ones I have developed take their inspiration from Carl Jung, Gestalt and Will Schutz. Each of these theories I have elaborated into a conceptual framework to apply to both the strategic and the emotional aspects of organizations. The particular conceptual framework described in this chapter is one inspired by an early theory of interpersonal behaviour devised by Will Schutz.[1]

Using a psychological theory for a very different purpose than it was created for

While each of the three theories mentioned above is invaluable if you want to understand an organization in a perceptual, psychological and subtle way, it is Will Schutz's ideas that I use the most in practice. This is because they help you put names to processes that are quite fluid and intangible and, as a result, help you be quite precise and well aimed in working with an organization, even though the overall approach is a psychological one. To create the dimensions of a theory from the outset is an entirely different order from merely elaborating and adapting them as I have done, and it is to Will that credit must go for the groundbreaking concepts themselves. The framework I describe in this chapter

[1] Will Schutz FIRO: *A Three-Dimensional Theory of Interpersonal Behavior.* Originally published by Holt, Rinehart and Winston, 1958. Issued in a reprint edition entitled *The Interpersonal Underworld* by Science and Behavior Books, 1966.

tries to stay true to his original ideas. Nevertheless, my purpose is quite different from his early theory.

I retain some of the key terms of his original theory, but their meaning is developed to describe organizations rather than individuals, and business rather than interpersonal dynamics. It is because Schutz's earlier work is so rich and profound that it can be elaborated in such ways.

Three core areas of experience for an organization: inclusion, control, affection[2]

One of the key missing aspects of working with or running an organization is an appreciation of the real significance of what occurs and an understanding of the meaning of events that arise during an organization's attempts to move forward. We have many ways of deciphering the business or marketing ramifications of the actions and decisions an organization takes but are often lost when trying to understand their unexpected or indirect effects. The main benefit of a set of ideas that provide a psychological viewpoint is to make those effects explicit and to be able to predict the larger and deeper significance of what an organization does and aims for. In a later chapter, I set out the exact parallel of these three categories in terms of particular feelings that exist in the organization. With that, we then have a way to understand both the hidden significance of what the organization decides and aims for and we also have a way to understand the feelings and atmosphere in an organization. First, let's explore a way of describing an organization in terms of the psychological significance of what it does.

The aims and activities of any organization can be described in terms of three areas of experience. These areas are the same for individuals,

---

[2] The Schutz theory states that three core areas of experience exist in any interaction between individuals, namely inclusion, control and affection. Schutz subsequently changed the term 'affection' to 'openness' but I retain the original term. In relation to individuals, the inclusion area of experience describes the frequency and style of one's interaction with others, as well as how one establishes an identity alongside these others. The control area describes that area of experience related to exerting influence and establishing effectiveness. Affection describes that area of experience related to the manner of direct engagement with others, and with the way in which relationships are sustained. Note that in Will's theory a key aspect is the difference between the amount of inclusion, control and openness (affection) behaviour that is wanted, and the amount which is received. In my own elaboration of his ideas to organizations in this book I leave out this aspect because of the extra complexity it adds. Nevertheless, it is an aspect that can be explored in some depth once the basics of the theory as it applies to organizations and business have been understood.

groups, business areas and the organization as a whole. I work with them primarily at the level of the organization and I define them as set out below. The conceptual framework simply gives you a new perspective that helps you integrate the strategic and the psychological, the business and the emotional world.

The three areas of experience are summarized in Table 2.1.

Table 2.1 Three areas of experience for the organization

inclusion aims	to establish that the organization exists and is comfortable with its own innate right to exist; to easily claim its own space and territory in the market-place; to comfortably interact with the environment and other organizations and customers; to set and maintain boundaries so that the organization stays intact and feels it can maintain its integrity; to create a unique individuality for that organization so it is distinguishable from others; to have a sense of presence so that others are aware of it and that it can claim attention when it wants to
control aims	to establish that the organization is effective in the world relative to others; to create a means of expressing the organization's power and talent so that it achieves what it sets out to; to influence others without being overbearing and to adapt to others without being a pushover; to maintain a feeling of being in control and on top of things; to establish a clear direction to aim for; to be comfortable with competing as well as with the risk of change; to have a deep rather than superficial confidence that it can meet its own goals
affection aims	to create a manner of engaging with others that is real and genuine rather than superficial; to create relationships with others, such as alliance partners and customers, that can be sustained; the organization relates to, and takes care of, itself in a way that ensures its wellbeing for the long term; to create positive long-term relationships with others that can be relied on; to engage genuinely with tasks; to establish a larger agenda that fulfils a sense of purpose and has meaning; to create loyalty, trust and commitment

A FRAMEWORK TO HELP YOU SEE THE ORGANIZATION 31

The inclusion area of experience for an organization

Every organization must establish that it 'exists' in the world alongside others. This is a primary goal for the organization in the **inclusion** area of experience. It needs to claim space for itself *vis-à-vis* others and to establish an identity that distinguishes it from others. It needs to project 'who' it is, therefore, rather than just what it does, in order to properly fulfil the requirements of this area of experience. One component of doing so is that the organization commands a certain presence, so that others register that it exists in the first place. A key aim of this area of experience is for the organization to claim space for itself, which includes a sense of its own 'territory' in the market. When an organization has a clear identity, a presence and a comfort with its own innate right to take up space and exist in its own way irrespective of how well it is performing, such an organization has a great advantage in being able to establish a niche, or space, for itself in the market.

These are the requirements, or capacities, of the organization that are covered by the inclusion area of experience. This area requires that the organization is comfortable with being visible, being seen by others, without either avoiding attention or seeking it excessively. In order to 'exist' alongside others, as a unique intact organization, it needs to establish boundaries between itself and others, and these boundaries may be quite open or quite closed. It needs to ensure that it can exist comfortably alongside others, and each organization therefore needs to establish for itself a satisfactory means of interacting with others, which may be by interacting a great deal with other organizations or only a little.

All these are requirements that any organization is faced with, of course, since these activities and aims occur in business in any case. The definition I have given enables you to see how these requirements are both business oriented and emotionally oriented at the same time. To fulfil an aim such as obtaining a clear sense of identity and presence for an organization requires various business activities and systems but it requires also certain psychological capacities, such as a comfort with being known and seen by others in its own right. For the purposes of the conceptual framework used here, they are grouped together under the term inclusion area of experience of the organization. The key purpose of this area of experience can be summed up as being that the organization feels an innate right to exist in its own way, and projects that identity in the world alongside other organizations, so that others are aware both of its existence and of what it is like. Every organization will have created strategies and promotions, systems and practices with which to function in these ways. What those different choices appear like we explore later in this chapter. How well the organization operates within this area of experience can be thought of in terms of whether it achieves these particular inclusion aims or not.

The control area of experience for an organization

The second area of experience is entirely different. The primary focus of any organization within the **control** area of experience is that it acts in a way that ensures that it gets what it wants or has the effects on others that it needs to have. The control area of experience is concerned with achieving goals and establishing a measure of success relative to other organizations. Every organization needs to express its power in some form and to express its talents and capabilities. All these aspects are governed by the control area of experience and, as you can guess, many organizations focus on this as their only, or primary, area of experience.

An organization can function in this control area in different ways. For example, it can be highly competitive and attempt to dominate other organizations, or it can achieve its own goals more successfully by adapting to the environment and reacting quickly to it. It can try to dominate customers, or it can have customers influence the organization strongly. Or it can adopt a mix of both control styles. As a result of its success in expressing its particular style of control, the organization establishes its effectiveness relative to other organizations. In order to do so it also needs to determine a direction in which to head, and each organization can do this in various ways. Some will do so in a planned way, and others will set and follow a future direction in a much looser way. Both of these approaches reflect different ways of operating in what, in this conceptual framework, is called the control area of experience.

The essence of this area, then, is how the organization expresses power, influence and its own capabilities in order to establish that it is effective and meets its own goals. Different organizations will do so in different ways. The different choices an organization makes to function and perform in this area – in its strategies, work practices and so on – can be described as its 'control nature'. The main ways in which this appears are described in more detail later in the chapter.

The affection area of experience for an organization

There is a third area of experience which every organization must pay attention to even though, like the previous two, the aims and activities that occur within this area will usually not be thought of by an organization in terms of their psychological significance. Nevertheless, the components of this area of experience are still always present and it is an acknowledgement of the existence and importance of this third area that often provides the missing piece in organizations because, while its

A FRAMEWORK TO HELP YOU SEE THE ORGANIZATION 33

needs are ever present, they are also often simultaneously ignored. It is paying attention to and cultivating the aims and activities of the third area of experience, called affection in this conceptual framework, that pays the most dividends, since the benefits that accrue from doing so are those that most organizations seek but do not apply the right measures to obtain.

The essential components of the third area of experience are that the organization develops a genuine and real manner of engaging with others, is able to create and sustain relationships as well as itself for the long term and provides a sense of meaning and purpose. Instead of aiming to establish that the organization exists (inclusion) or is effective at achieving goals and expressing power (control), the affection area aims to establish a sense of purpose within the organization and a belief and engagement in what people are doing. This is the deepest of the three areas of experience and sometimes the hardest to see in relation to a business.

One indication of the fulfilment of the affection aims, and of an organization that functions well in this area, is a strong level of commitment to the organization as a whole, to a larger agenda. Another is that people, such as the organization's customers, are very loyal and, in general, that others care about the organization and have a profound belief in it. An unmistakeable sign that the organization is fulfilling the aims of this affection area well is that it is seen and felt to be trustworthy and it is, in fact, trustworthy and truthful. Creating this requires a certain stance in relating to people as well as tasks. It is necessary that the way in which the organization 'engages' is real and genuine rather than superficial. This applies both to relationships with other organizations, such as customers, and to relationships within the organization itself. Fulfilling this affection purpose means there should be little dishonesty and little manipulation, and people should get on with each other directly and straightforwardly. This is not the same as being sociable, however – what is important is that the relationships are genuine and 'engaged'. When the affection area is functioning well the organization will have developed strategies, processes and styles that serve to meet these aims well, but it requires also a psychological capacity for genuine engagement with both tasks and other people, and an appreciation of people's need for a sense of purpose and to feel that what they do is 'real'.

In essence, therefore, the affection area is about the organization's capacity to engage directly and truthfully with anything in order to create the sense that there is a purpose and value to what the organization does and, therefore, others care about it, believe in it, trust it and want to engage with it. This area of experience also corresponds to the organization doing what is needed to look after itself for the long term. It refers to how well the organization engages honestly with itself, or whether it does so at all. All these aspects relate to the affection area of experience for the organization.

Different organizations will vary in their success at meeting these three aims

Not every organization will achieve all three of these purposes well, so most of the chapters in this book are aimed at illustrating how to do so. What should be clear, however, is that organizations will fulfil these three aims in very different ways and with varying degrees of success. The overall objective, of course, is to be effective in all three areas otherwise one of the three purposes or aims will be unfulfilled. The organization may have an unclear identity in the eyes of others and find it hard to claim space for itself in the market if it fails to attend to the inclusion area of experience. Similarly, if it fails to attend to the control area of experience and its aims it will be ineffective at expressing its power and capabilities and exerting the influence it needs in order to meet its own goals. Finally, if it neglects the affection area and its aims, then the organization will have poor levels of commitment, relationships will be shallow, tasks will be superficially done rather than truly done and it will find it hard to get others to care about or believe in it. Even though, therefore, the conceptual framework is one derived from psychology, the aims it describes are perfectly valid in terms of a business agenda.

Different organizations will also vary in the way they function within each of the three areas of experience

In order to understand whether any organization is successful at meeting these aims, it helps to fine-tune our knowledge of what each organization actually does within each area of experience. One level of analysis is to directly assess the organization's performance in each of the three areas, as I have mentioned above, and the other, which we turn to next, is to describe the particular way or manner in which it functions within each area – *how* it does so rather than how well it does so. This is equivalent to describing 'who' an organization is because the latter concept, in this particular framework, includes far more than the identity of an organization but includes also all the various ways in which any organization functions in terms of its strategic stance and such things as its orientation towards customers. In the next sections I describe the different ways in which we can describe 'who' an organization is within this larger context.

Describing 'who' the organization is

The medical–bionutrition company described earlier in this chapter functioned within each of these three areas of experience in a particular manner. The way in which each organization does so is called that particular organization's **psychological nature**, in other words 'who' an organization is, and in what follows I describe what the main psychological natures of any organization are, and identify explicitly those that define the medical–bionutrition company. As you will see, I focus only on the two main ones in each area of experience. While this is a simplification, since there is an infinite variety within each area, by limiting the description to the two most characteristic ways in which an organization functions in each area, we get a sense of all of the natures very easily.

When you apply the ideas to a real company, you can assess an organization as having a bit of this psychological nature and a bit of that nature, rather than being one particular nature consistently. You need to adapt the ideas to fit your organization, rather than force your organization to fit the framework.

Using our right brain with an image and our left brain with a name

The two main psychological natures that describe the different ways of functioning in each area of experience are illustrated by a visual picture of two images, as well as two names that can be associated with them. The images make use of our right brain, whereas the name is a way to get across the key meaning with one word and makes use of our left brain. Both the images and the names set out the essence of the two natures in question. Remember that they describe two ways of meeting the aims of each area and that my explanations assume that each of those ways is functioning well. In other words, in terms of the inclusion area for instance, that the organization really does feel that it exists in its own right, that it can take up space in the market and establish a sense of its own psychological territory, that it is comfortable interacting with other organizations and has an innate kind of presence when it projects itself. When you look at the images and names, therefore, pay attention to both whether one image rather than the other is a better fit for an organization, and also whether that image and name fit that organization with some ease and with a sense that it is an asset of that organization, not a rigid part of its character or a weakness. It is only when you go this next step that you will be able to gain an evaluation of how well the organization is performing in that particular psychological area. The different natures only help you determine *how* it does so, not how well.

Identifying the way the organization projects itself to establish that it exists and has presence

Figure 2.1 shows a pair of images that depict the two main psychological natures associated with the inclusion area. The two names applied to these images are the Connoisseur and the Populist. As you look at each image and think about the name, you can try to determine the inclusion nature of companies that you know.

Connoisseur　　　　　　　　　　　　　**Populist**

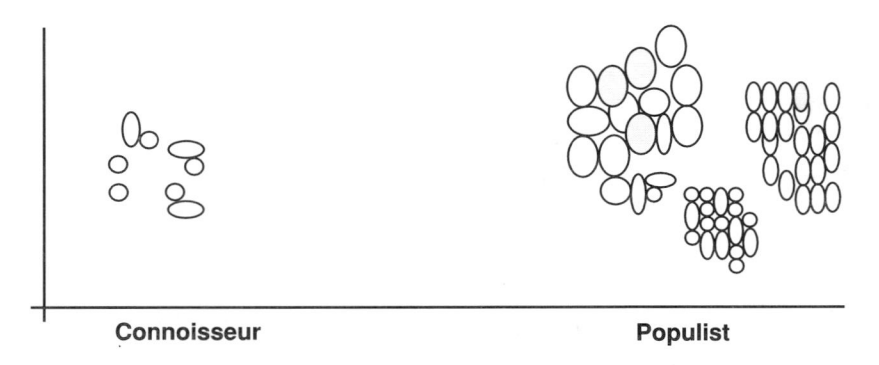

Figure 2.1　The images of the Connoisseur and Populist

Organizations that adopt a more Connoisseur approach in the way they act in the inclusion area of experience are represented in the figure by single circles, or quite small groupings, rather than as belonging to one large group. There is also a distance between each small group and its neighbour. Each one consequently has its own space, and there is an overall sense of there being more space on this left side, where the Connoisseurs are represented, than there are circles. These circles also stand out more individually, and within each small group the circles can look quite different. In contrast, the organizations that adopt a more Populist approach are shown in the figure as lying quite close together, and the circles representing them are part of much larger groups. There are more circles than space in this right-hand side of the figure, and the Populists look as though they prefer this greater interaction than do the Connoisseurs, who seem to prefer less interaction with other organizations. Unlike the Connoisseurs, the Populist organizations have circles within each group that are quite similar to one another in size and shape. This is because Populist organizations are defined more by the group they are in rather than as individuals. This is how a Populist organization feels that it 'exists' – by being 'like others' or part of a group. The Connoisseur organization, on the other hand, feels that it 'exists' when it is unique, and it is consequently more aware of a need for boundaries in order to feel it will remain intact as an organization. Both types of circle have their own space, and they know where 'their' territory is. They are simply trying to meet the aims of this inclusion area of experience, which are the same for each, in very different ways. These are the same basic principles that apply to every other feature of the Connoisseur and Populist organization that you will see in any organization.

The medical–bionutrition company described earlier was a Connoisseur in the way it functioned within the inclusion area of experience because it stood out as a building, was distinctive in its style and was restrained in its interactions within the organization. It was relatively quiet and sedate. Its interactions outside the organization – such as networking or attending conferences, the few strategic alliances it formed and the preference for using its own sales force – also reflect the Connoisseur. Other details – such as the fact that the organization was hard to find, with its name invisible, or that the work space within the building was divided into clear territory and involved personal ownership of desks – support this same assessment of the organization as being a Connoisseur.

Assessing whether the organization was fulfilling its inclusion aims

Let's consider, though, how well this company was meeting the aims of the inclusion area. It is easy to determine that the way it projected its identity in the world and claimed space was more as a sedate Connoisseur than a boisterous Populist. However, the real question was whether this Connoisseur nature or style achieved the aim of establishing the company's presence and creating an impression that it was comfortable existing and claiming its own space. In other words, were others sufficiently aware of the company's existence? Did it find it easy or hard to project itself? The advantage of using an approach like the one described here is that, instead of simply categorizing organizations by 'type', we can understand what the point of it is.

If you consider the details I gave you earlier about the medical–bionutrition company the answer to this deeper question is that, while the company was a refined Connoisseur, it could have established its presence and existence in the eyes of others in a far clearer way than it actually did. For example, the detail that indicated that it was hard to even find the building supported the more businesslike detail that people outside the organization had little idea about 'who' it was, its identity, even though they knew what it did. These are small details that alert you to wonder whether the company was adequately fulfilling the aims of the inclusion area. The advantage of the psychological framework is that you can connect these disparate details together because they have the same underlying significance. Meeting the inclusion aim of this company should, therefore, have received some management time and attention even though it may not have been an acutely serious or evident problem.

So far, all we have used to determine whether an organization is a Connoisseur or a Populist in its way of functioning in the inclusion area is an image and a name. We can also categorize many features of an organization in terms of their significance for its psychological nature, and it is to this that we turn in the next section.

Some key features of the Connoisseur and Populist approach in an organization

The different ways in which these two natures can emerge is infinite and so the descriptions that follow highlight only some key factors. The important thing is to grasp the essential meaning of the particular nature and then you will be able to identify any aspect of any organization that you come across. Table 2.2 sets out a summary view of the various features of the Connoisseur and the Populist approach which you can use as an orientation.

Key qualities

The main qualities that will characterize the Connoisseur nature will be being distinctive, interesting, innovative, refined and stylish. The qualities that characterize the Populist nature are, instead, being inclusive, social, modern, exploring and outward-focused. These are the key qualities that help to define 'who' an organization is to others. The qualities of the Connoisseur signal a focused approach and a distinguished style, while those of the Populist signal a diverse, stimulating style. They tell you that the way the thoughtful, distinctive company (the Connoisseur) is establishing space for itself in the market will be very different from the way the exploratory, varied company (the Populist) will be establishing its own space.

Work practices

In terms of work practices, the Connoisseur approach is to prefer more selective interaction between people and boundaries, and there will usually be a clear demarcation of territorial space or some way of creating a physically distinct sense of having their own space even if that is created by cabinets or the strategic placing of wall pictures. To a

A FRAMEWORK TO HELP YOU SEE THE ORGANIZATION

Table 2.2 Key features of the Connoisseur and Populist approaches

Connoisseurs	Populists
– dignified, elegant, distinctive, innovative	– inclusive, sociable, modernizing, exploring
– like a lot of space, territory, clear boundaries	– vague boundaries, communal space
– discreet in public presentation, name/logo	– high impact in presentation, name/logo
– atmosphere quiet and thoughtful	– atmosphere active, bustling
– more comfortable one-on-one than in groups	– prefer large groups, presentations, events
– prefer to focus on a few things they do well	– prefer to try many things, variety is better
– choose a few strategic alliances, networks	– seek out many strategic alliances, networks
– aim for quality in brands, products	– aim for appeal in brands, products
– priority is on products more than markets	– priority is on markets more than products
– think innovation, design, R&D are key factors	– think sales, promotion are key factors
– think instinctively in terms of focusing	– think instinctively in terms of diversity
– aim for structures that allow individuality	– aim for structures which have commonality
– reward distinctiveness and originality	– reward social skills, participation
– want products to be innovative, leading edge	– want products to be fashionable, accessible
– discriminating between each customer	– aim to treat all customers equally
– assume customers want to feel private	– assume customers want to feel included
– like to create a feeling of tranquillity	– like to create a feeling of stimulation

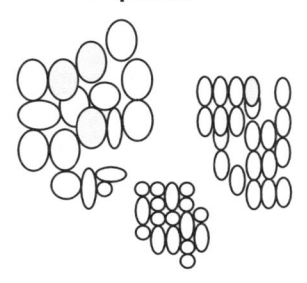

Both Connoisseur and Populist approaches are ways to achieve the same inclusion purpose:

Establishing the presence of the organization, creating space and territory alongside others in the market, establishing a means of interacting across boundaries whether with other organizations or within the organization, maintaining a sense of integrity or intactness, establishing a sense that the organization truly 'exists'

Connoisseur, this is a way of maintaining and projecting their uniqueness rather than having it disappear in the general morass. Since Populist organizations, by contrast, prefer high levels of interaction and they are more boisterous, they will mingle people together in various ways. There will be fewer private areas and more shared territory because, to a Populist, this creates the high level of interaction they think is 'normal' and it creates for them the sense of being 'one of a group', which is how that particular nature experiences that they 'exist'. The Connoisseur nature within work values innovative thought and considered ideas and believes that, by adopting this approach, they will create products that give the organization a distinctive edge in the market. Populists try to achieve the same aim but do so by creating a higher level of interaction between people, group activity and fostering a sense of constant activity, instead.

The overall basis for evaluating people within a Connoisseur organization will focus on their distinctiveness, their originality, individuality and uniqueness. These criteria will be reflected in many ways, such as the performance systems, and form the real basis for promotion. In contrast, the overall basis for evaluating people within a Populist organization will focus on their group skills, participation with others, and their general ability to fit in. These principles will also be reflected in numerous formal and informal ways within a Populist organization.

Strategic or business stance

The strategic or business stance of organizations will reveal exactly the same kinds of differences. The business priority for a Connoisseur organization is usually focused on the product more than the market, as they believe in innovation as the key to success. The watchwords here are quality, design, engineering, R&D – anything in short that reflects the principles of selectivity, refinement and thought. The Populist organization, on the other hand, will prioritize marketing, sales and promotion more than design or quality. They talk in terms of the market relatively more than the product because, as with everything, their orientation is towards reaching out and expanding.

A Connoisseur will tend to have fewer alliances and strategic partnerships than a Populist within the same market environment would. Microsoft reflects this Connoisseur approach, creating alliances out of business necessity more than out of a natural impulse to do so, and it is very selective. Connoisseurs prefer to have their own sales force and more focused distribution channels, partly in order to ensure they retain their unique ways. Populists tend to actively seek out alliances and they need to constantly try new and different things. Their key words are variety and quantity, in contrast to the focus of the Connoisseur on

A FRAMEWORK TO HELP YOU SEE THE ORGANIZATION 41

quality and doing a few things very well. The orientation of the Connoisseur reflects the fact that they establish their existence and space in the market through clear boundaries and projecting distinctiveness. The orientation of the Populist reflects the fact that they establish their existence and space in the market through a great deal of interaction and alliances with other organizations and through projecting themselves in a way that makes a high impact.

Approach to customers

Connoisseurs try to project their distinctiveness and uniqueness with customers as well. A Populist, however, will be very inclusive and expansive with customers and they like to project the idea that they are popular. They sell on the basis of having products 'everyone' is buying. Many consumer product companies are Populists, such as Pepsi or Disneyland. Companies like Nike are Connoisseurs, as they aim to sell their running/training shoes to people who are serious about running and training, and consequently sell to a certain customer niche. This contrasts with the approach taken by Reebok, where the selling pitch is more that of buying the product because of its general popularity rather than being exclusive. If many other customers have bought a given product, then that, to a Populist, is a sufficient rationale with which to sell that particular product. Such a sales pitch will reach Populist customers, who will buy for such reasons as doing what others do, but it will turn off Connoisseur customers, who want to feel distinctive and selective in some way.

Different ways of meeting the same aim

These descriptions of the features that can identify each of the two inclusion natures have been presented as contrasts in order to make the two natures more visible. In fact, most organizations will have a mix of the two natures. What is important to bear in mind is that these two very different approaches are aimed at meeting the same goal even though, if you look only at their outer or surface appearance, it is often hard to see that that is the case. The 'outer appearance' of each nature is these various features of the organization we have just explored. These are nevertheless simply ways of attempting to meet the same inclusion aim, which is to project the identity of the organization in a way that makes sure that others are aware of its existence, the organization finds it easy to claim space for itself, interacts as needed with others, and has a certain presence. Examples of companies that reflect these two natures are set out in Table 2.3. These appear as examples because they reveal

Table 2.3 Companies that reflect the Connoisseur or Populist

Connoisseurs	Populists
exclusive high-class jewellers: Omega watches	accessible, popular jewellers: Swatch watches
Swiss banks, providing privacy, anonymity	Citibank, aiming to be global, diverse
Daimler-Benz	Chrysler
computer companies like Digital, Hewlett Packard	computer companies like Compaq, Dell

the differences in approach rather than because they are necessarily examples of excellent companies.

Identifying the way the organization expresses its power and effectiveness

The other two areas of experience, control and affection, each have their own purpose, and quite distinct ways of fulfilling it. In what follows, we adopt the same approach we used earlier with the inclusion area, only this time to help us understand the different ways organizations function within the control area of experience and try to fulfil the aims of that area. As before, we start with the images and names of the two main natures and then move on to the general features within the organization that reflect the two control natures. The images that capture the different ways of expressing this are represented in Figure 2.2, and the two names corresponding to these images are the Juggler and the Boss.

One requirement of the control area is that the organization creates some idea of where to head. Both the Juggler and the Boss provide a sense of direction and knowledge of the way ahead, represented by the arrow in the images in Figure 2.2, but they do so in quite different ways. The control area of experience also relates to achieving things, so both natures establish some kind of goal that will tell the organization that it has been successful, represented by the cross or marker at the end of the arrow. However, the Juggler path towards this goal is less definite. This is because the Juggler way of attaining a sense of control is by being open to the environment and they are always alert, along the way, to new ways of doing things, or changes they may decide to adjust to. At any point in time, they have a clear idea of how to get to the end point, but they make a priority out of being ready to make a better plan

A FRAMEWORK TO HELP YOU SEE THE ORGANIZATION 43

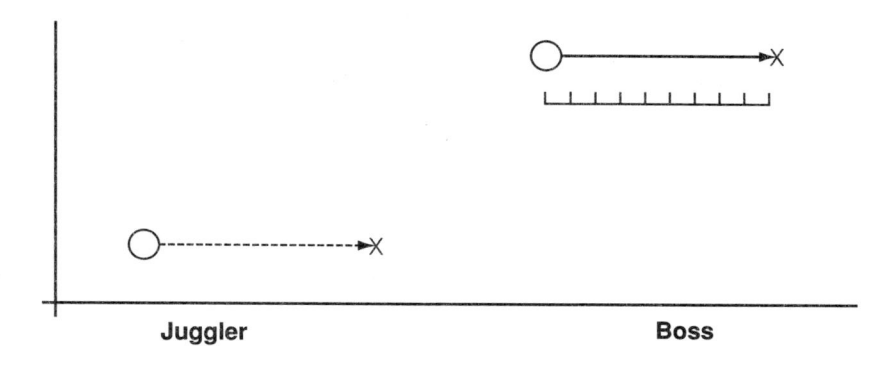

Juggler **Boss**

Figure 2.2 The images of the Juggler and Boss

if they see fit at a later time and, indeed, a different end point. Once they have a definite final path, you see the speed that such organizations are capable of, which is one of their key assets. The Juggler circle is positioned lower down in the figure than the Boss circle as they believe in staying 'close to the ground'. The information in such organizations is often qualitative, but they trust this as it is usually more immediate. It is just as real to them as quantitative data. They gain a sense of control in this way, which is why they find extensive management differences and status get in the way of achieving goals most effectively. All these aspects are reflected symbolically in the part of the figure representing the Juggler and show how that approach tries to attain the aims of the control area of experience, achieving goals, releasing talent and feeling that they can stay 'in control'.

The Boss circle, in contrast, attains the same aims and a feeling that they are staying 'in control' by a very different approach. The Boss circle has its direction planned clearly and definitely all the way to the end goal. These organizations need to have the way ahead mapped exactly and in detail so that they can plan properly and have resources ready. They 'know what they are doing' this way. They want to be able to stay with the same plan to the end and they focus on being able to do so, even though, like the Juggler, they can make changes, but only if they really need to. The difference between the two natures lies in the assumptions and priority that each gives to 'sticking to the plan and knowing exactly where you are in relation to it' or, alternatively, 'being able to change the plan if a better way of doing things is found'. The Boss circle shown in the figure has a ruler or measuring stick from beginning to end, since this is how Bosses feel in control. They measure where they are at all stages and assess their progress primarily in relation to this prepared measuring stick. They measure in a quantitative way, and are much less likely to trust, or decide, on the basis of qualitative data.

Their circle is also further from the ground, because they need to amass together all the data they collect. This gives them the sense that they are on top of things. It is because this is the way they feel in control that Boss organizations create more predictable and defined management levels and have a greater reliance on planning and measurement systems.

The medical–bionutrition company described at the start of this chapter is a Boss because of the emphasis on planning and needing a definite direction. They devoted a lot of resources to developing a good strategy. They liked to know in advance what was going to happen, and they were uncomfortable with changes to plans or diary arrangements. They liked a clear management hierarchy, with separate offices for managers. Even their main building was tall, towering over other buildings. These are the details that suggest the company's control style was that of the Boss more than the Juggler. By being like this, the company was attempting to meet the purpose of the control area. Other organizations can have a more complex mix of the two approaches.

Assessing whether the organization was achieving its control aims

The primary question that we need to address, however, is whether this company was fulfilling the aims of the control area with its particular Boss nature. The concern in the company itself was that they should reduce the management hierarchy and lessen the formal control that we could identify as part of its Boss nature. The reason they focused on this issue was not because they were poor at fulfilling the control purpose, that is, being effective at expressing power and establishing their effectiveness at meeting goals or releasing competence in the organization. The reason they did so was because they had assumed that any hierarchy was incorrect given the prevalent assumptions in the management and business press which tend to promote the approach of the Juggler. However, both the Juggler and the Boss approaches can be equally successful. The real test is whether an organization achieves the control purpose, rather than whether it does so with a hierarchy or a flattened management structure. In the medical–bionutrition company they were very successful at achieving their goals and did so through an easy and natural release of talent and competence. In this company it was correct for them to be a Boss in terms of their control nature and it helped them achieve their control purpose. They should, therefore, have focused their time and attention on other aspects of the business.

A FRAMEWORK TO HELP YOU SEE THE ORGANIZATION

Some key features of the Juggler and Boss approach in an organization

We have access, though, to more than these images and names to help us understand these two very different ways of attaining a sense of control. General features that will identify an organization's control nature are described in the following sections and the key features are summarized in Table 2.4, which you can use as an overall orientation.

Key qualities

The key qualities associated with Jugglers are those of being fast-footed, adaptable, resourceful and dexterous. With Bosses, on the other hand, the key qualities are those of being directed, measured, forceful and prepared. These are the contrasting sets of qualities we would immediately use to distinguish between the two main approaches to attaining a sense of power and effectiveness in the organization's control area of experience and they create organizations, or parts of organizations, that have a very different tone and feeling to them.

Work practices

One immediate arena within the organization where the differences between these two control natures is very obvious is in its work practices. Jugglers dislike formal power distinctions, so offices, parking spaces and amenities will be open to all. Boss organizations, in contrast, tend to place the various management levels on separate floors, or in different kinds of offices, and need to create some kind of distinctions between people within the organization that will reflect the amount of power they have. Many of the trends that organizations have been engaged in in recent years – lessening the degree of formal control, for example – can be described as an attempt to move from the Boss style of control to a more Juggler style. However, many of these changes are superficial and you need to pay attention to other aspects of the organization than its organizational chart or hierarchical levels in order to determine its true control nature.

One sign of an organization being a Boss in its control nature is many instructions and written commands put up on walls and notice-boards telling people what they should do. Jugglers rarely have signs up telling anyone what to do because they expect you to disobey rules or to ignore them. If they do have instructions up, it is so that you take individual responsibility for what you want to do. Minutiae such as these indicate that the real nature of the organization is more the Boss, even if the

46 READING THE MIND OF THE ORGANIZATION

Table 2.4 Key features of the Juggler and Boss approaches

Juggler	Boss
– resourceful, adaptable, dexterous, collegial	– powerful, prepared, directed, ambitious
– keep 'close to the ground', opportunistic	– devote a lot of time to planning ahead
– adapt to or challenge industry rules	– like to set or dominate industry rules
– focus on being resourceful	– focus on obtaining resources
– think instinctively of delegating	– think instinctively of decision making
– feel in control by letting go of the reins	– feel in control by monitoring and knowing
– atmosphere is adventurous, playful	– atmosphere is orderly, deliberate
– key success factor is to adapt and respond	– key success factor is to be prepared
– develop strategies by trying things out	– develop strategies by thinking ahead carefully
– like buildings that blend into environment	– like buildings that are tall or dominate
– work practices more important than structure	– spend a lot of time on structure and systems
– aim to maximize options	– aim to provide answers
– need to define roles loosely	– need to specify reporting lines
– products focus on providing choices	– products focus on providing stability
– often delegate to customers	– like to give customers advice
– believe the priority for customers is flexibility	– believe the priority for customers is certainty
– like to create a feeling of freedom	– like to create a feeling of confidence

Both Juggler and Boss approaches are ways to achieve the same control purpose:

Establishing a way of exerting influence on other organizations and the environment that the organization needs in order to achieve its aims, being effective and successful at meeting its goals, achieving results and winning, being comfortable in both influencing and adapting

A FRAMEWORK TO HELP YOU SEE THE ORGANIZATION

professed strategy is to be 'low' in terms of formal control, in the manner of a Juggler. The visible signs of formal control can be lessened yet the underlying psychology can stay exactly the same. I once worked with a client running a series of programmes on loosening the grip of management control. While the client watched the ratings on the workshop sheets to judge the success of the programme, I watched the notices of instruction stuck up in the elevators and on walls to monitor the success of what I was doing. The real state of the organization, in terms of whether it genuinely was changing its way of attaining control, was reflected in these things rather than in the redrawn organizational chart.

The real control nature will also be reflected in the actual values and criteria by which people are valued and appraised. The Juggler nature will value such factors as risk taking, speed and a sense of adventure within the overall approach to work, whereas the Boss nature values such factors as being certain, looking far ahead and making the right decision more than a fast decision. These are the implicit assumptions and values that will be reflected in many of the formal and informal systems within the respective organizations.

Strategic or business stance

The strategic or business stance adopted by different organizations will also reflect these same control natures. You will be able to see this by the way in which the organization tries to exert influence over other organizations and the environment in general. The primary distinction will be that the Juggler will focus first and foremost on adapting to their market and the Boss will try to actively shape or influence it. To achieve this, Bosses make use of extensive information systems, as well as detailed monitoring and budgetary systems, and these are aimed primarily for the use of those at the top. They find it difficult to move forward without a strategy. With these in hand, the Boss organization feels it can exert its power and influence and it will focus also on obtaining the 'leverage' it needs to attain its goals. Jugglers have a very different set of assumptions and they determine a strategy by first moving forward and testing what happens. This gives them the information they need to know in order to stay in control. They rely on resourcefulness and on being clever rather than on having leverage, a strategy or planning systems to achieve the influence they need to attain their own goals.

Some Bosses try to dominate the game they play in and to set the industry rules, or, at least, they like to have clear rules or standards in the industry. Then they feel they are 'in control'. Jugglers do their own thing irrespective of anyone else and evade the industry rules or they openly challenge them. Sun Microsystems is a good example of this, as is the Virgin Group. Both have been successful in positioning themselves in their respective markets as an alternative to the 'big boys' in the industry – the 'establishment' – and in appealing to customers' ideas of breaking rules set by others. Any company that promotes itself or its products along the lines of 'You don't really trust what these fat cats of the establishment have been telling you all these years, do you?' will be a Juggler. The Boss approach, in contrast, will be to position themselves as a leading and authoritative figure in the industry, one that knows the rules and has experience that others can rely on. In this way, the Boss control nature aims to provide reassurance and, by so doing, establish a sense of being in control.

Approach to customers

The assumption of a Juggler is that the customer is an equal, and they often delegate part of the process of purchase to customers in the same way that they rely on internal delegation as a key way to run the organization. They focus on giving customers as many choices as possible, and freedom of choice. The Juggler is likely, for example, to provide a facility for customers to ask questions on their own initiative, while the Boss organization, on the other hand, will assume customers want them to take responsibility and take care of everything. The Boss would prefer to deliver complete reliability, rather than freedom of choice, if they had to make a trade-off between the two. Their approach is based on providing to customers exactly what the latter ask for, and this should, if possible, be known ahead of time. Jugglers may talk of surprising customers, as a way of pleasing them, rather than stress the importance of being completely reliable, safe or certain, which is the Boss's way of pleasing customers.

Different ways of meeting the same aim

As with the features of the Connoisseur and Populist natures, those that reflect the Juggler and Boss natures also appear very different if we look at them only from the point of view of their surface appearance. It helps to remember that the two different approaches epitomized by the Juggler and Boss are still nevertheless both aimed at achieving exactly the same goal – the feeling of being in psychological control and an awareness of their effectiveness at achieving what they aim for by expressing their power and competence. Neither of these two approaches is better.

However, what the framework adds to our understanding is the idea that the control area is only one of the three areas of experience that need to be paid attention to in the organization. Examples of companies that reflect these two natures are set out in Table 2.5. These appear as

A FRAMEWORK TO HELP YOU SEE THE ORGANIZATION 49

examples because they reveal the differences in approach rather than because they are necessarily examples of excellent companies.

Table 2.5 Companies that reflect the Juggler or Boss

Jugglers	Bosses
computer companies like Sun Microsystems	computer companies like Microsoft
Virgin Group, Easy Jet	BA, American Airlines
finance companies like J P Morgan	finance companies like Chase
customer service companies that respond to client needs, such as small legal or accountancy firms	customer service companies that 'deliver solutions', such as the big five consulting companies

Identifying the way the organization establishes a sense of purpose and genuine engagement with what it does

We move now to the third area of experience and the two natures that characterize that. This area of experience, affection, describes the manner in which the organization engages directly and genuinely with people as well as with tasks, as a result of which it creates a sense of purpose and meaning, others care about it, believe in it and trust it. Once again, we follow the same process by starting with the two images and names that represent the two main natures described here. The names are the Professional and the Attractor, and the images are illustrated in Figure 2.3.

One key difference which Figure 2.3 shows is that the image of the Professional organization has square edges, whereas the Attractor organization has soft edges with no corners. The former conveys feelings of sharpness, of everything being cut and dried. These organizations like everything to be serious and matter of fact, without too much volatility. The Attractor image, in contrast, is that of an oval, and conveys a sense of simplicity and gentleness. The soft edges have no connotation of weakness, however, since ovals can be enduring, tough and resistant. Ovals are a more natural shape, whereas squares are usually deliberately constructed. These differences reflect the fact that Professionals are concerned with presenting themselves in a particular way, whereas Attractors believe it is better to present themselves as they are, and say what they feel more easily. Professionals are more direct about what

50 READING THE MIND OF THE ORGANIZATION

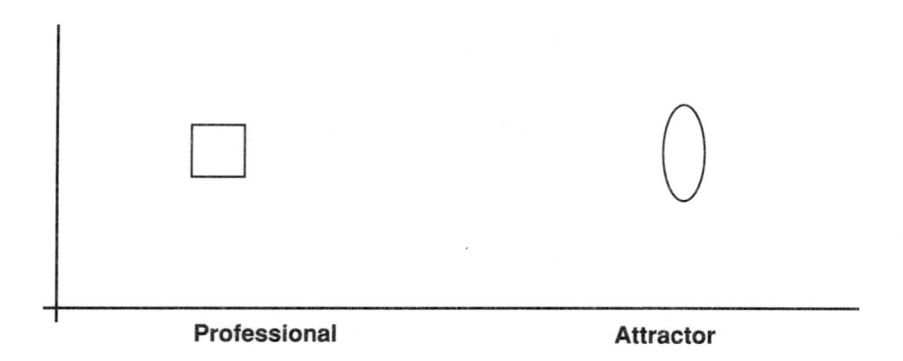

Figure 2.3 The images of the Professional and Attractor

they think and are focused on getting on with the task at hand, efficiently. Attractors are more focused on getting on with their work in an intense and committed way. The true Attractor nature is always revealed by a passion for what they do.

Both images also convey a sense of the different ways each organization establishes a sense of purpose and meaning to why they exist. Professional organizations are in business for the sake of the business itself, although this deeper aim often remains unsaid since, to a Professional, existing as a business for its own sake is such an obvious rationale that it need not be stated. Their sense of being serious and businesslike reflects this deeper understanding of why they exist. The Attractor, in contrast, has a purpose that is often focused on a real agenda of expressing creativity, developing people, or they have a larger social aim alongside their business aim. Such organizations are not in business only for the sake of business *per se*.

The medical–bionutrition company mentioned at the start of the chapter is an Attractor in its affection nature, and the main reason this can be gauged is the emphasis the company gave to engaging directly with people, both within the company as well as with customers. Their priorities were to create a sense of trust and they gave a high priority to developing their human assets. The Attractor nature was also apparent in the fact that they had a personal rather than an impersonal manner. People guided me to offices, for example. They kept central resources and offices that a Professional would have said were a waste. They were easy to develop a rapport with. Their business and marketing stance emphasized trust, and they had long-term customers, with a lot of repeat business. All of these details support the idea that they functioned within the affection area of experience as an Attractor rather than a Professional.

A FRAMEWORK TO HELP YOU SEE THE ORGANIZATION

Assessing whether the organization was fulfilling its affection aims

Many of these aspects tell you at the same time that this company achieved the aims of the affection area. We know that its Attractor nature was in keeping with the marketing message conveyed, that its customers should trust it and ring a certain number to speak 'personally' with the company, and this fitted with the direct and personal way in which individuals themselves were treated within the organization. The fact that they found it easy to create a rapport with others and had long-term loyal customers were both signs that the organization was really meeting the aims of this area of experience rather than just going through the motions of doing so. People cared about the organization and believed in it, which is another key test of whether the aims of the affection area are really being fulfilled or only appearing to be so.

It may seem that I have overplayed my assessment of this company and that it is impossible for a company to achieve these aims in a truly genuine way. However, the whole point of my using this company as an example is because it actually did meet the aims of this affection area in a real way. My description of this company is not overplayed, but we are accustomed to organizations that engage with others, their tasks and themselves in merely a superficial way, paying lip service to it all. The reason why this company functioned in the way it did was not because of a stroke of luck or because they happened to have the 'right' chief executive, a panacea that organizations often look for. Obtaining the benefits that accrue from the affection area, such as the loyalty others have towards the organization and the belief and trust they have in it, can hardly arise from one single person at the top but only from a general stance within the organization as a whole. In the medical–bionutrition company, their affection area was probably their greatest psychological asset yet this company only achieved this because the whole psyche of the organization was oriented in that direction. The activities that comprise this area needed to have been attended to actively, on a daily basis, and in a spirit of honesty, or the organization would never have acquired such benefits as loyalty, belief and trust in the first place. Many organizations want their people and customers to be loyal but pay little attention to the daily necessities that deliver these benefits, or they simply have never been taught how to do so or what actions and stance will actually achieve those ends.

Some key features of the Professional and Attractor approach in an organization

In order to be able to pay more genuine attention to the affection area, it helps to know what the different features are that you might see in an organization that reveal whether it is a Professional or an Attractor. General features of an organization that identify these two affection natures are described in the sections that follow and are summarized in Table 2.6.

Key qualities

The most distinct qualities that are associated with being a Professional are those of being cautious, formal, professional, serious and straightforward. The qualities of the Attractor, on the other hand, are those of being genuine, personal, committed, creative and open. These respective qualities also suggest how the two affection natures engage, both with others and with themselves. They reflect also the different assumptions about why the organization exists in the first place.

Work practices

In keeping with these qualities, in terms of work practices a Professional tries to present a particular, deliberate face to the world, and this is seen also in the serious and deliberate way in which people interact with each other and go about their work. EDS, the computer service company, is a classic example in this respect, with a great deal of caution in the way it presents itself and great seriousness and deliberation in the way in which people engage with each other and their work. The issue of trust is usually a crucial one in relation to the affection area. An Attractor organization, on the other hand, is more likely to emphasize the importance of being dedicated and committed and to engage in a more passionate and personal way with their work, and to be more open and natural in the way they engage with people. In Professional companies, for example, people tend to speak in a calm way, as it is important in such organizations to stay 'level-headed' or appear to be so. In Attractors, however, there is a greater level of comfort with people expressing what they feel.

The primary values that underlie many of the informal and formal systems in a Professional, such as promotion and performance systems, reflect their concern to appear professional, and reveal an emphasis on education level, abilities and trained skills. In an Attractor, the focus

A FRAMEWORK TO HELP YOU SEE THE ORGANIZATION 53

Table 2.6 Key features of the Professional and Attractor approaches

Professional □	Attractor ○
– serious, distant, impersonal, straightforward	– personal, giving, creative, committed
– focus on information secrecy, confidentiality	– focus on how much information to disclose
– like businesslike relationships	– like humour, genuineness in relationships
– like things to be efficient, no wasting time	– like things to be personal, spend time
– manage relationships with clear contracts	– manage relationships by establishing trust
– key success factor is delivering results	– key success factor is people, relationships
– clear separation between work and personal life	– accept an overlap of work and personal life
– tend to maximize technology	– tend to make technology user-friendly
– atmosphere is serious, hard-working	– atmosphere is warm, committed
– focus on rewarding skill, ability, results	– reward person's approach, contribution
– use central resources only as needed	– believe in having central resources
– believe that being professional is key	– believe that creating commitment is key
– create alliances when good for the business	– create alliances to have long-term allies
– assume customers want efficiency, rapid service	– assume customers want personal service
– talk of creating good business relationships	– talk of creating trust and loyalty
– focus on presentation of products and company	– focus on products/company making contact
– try to create a feeling of dedication	– try to create a feeling of kindness, gentleness

Both Professional and Attractor approaches are ways to achieve the same affection purpose:

Establishing a satisfactory means of engaging with others, of creating relationships, creating the means by which the organization maintains and sustains itself for the long term, creating an accepted way to relate to customers and others, providing a sense of purpose and fulfilment

shifts slightly to emphasize personal attributes such as enthusiasm, integrity and also whether there is a commitment to the overall organization.

Strategic or business stance

The strategic and business stance of organizations will reflect the same principles. One of the key aims of the affection area is to sustain the organization for the long term. Various features of an organization will reveal whether it does so more in the manner of the Professional or the Attractor. The Professional nature relies on a more contractual and instrumental stance in general, whether with suppliers or strategic partners, as well as with customers. Since, to Professionals, business is business, they conduct relationships as business deals and make no assumption of staying together with a supplier or partner for the long term. It is part of the game that they, and other organizations, operate in a matter-of-fact way that can be quite impersonal. To an Attractor organization, on the other hand, relationships with suppliers or strategic partners, as well as with customers, are based on an assumption of loyalty and common interest over and above the immediate or current business transaction. An alliance, for example, will not be just a business deal but a stepping stone to furthering a longer-term relationship. Attractors will seek to establish a greater level of personal rapport and trust because, to them, sustaining their organization over the long term is based on such foundations.

Within the two organizations, the business assumptions also vary. Professionals focus on their capital base from the point of view of financial assets. This is their priority. Attractors, on the other hand, focus on their human asset base and count on having good people and commitment to ensure the company's future. Both kinds of approach are aimed at achieving the same psychological aim, of feeling that the organization is taking care of itself in a way that will sustain it for the long term, and, at the same time, they reflect the very different assumptions these two natures have about why they exist as an organization and what their underlying purpose is.

Approach to customers

Both affection natures have different ways of relating to customers as well. Professionals assume they should present themselves as efficient and businesslike, because they expect customers to want an impersonal exchange that does not require anything more than the same kind of response from the customer. Attractors, in contrast, assume they should be personal and warm. Humour and fun are hard-to-mimic indicators of this nature and, for Attractors, being distant is inappropriate and

A FRAMEWORK TO HELP YOU SEE THE ORGANIZATION 55

they aim for loyal customers. Both are simply trying to achieve the same purpose, of creating a manner of engaging that they think is appropriate and real. In Attractors, it is important that something of the person – the supplier or the creator – is conveyed in the service or product. In Professionals, on the other hand, it is important that the person, or the personal element, is deliberately covered up. These different approaches also reflect the different assumptions each nature has about an appropriate way to engage with others.

Different ways of meeting the same aim

As with the two main natures in the inclusion and control areas, the features of the Professional and Attractor represent the outer appearance that you can observe in an organization. However, both natures are attempting to meet exactly the same aims, those of the affection area. Examples of companies that reflect the Professional and Attractor natures are set out in Table 2.7. As before, these are chosen simply to illustrate the different affection natures rather than because they are necessarily good examples of achieving the aims of the affection area.

Table 2.7   Companies that reflect the Professional or Attractor

Professionals	Attractors
Pepsi – key lever was to change the packaging	Coca Cola – the 'real' thing, loyal customers
Calvin Klein, selling on the basis of clear, tailored lines	Companies like Gap, which sell on the basis of touch
Companies devoted to spin doctoring, PR	Companies devoted to creative expression
Professional service firms that try to appear 'seamless'	Professional service firms that try to be 'real'

Using the conceptual framework

As you can see from the descriptions of both the different psychological natures as well as the three areas of experience, we can use the conceptual framework in several ways. I have tried to set out the key terms so that they are easily remembered, rather than portraying the infinite complexity of the three areas or the different natures. The framework as I have outlined it has given you the basics, the common words in the vocabulary which will help you make sense of the remaining chapters of the book as well as your own organizations. However, it is probably only when you start to apply these ideas that you will feel able to 'speak' or really use this new language.

Perhaps the two key aspects to bear in mind is that you can use the conceptual framework to assess both who an organization is, what its particular 'way' is, and how well it is performing. Note too that the framework is simply a way of understanding what the business is doing anyway from another perspective. The framework is another way of seeing the organization which allows you to interpret the deeper significance and meaning in its everyday actions and goals and, by so doing, you can understand many events that seem otherwise to be incomprehensible. It allows you to run organizations in a way that takes into account their emotional and subtle realities as well as their business realities.

One advantage of using it is that, as you could see, we can refer to both the qualities of an organization as well as its strategy in one sentence. We can draw together an aspect of the organization's approach to customers and work practices under the same set of terms. It is this that affords separate parts of the same organization the opportunity to make sense of each other. They can start to talk the same language or, at least, understand that their objectives are often the same, even if they have very different ways of achieving them. From this we can see how the organization is connected together in a subtle and psychological way.

For example, we could make sense of the medical–bionutrition company with details that varied from its furnishings, to the way people behaved, to its business priorities. We used these details to determine the particular way it functioned within each of the three areas of experience, and we used the same details to help us understand, at a broad level, how well this company was performing in the three areas. This could help us determine whether it was paying attention to the right concerns in its business although, in practice, the kind of analysis I have shown you here would need to be more extensive. A summary of the different psychological natures we could discern in this company, as well as its fulfilment of the aims of the three areas of experience, is set out in Table 2.8.

Perhaps the most useful component of the framework is that it helps you see that there are many different ways to run an organization well. Using it can lessen the tendency to think that there is one right way to function successfully. Staying focused on the idea that these natures fulfil a purpose or achieve a goal helps organizations evaluate for themselves what is working for them, even though that may be different from the norm or current fad. Their own style may be effective for them as a unique company. This is, in fact, exactly the scenario we explore in the next chapter.

Table 2.9 summarizes some of these advantages of using the conceptual framework.

A FRAMEWORK TO HELP YOU SEE THE ORGANIZATION 57

Table 2.8 The meaning of the details on the medical–bionutrition company

area of experience	details	aims of that area
inclusion	distinctive-looking building, logo and name low key, networked infrequently in industry, relied primarily on own sales force, territorial workplaces, atmosphere sedate and people stayed focused, careful in recruitment, 'name' brand associated with quality, innovative products, unusual and stylish furnishings, few strategic alliances, reception area designed for privacy, aimed to be global, name of company known but 'who' they were was less so	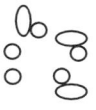 It functioned in the inclusion area as a **Connoisseur** but it should have been better at fulfilling the inclusion aims, of projecting its identity, claiming its own space and having a definite presence. This was an area that should have received management attention
control	clear management hierarchy, separate offices for managers and separate floor for executives, spent a lot of time and money to create a clear strategy, had a dominant voice in the industry, liked to plan ahead both strategically and individually, uncomfortable with changes in diary arrangements or plans, had extensive budgeting systems, pricing tactics were to price above average, well established in industry	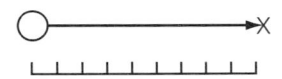 It functioned in the control area as a **Boss** and was effective at releasing talent and capabilities and meeting goals. Its concern to reduce the hierarchy was an unnecessary issue in this company
affection	personal approach, focused on developing human assets in company, devoted a lot of resources to personal development, furnishings designed for comfort, extras like creative flower arrangements, lot of empty offices, easy to create rapport with people in general, customers were long term, lot of repeat business, people often laughed – evidence that humour was acceptable – trusted in industry, structured with home base in Europe	 It functioned in the affection area as an **Attractor** and it fulfilled the affection aims, of creating a sense of purpose, loyalty and trust, quite effectively. The aims of this area were well met

Table 2.9 Advantages of using the framework

> it extends the focus of attention to a wider brief than only **the control area** of an organization
>
> it is easier to figure out the organization in a **dispassionate** way rather than judge it
>
> you can read the organization with a **range** of details without being an expert on psychology or strategy

Understanding the emotional change required in the organization

CHAPTER 3

Making the deeper change required to accompany the strategic response

In this chapter, I show you one way you can put the framework we explored in Chapter 2 and the ideas behind the psychological natures to good use. One of the main benefits of the approach is that it explains what is going on under the surface of an organization, and links the business world with the more invisible realities that exist. We can use it, in particular, to interpret the implications of any new set of external or market circumstances. Any change in the external situation facing an organization or a shift in the nature of its market often requires a corresponding adjustment within the organization itself. Typically, we focus only on the changes needed in terms of the organization's products, systems and structures, but we can understand them also in terms of the internal emotional and psychological change that is required in the organization. Sometimes, organizations make these adjustments quite readily and simply, but at other times it can seem absurdly hard to get the change within the organization that is so obviously required of it. When such an adjustment fails to occur, or does so only with great difficulty, you can be sure to find a dynamic within the organization that has an emotional basis.

Much of my time as a consultant is spent trying to explain and sort out such a dynamic in organizations. A psychological and perceptual perspective can cut through the surface appearance and make what seems incomprehensible, quite comprehensible. The purpose of this chapter is to illustrate this is so and we focus on the theme of making the internal adjustments within the organization that are necessary in order to meet a change in the external market conditions.

Seeing the connection between the strategic events and their deeper meaning

The example we focus on in this chapter in order to illustrate this theme is that of a pharmaceutical company where the internal organizational changes that were required were seemingly impossible to make, no matter how much they talked of their desire to make them. The framework of different psychological natures can explain why this was so.

It can also explain why the exhortations of the financial analysts and the media made little sense and had little impact on the company. They were being encouraged to make changes that represented a shift in 'who' they were that was not only unnecessary in order to meet the external requirements, but also contrary to the changes that should have been made. They needed to work with 'who' they were, rather than against it. It was only when they started to do so that they were able to make the transition that was implied by the strategic requirements, but in the interim the organization suffered both internal strain as well as some damage financially. It was one of those mysteries we often figure out later than we should, because we are so focused on the formal goals and requirements that we discount the deeper or emotional meaning of what is happening. The framework helps us identify and label what those meanings are.

The other benefit of using this approach to understand such events is that it explains the normal set of business activities from a different perspective than usual. One of the basic tenets of the framework is that an organization needs to attend to all three psychological areas. This seems straightforward and logical, and you can predict the effect on the business if the purpose in any one area is unmet. It could mean that the organization will have an unclear identity in the market if it fails to attend to the inclusion area and its requirements. Or, the organization may be unable to exert the influence it needs to have on the environment if it fails to attend well to the control area and the activities and requirements associated with that area. Or, the organization may be inept at building and sustaining relationships if it fails to attend to the affection area of the organization. However, this idea of needing to attend to all three areas of experience can still seem a bit abstract even though it makes logical sense. So the particular example we explore in this chapter is used to illustrate this idea more specifically. In this company it was the inclusion area which they were less comfortable with than the other two areas of experience, particularly the control area.

Applying this overall perspective helps you to see how the two worlds, the emotional and the strategic, are entwined. The connections between them may be invisible but, if you have seen the relationship once, you can easily use the ideas to explain the dynamic in any organization, and create the organizational adjustments you need more easily.

A brave new world for the pharmaceutical company

It is often the case that a new set of circumstances in the environment or in the nature of the market forces an organization to make a change that affects 'who' it is, its psychological nature. In the example described in this chapter, the new development in the market that I want to describe is that which occurred at the time Aids came to the forefront of the news and public consciousness. This had a dramatic impact on this company's market, since one of its products was considered to be helpful in the early treatment of Aids, and one of its subsidiaries was involved in the distribution of sexual protection aids.

On the surface, such a situation would be the envy of most organizations. It represented a potential bonanza, as the market need escalated dramatically without the company having to do anything to bring this about. However, the situation facing this company was not so simple, and in fact many companies faced with a dramatic change in their market adjust to this in complicated ways, rather than in the straightforward ways a more businesslike analysis often suggests. Organizations do strange things sometimes. Let's see what the pharmaceutical company did.

In the pre-Aids environment, both the company and its products were very discreet, and their profile in the external world was low. They advertised relatively little and they disliked attention in the media, except through the annual presentation of financial results. They had little need to do anything else. We can interpret such an approach as that of a Connoisseur, one of the two natures that fulfil the inclusion purpose of the organization and help to establish its identity, territorial space and presence. In such an environment, being a low-key and quite withdrawn Connoisseur was something they were required to be. To be more visible and impactful was impossible at that time because they were tightly regulated and their customers would have 'punished' them financially if they had promoted their products with bright colours or bold packaging. In addition, they had few other companies alongside them in that market niche and there is often less need to attend to any of the requirements of the inclusion area when that is the case rather than when there are numerous companies in the same market. Both the strategic and the psychological rules of their old environment, therefore, were very different from their new rules.

A challenge to the way the company fulfilled its inclusion purpose: being known

It was the company's inclusion area of experience, therefore, that was most affected when Aids hit the headlines. This was because the challenge, or opportunity, that the change in the market gave them involved an adjustment in the way they interacted externally, in how they projected their identity and promoted their products, and in the subtlety or impact of their advertising. The new environment required that people in the company should network actively with the media and external groups, and talk about social issues in public rather than just discuss their business results or financial performance. They now needed to actively promote the company itself as well as their products, and to use identifiable names to describe their products that would be remembered and get people's attention. Promotions had to be noticed all of a sudden, whereas before they didn't matter in quite the same way.

The company was faced with creating space for itself and establishing its identity in a market that now had far more companies in it. In their earlier market, since they had few other companies to compare themselves with, they had little need to create a really distinctive identity or fine-tune their way of projecting that identity. They needed to learn to do so in a far more sophisticated way. For all these reasons, the market change could be characterized in terms that correspond with what we would call the inclusion area in the framework I am using. It required new solutions to the way in which that particular inclusion purpose of the organization was fulfilled. Companies need to constantly rework and re-evaluate their particular solutions in any of the areas of experience. As a result, they may need to enhance or alter the way they express themselves and their nature.

In the pharmaceutical company, the shift in the market which they needed to adjust to was not a gradual one, but a sudden one. The change required was to become a higher-profile, more 'colourful' Connoisseur, but not necessarily to become a Populist in nature, however. Unfortunately, as we shall see, just setting strategic priorities that reflect such an adjustment is the easy part. In the pharmaceutical company and its subsidiary they did set such priorities, but they were undermined by the inner and emotional stance of the organization, which did not change for quite some time.

What happened? What you would expect is that they would make the necessary changes in the business and emphasize anything that we would characterize as part of the 'inclusion area'. For example, you might expect to see a more diverse set of distribution channels. You would expect greater priority to be given to marketing and sales, more money in the advertising budget, a higher level of product promotion, deliberate cultivation of a more public identity, and so on. All these activities needed to be performed in a more sophisticated way than previously. They represent parts of the business that fulfil, in a specific way, the inclusion area of experience since they are constructed in order for the organization to interact externally, to create a space for itself in its market-place as well as to obtain a sense of presence. They are quite normal components of running a business, but interpreting them in terms of the three psychological areas allows us to see their underlying meaning and to decipher what they imply for the psyche of the organization.

Feeling forced to do things instead of willing to do them

While the company did determine goals very similar to those logical, 'correct' ones I have mentioned above, few of those goals were met, and very little genuinely changed for quite a while. Their response to any external advice or to comments about them in the media was defensive. This in itself tells you that there is a far deeper inner change needing to be made that, for one reason or another, the organization is finding it hard to make. And, if you had been expecting an orderly, straightforward adjustment in the organization, you would have been somewhat bemused by what actually happened.

The company complained that promoting the organization and being 'in the public eye' was 'making a show of yourself' rather than doing business. They wanted to start legal action against one competitor that was highly publicity-oriented and which actively sought attention in the media. They saw this competitor as 'unfair', and many bitter comments were made about what seemed to be that company's 'favoured status' in the eyes of the regulatory authorities. I watched several managers showing me with fury the latest advertising 'gimmick' of this competitor, assuring me that it was 'not the proper way to advertise such products' and that 'they' would never have been allowed to get away with it. This seeming 'favouritism' was interpreted in the pharmaceutical company as being the result of that competitor's 'cosy' relationship with people in the media, something which they themselves scorned. The high profile of the chief executive of the rival company was seen to give them an 'unfair advantage', and they resented it.

That networking with external people was not only a legitimate but an essential part of normal business activity was something they found hard to accept emotionally, even though such activities were specified as part of the new goals and objectives they had set themselves. The right goals may have been on the right pieces of paper, but how could such goals be properly met if the approach under the surface was that these were something that 'had' to be done, as if they were forced to do them against their will? This is the emotional reason for the fact that their goals, their explicit intentions, were specified but never really or well fulfilled.

Other aspects of their agenda as a business also changed dramatically, and demanded changes that seemed straightforward but were, one way or another, never fully carried out. For example, the new environment required that the company talk about Aids as a social issue, in public. Other companies would have made the maximum use of this open door to publicize themselves. This was free publicity, after all. However, that was not how it seemed to the pharmaceutical company. These requirements, to promote the company itself rather than just the products, and to promote in this indirect, tangential way, seemed 'wrong' to them, fundamentally out of kilter. To perform any public role which was not confined to reporting straight business performance or their financial results felt strange, even though they dutifully 'went along with' performing these more public roles.

Although the previous environment had not demanded any great attention to be paid to the inclusion purpose of the organization and the company had previously been required to function in a self-effacing, almost invisible way, each psychological purpose is still there in any company, at any time. The inclusion purpose requires some fulfilment of activities that relate to interacting externally, projecting the identity of the company, setting up ways to interact with the external environment as well as establishing a satisfactory level of joint interaction within the company. The need to perform these activities in some way is always present, and was so in the pharmaceutical company and its subsidiary even in the pre-Aids era.

The company had been fulfilling the purpose associated with the control area, establishing its effectiveness and exerting its power and talent, reasonably well. However, within the new set of external requirements, fulfilling even this purpose would be a challenge if the company failed to adequately make its presence known alongside other organizations which had started entering this same market. Moreover, when a company is uncomfortable claiming its own right to exist as itself, this will affect its ability to meet its affection purpose, namely to engage in genuine and satisfactory relationships with others. As a result, in the pharmaceutical company their affection purpose was only partly fulfilled and they used a mask of the Professional nature with which to engage with others in a very cautious and quite distant manner. What their true affection nature was under this mask was very hard to gauge.

Figure 3.1 illustrates these three natures of the pharmaceutical company.

EMOTIONAL CHANGE IN THE ORGANIZATION 65

inclusion area	control area	affection area
to establish a clear identity and presence, interact with other organizations, claim space	to exert influence, establish its effectiveness *vis-à-vis* others, express competence and achieve results	to establish a satisfactory way of relating to and engaging with others and sustaining itself
self-effacing Connoisseur	clear Boss	real affection nature unclear
too low key and withdrawn with neither products nor company having sufficient presence or impact in the new set of external conditions. Their inclusion purpose needed to be more easily and naturally fulfilled so they felt they had the innate right to exist and claim space	achieved this control purpose since they obtained good financial results. They did so by having effective products and a hard-working organization, but in the new environment they could no longer fulfil this control purpose unless they started to fulfil their inclusion purpose also	tried to achieve affection purpose by being cautious and reserved when engaging with others. This area of experience was affected by the fact that the organization found it hard to exist as itself, so it was difficult for it to trust others or sustain genuine long-term relationships

Figure 3.1 The areas of experience of the pharmaceutical company

Understanding why the company found it so hard to make the transition

It often helps to understand why a company finds it so hard to do what seems so obvious and easy if we are focused only on the surface appearance and the logically correct solutions. The change that needed to be made in this company was an emotional one. They had absorbed the psychological rules of the earlier market-place very successfully, but they now needed to learn what these rules were in their new market-place, not just what the new strategic rules of the game were. However, they viewed all of their new demands and activities, this whole new way of thinking, with a slight contempt. I would see some of them state an objective related to promoting the company and its products in a more visible and impactful way, for example, yet they would state this with a hint of a sneer on their faces, or a rise in their voice that was inappropriate, that 'said' far more than their words. They didn't really want to do things in that new way for the simple reason that, in the past, they would have been 'penalized' for doing so, and also because they simply didn't know how to as they had never had to learn to operate in this area of experience in a sophisticated or clever way. They continued to promote their products and themselves in a way that was too low-key. It was as though they simply couldn't help it. Emotionally, they were faced with something very different from the wide open world, the beneficent market-place, that the analysts, consultants and journalists saw. Telling them to be bold and impactful, which was the advice they were given, was a waste of time.

There were two key things that they should have been helped with, instead. First, it required a deeper level of acceptance of what was actually needed than simply formulating strategic or production requirements. The company had 'played the game' in their old market environment very well and had been rewarded for doing so by a commensurate financial success. However, what they found hard to do in the new set of circumstances was to interpret the external demands in terms of their deeper implications. As a result, the changes they focused on were too superficial. They needed help to work out what these implications were, however, since this kind of analysis is rather difficult, especially when it is an unknown area of activity in many organizations.

The second key thing that the company should have been helped with was to let go of the key emotional reason why they found it so hard to make the adjustment required of them. The company was used to being self-effacing. It was the reference point for what was 'normal' to them as well as what was 'allowed', since the external environment had required this kind of stance from the company before. This orientation was something that most people in the company were unaware of, of course, but it was this reference point that had to be altered. They needed to acknowledge that having more presence, promoting themselves as a company, and interacting and networking more widely was not only 'normal' but 'allowed'. They needed a new reference point that said it was OK for people to be distinctive and stand out within the company as well, and that it was perfectly OK for people to be out and about with the authorities and people in the media without having to justify this to their colleagues. This is a completely different requirement than simply accepting that they 'needed to be more widely known'. There is an extra step implied. The difference is reflected in a mental reframe that replaces the phrase 'we need to be more colourful and impactful' with the phrase 'it is perfectly OK to be more colourful and impactful'. It is only the latter mental orientation that will remove hidden tension in an organization faced with the kind of conflict that the pharmaceutical company was faced with.

Implicit in these changes is the requirement that they think in terms of who they needed and wanted to 'be', not just what they were required to 'do'. It is often the case that change in an organization must first come at this level before the tangible efforts bear any results, and that the organization must change its understanding of who it is, its sense of itself, before any actions will work as intended. Without doing so, an organization will often strain and struggle but make little progress. By doing so, an organization's practical solutions work far more smoothly and in a way that seems natural.

Thinking about such changes in terms of psychological natures helps you pinpoint quite precisely, rather than generally, what their underlying meaning is in terms of who the organization needs to be. Unless you are precise in figuring this out, your recommendations or actions may miss the mark, as we shall see.

Being able to ignore incorrect and damaging advice

One of the problems with getting the pharmaceutical company to change was that its analysts and consultants were recommending solutions that went beyond what was needed to deal with the new situation. They correctly identified that the company needed more interaction, visibility, networking, publicity, and so on, but they recommended solutions involving a lot of interaction, massive fanfares of publicity, media courting and politician handshaking. This implied the company having to make a gigantic and abrupt leap from being a shy, avoiding semi-Connoisseur to being a high-octane Populist. This was one of the reasons why the company reacted in the way it did and why there was fierce but unconscious resistance to the advice they were given.

The real answer is so much simpler than that which is often considered necessary. If the key emotional reason behind such unwillingness to make the change needed relates to the fact that the company, unknown to itself, feels normal and comfortable when low-key and relatively withdrawn, it is a waste of time trying to get that company to become a Populist in its approach. If you carry out a strategic analysis such as a strengths/weaknesses/opportunities/threats analysis, which the company did, you will typically come up with aims that do reflect such a highly Populist approach. That is, an apparent need for massive publicity and self-promotion of the company as well as their products. But if you take into account the emotional reality of the organization, such an approach won't work. It might look right, but it isn't right. Even more relevant, it isn't necessary. This degree of change was not needed in this situation to deal with the new market requirement.

Figuring out the degree of change a company needs to make

Distinguishing between the different psychological natures helps you be precise in figuring out the degree of change a company needs to make. We can see that the pharmaceutical company needed to better fulfil the inclusion purpose of the organization, but we know that there are other ways of fulfilling exactly the same purpose. We are not restricted solely to the Populist approach to dealing with this area of experience.

The market challenge facing the pharmaceutical company could be met by fulfilling their inclusion purpose as a Connoisseur, albeit a clearer one than before, rather than as a Populist. This would have met the changed external requirements. It would have been perfectly adequate for the company to have been selective in their networking and in the people they courted, and to have been artful, subtle and high-class in their promotions. In other words, to have been a crystal clear, well-functioning Connoisseur rather than a hidden, self-effacing one. If the advice they had received, the articles written about them in the media or even their own view of themselves had highlighted the fact that all they really needed to do was build on their existing nature and to express it in an assured rather than a tentative way, and not to become a totally new kind of organization, then their reaction would have been more straightforward. What the company needed was simply to enhance their existing nature and to learn to apply it in a clever and sophisticated way. They needed to project a sense of refinement more than the loud active stimulation of a Populist company. Their main new competitor projected themselves, and acted, as such a Populist. Creating a distinguishing presence for itself in others' eyes required that the pharmaceutical company discover its own innate style rather than follow those that fitted other companies.

However, initially, the company accepted the recommendations of their analysts and consultants and incorporated them into their objectives. When few of these were met, the defensiveness in the company grew. Managers came and went. Advisers came and went. The new managers left. The media got irate with them. It was not until they started to develop the approaches and style that we would associate with the Connoisseur nature that the changes they needed to make began to unfold. Strange as it may seem, it was when they realized that they needed to change less than they had thought that they genuinely and fundamentally changed. Once they had been helped to take their own

EMOTIONAL CHANGE IN THE ORGANIZATION   69

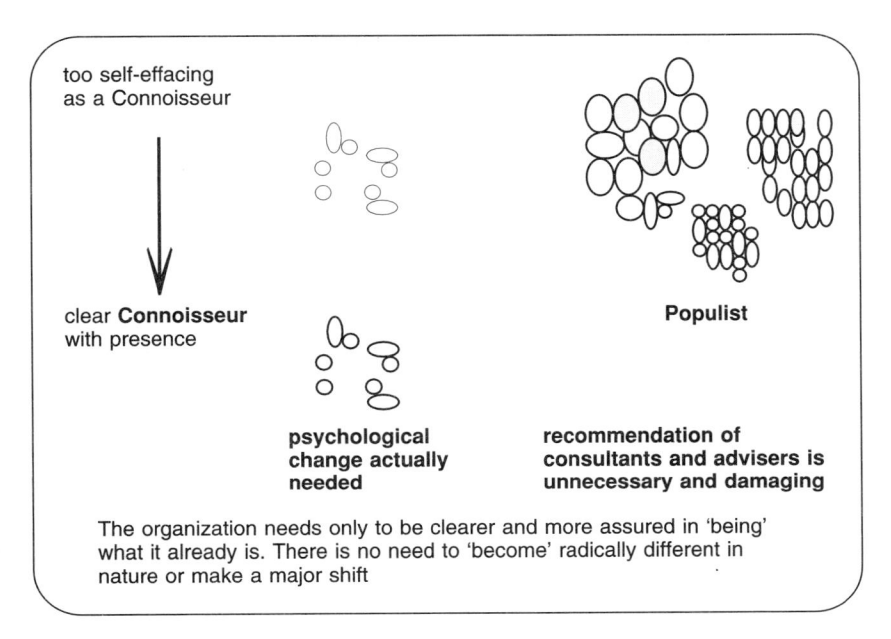

```
too self-effacing
as a Connoisseur

        |
        |
        ↓

clear Connoisseur                                    Populist
with presence

                     psychological        recommendation of
                     change actually      consultants and advisers is
                     needed               unnecessary and damaging

The organization needs only to be clearer and more assured in 'being'
what it already is. There is no need to 'become' radically different in
nature or make a major shift
```

Figure 3.2   Bringing out the Connoisseur more

'stance' as a company and had received clarification of the meaning of what was happening to them, they were able to make the business-level changes that were necessary, and yet still retain their sense of who they were. To do this they had to ignore the bias that is so often present, namely that any organization should behave in public like a high-octane, expansive Populist.

Figure 3.2 illustrates the degree of change actually needed in the pharmaceutical company.

Receiving the support they needed in order to make the transition

Being able to unhook the emotional reference point that said that the company should be hidden and self-effacing came from a gradual build-up of contact with other companies and other people in that industry. The main change occurred when they hired external promotional people who were Connoisseurs, like themselves. These people validated and 'proved' that it was OK to promote the company as well as its products in a more subtle, distinctive and refined Connoisseur style. They hired people with this nature into their top management levels, and eventually this built up the kind of experience and skills that meant they could

70 READING THE MIND OF THE ORGANIZATION

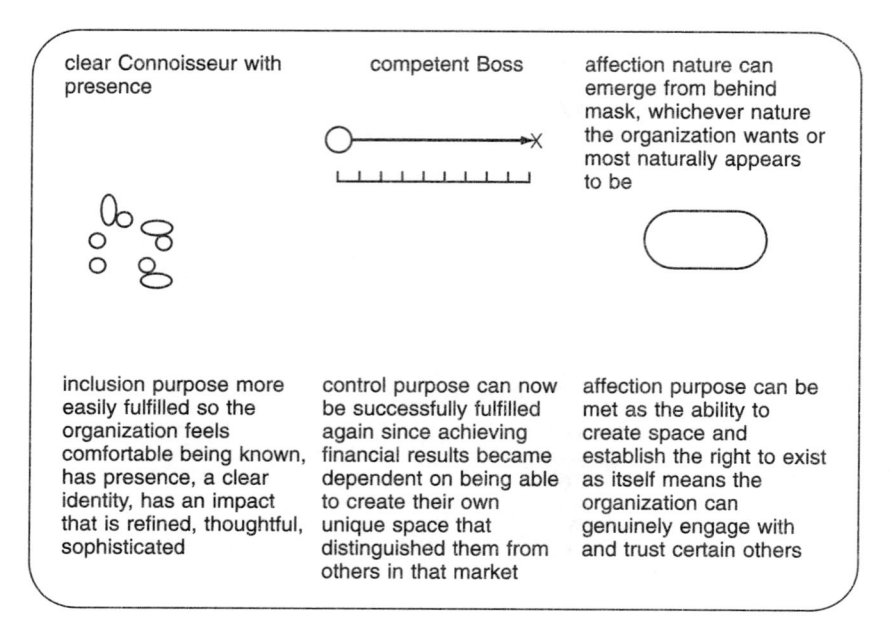

clear Connoisseur with presence	competent Boss	affection nature can emerge from behind mask, whichever nature the organization wants or most naturally appears to be
inclusion purpose more easily fulfilled so the organization feels comfortable being known, has presence, a clear identity, has an impact that is refined, thoughtful, sophisticated	control purpose can now be successfully fulfilled again since achieving financial results became dependent on being able to create their own unique space that distinguished them from others in that market	affection purpose can be met as the ability to create space and establish the right to exist as itself means the organization can genuinely engage with and trust certain others

Figure 3.3 **The psychological change in the pharmaceutical company**

successfully fulfil the inclusion purpose of the organization. The identity of the company was projected through being skilful and artful in their style and branding, and focused in their well-chosen interactions.

Another key aspect of the transition was that it gave the company the ability to again fulfil its control purpose satisfactorily and to achieve the financial results they aimed for. It gave them also the potential to genuinely fulfil the affection purpose of the organization for the first time. It is only when an organization feels it has the innate right to exist and take up space that it can engage with others in a truly trusting way instead of being too cautious. Such a simple change as enhancing the Connoisseur nature they already had in terms of fulfilling their inclusion purpose had the potential of allowing many other positive changes to unfold for the company.

Figure 3.3 illustrates how this pattern could be seen to create a positive effect in the other areas of experience of the pharmaceutical company.

Figuring out the meaning of the situation the organization is faced with

If you looked at this situation only from a traditional marketing or strategic perspective, you would never be able to understand why this company reacted as it did. Getting the change you need often requires an emotional explanation, not just a strategic one. We need ways of making these explanations clearer. In the case of the pharmaceutical company we started by figuring out the meaning of the strategic shift in the environment. The first aspect of my description of events characterized the situation in a way that made it obvious that the demand on the company affected its inclusion purpose. You can figure out the implications of any external situation or demand, and in the tables that follow I illustrate this with some general examples.

If the environment changes in a way that demands an adjustment in the way the organization interacts externally or a new way of establishing space or a niche in the market, or if the organization is required to promote itself in a new way, the demand can be characterized as one requiring new solutions to fulfil the inclusion purpose of the organization. Other changes in the environment which also relate to the inclusion area are less obvious, such as an increased demand for truly original products rather than products which are simply updated or modernized. There may be an increased expectation from customers to feel left alone and uninvaded by organizations in order that they experience a sense of tranquillity and quiet. Any such external changes imply either a relative shift in the balance between the Connoisseur and Populist natures, or that the organization is simply better at being a Connoisseur or Populist.

If the demand from the environment affects the degree of influence the organization has or the kind of influence that is needed in the company's market, or if it affects such things as the speed of response needed, then all these changes have implications for the way in which the organization fulfils its control purpose. Customers may demand that they are treated as intelligent or they may increasingly want information about products instead of high-pressure selling techniques. These particular external changes often imply either a relative shift in balance between the Juggler and Boss control natures, or that the organization is simply better at being a Juggler or Boss.

Finally, if the demand from the environment affects the nature of people's relationships, or the way the company engages with customers, suppliers or outside organizations, or if it affects the deeper purpose of the organization, these changes have implications for the way the organization fulfils its affection purpose. Customers may increasingly demand that people in the organization are spontaneous rather than that they are simply polite and well trained. They may demand that the organization engages with them in a more natural way. These changes often imply either a relative shift in balance between the Professional and Attractor natures, or that the organization is simply better at being a Professional or Attractor.

A reference point to help you see if the organization is really in tune

In Table 3.1, Table 3.2 and Table 3.3 examples of external changes are set out in terms of their meaning in terms of the three areas of experience respectively. You can use these as reference lists to identify the implications of any shift or change.

In order to illustrate whether any solution or approach by the organization is truly appropriate, I have also set out in each table the kinds of qualities or principles organizations often use as a reference point for themselves when making changes. These can be categorized in terms of the psychological natures they reflect. In addition, since many organizational changes are accompanied by attempts to rebrand the company or change its logo and outer presentation, you can also use the list of colours specified for each psychological nature to see if the organization genuinely knows what it is doing to itself. Such factors as qualities and colours often seem trivial in contrast to such serious things as the strategy and structure of a company. However, it is precisely such trivia that are a good test of whether the organization has got the point or has missed it completely. Changes may seem right intellectually but the tell-tale signs of whether they are emotionally in tune with what is going on in the organization and what is needed at a deeper level will be displayed in such details. If the meaning of the external demands the organization is faced with does not relate to the kinds of qualities or principles used as a reference point for itself, or the colours used in any rebranding exercise, you know that the organization is operating only at the level of surface appearances. If, on the other hand, such details as the qualities and colours that the organization uses to identify itself are in tune with the real meaning of what is required from the environment and the change needed, then you can be more assured that their comprehension of the situation is at a deeper and truer level.

Table 3.1 The meaning of changes that reflect the inclusion area of experience

	changes that reflect the **inclusion** area of experience	**Qualities** companies often use to redefine themselves	**Colours** companies often use to rebrand themselves
each change implies a greater emphasis on the **Connoisseur**	demand for more innovative, truly original products rather than simply modernization clearer differentiation between products needed or they are seen as just the same as others need for greater selectivity and focus in what is offered to customers there is a shift in favour of high-quality, high-value products more than low-price standardized products customers want to feel uninvaded by the organization and have an atmosphere of tranquillity and calm more than stimulation	distinctive, original, innovative, considered and considerate, high-quality, refined, serene	subtle or distinctive colours such as aqua, shades of violet, magenta rather than red, silver, plum, white, an emphasis on colour coordination
each change implies a greater emphasis on the **Populist**	customers want products because 'everyone else is buying them', or to feel that they are like other people customers want products that are compatible with other products or so they fit with a standard an increased need for easier accessibility of products to customers there is a shift to standardized, lower-price products rather than high-quality, high-price products customers want to be stimulated or entertained by the organization or want a higher frequency of interaction	lively, active, open-door, sociable, conversational, entertaining, on-the-go	bright red, blue or yellow, any colours or shades that are considered to be either up-to-date, current or 'appropriate' for that kind of organization

Table 3.2 The meaning of changes that reflect the control area of experience

	changes that reflect the **control** area of experience	Qualities companies often use to redefine themselves	Colours companies often use to rebrand themselves
each change implies a greater emphasis on the **Juggler**	changes in the environment are faster or more numerous customers require greater flexibility in what is delivered or how it is delivered there is an increased need for more expertise, or skill built into the product itself customers want to be treated as intelligent and can make up their own minds, they want information more than pressure selling customers want a sense of playfulness, adventurousness, from the organization or they will see it as too strait-laced	flexible, daring, adventurous, free, intelligent, expert, fast, collegial, egalitarian, playful	any unusual combination of colours that breaks the rules but works, as well as shades of green or tan as a general rule because these signify balance, an essential part of the Juggler approach
each change implies a greater emphasis on the **Boss**	an increased demand for products which have a longer lead-time to develop a need for increased amounts of investment or R&D expenditure in general within that organization, in order to stay successful demand for increased reliability, certainty or precision of the product more aggressive competitive tactics such as pricing transitional shifts in the environmental rules such as overall product standards or rules in the industry	forceful, measured, steady, reliable, certain, prepared, powerful, insistent, aggressive	black, or black and white, crimson, any colour that is predictable or chosen because it is strong or forceful in impact

Table 3.3 The meaning of changes that reflect the affection area of experience

	Changes that reflect the **affection** area of experience	**Qualities** companies often use to redefine themselves	**Colours** companies often use to rebrand themselves
each change implies a greater emphasis on the **Professional**	an increased need for more distant, impersonal or transitory relationships with the organization customers want more efficient service at the expense of personal contact, and want to simply get on with their business as fast as possible the product needs to be more sophisticated or slick in its outer presentation or packaging in order for it to be successful there is an increased need for technological ways of interacting organizations increasingly engage with each other through contracts, formal means, instead of on trust or personal relationships	efficient, professional, tailored, business-like, rational, pragmatic, serious, even-tempered	navy blue and grey are their primary colours, any colour that is 'serious' or chosen because it masks rather than reveals, or suggests an absence of emotion or volatility
each change implies a greater emphasis on the **Attractor**	need for more loyalty from people outside – suppliers, customers, alliances – who stay for the long term, no matter what customers need time to ask individual questions customers prefer something creative or genuine in the product or company or want to know it means something customers want a real engagement with people in the organization rather than polite or well-trained people who feel like robots rather than human beings people the organization engages with expect a mutually beneficial relationship, rather than each trying to get the best deal for themselves	honest, warm, personal, spontaneous, humorous, trusted, natural, genuine, committed, creative	warm or attracting colours such as lemon, any shade of pink, apricot, peach, turquoise, orchid, spring-like colours that suggest 'life'

A process you can use to help the organization understand what is happening

These tables help you also in making use of a process that can be applied to any situation in which an organization is needing help to make an internal or emotional change. You may have discovered that the approach of the organization does not fit with the meaning of the external change. The process that follows in Table 3.4 can guide you in delving more deeply to understand why that is so. Not every strategic challenge will require this kind of analysis. Often, the change demanded is straightforward and can be obtained in an orderly, logical way. The focus in this chapter has been on illustrating what you can do when this orderly and logical process does not occur or whenever the degree of effort required to move forward seems disproportionate. This process can be helpful if the changes needed in an organization are not forthcoming in a reasonable period of time. At that point, you need to try to understand the organization in a more subtle way. You can use this process to help you either to think through what is being asked of the organization and what change is needed, or to talk through with others the same sequence of questions.

Applying the process to the pharmaceutical company

Table 3.5 summarizes the situation in the pharmaceutical company so that you can see how the process can be applied in practice.

Understanding the organization as if it were an individual person

The part of the process that people usually need to think about or talk through most is figuring out the internal change needed, and the emotional reasons for what is happening. This part of the process requires that you adopt a fresh stance and imagine the organization in rather a different way than most people are used to. There are no pat formulae for working through this part of the analysis, but one way that helps is the following. When you are trying to understand why an organization is doing something that seems odd, or why it is not doing something that you think it should, think of the organization as if it were a person. This is only a metaphor, a way to help you put the events in perspective. However, if you think of what is going on as if those same events, those same responses, were occurring in an individual, it

EMOTIONAL CHANGE IN THE ORGANIZATION

Table 3.4 A process to use to think through the implications

a process to clarify the psychological rules of the game the organization is faced with

1. what is the external demand, market change or strategic aim of the organization in this situation?

2. what psychological purpose or area does this correspond to? How well does the organization fulfil this purpose at present?

3. what internal organizational changes need to be made or could be made within this psychological area in order to meet the strategic aim?

4. what is the existing psychological nature of the organization in that area of experience? How well does the organization use this nature at present? Is it expressed well, tentatively or forcefully, flexibly or rigidly?

5. what are the psychological implications of these surface-level business changes? What do they seem to imply in terms of the psychological nature of the organization in that area of experience – should the relative balance between the two main natures in that area shift, or can the organization simply be better at expressing or being its existing nature?

6. what emotional factors might have to be taken into account in making this change? Is there a change in the psychological rules that needs to be clarified? Is there some past event or set of circumstances that the organization might need help in letting go of?

7. if there is difficulty in the organization genuinely making the changes required, or they make every effort to do so but do not seem to make much progress, what reasons, emotional or otherwise, would explain this? How would you help the organization successfully deal with these factors?

8. what specific solutions and options are there for the organization to enhance the psychological nature needed to meet both these psychological aims as well as its strategic aims? What specific solutions and options are there to change or shift the organization's psychological nature in that area of experience to meet both these psychological as well as strategic aims?

9. what impact will these changes and solutions have on the way the organization fulfils the other two areas of experience? In what ways will the organization now be better able to fulfil these?

Table 3.5 Applying the process to the pharmaceutical company

clarifying the psychological rules of the game for the pharmaceutical company

1. **The external demand and strategic aim** was to take advantage of the increased demand for their products that arose at the time Aids came to the forefront of the news and public awareness.

2. **The psychological purpose or area this corresponds to** is inclusion. The organization had paid little attention to this area because the market environment had not required it.

3. **The internal organizational changes that needed to be made** were to be more high-profile in the wider public arena as a company and to be far more impactful and colourful in terms of their products. They needed to interact more widely with the media and other external organizations.

4. **Their existing psychological nature** in this area of experience was the Connoisseur. The organization hid themselves from public view and were discreet in their promotion of their products because they would have been penalized for being more impactful.

5. **The psychological change needed** was to enhance their existing Connoisseur so that it was clear and assured. They needed to avoid trying to be a Populist. Their existing nature did not need to change, but their underlying discomfort with this whole area of experience needed to be dealt with so that they could cope with the external change which demanded a new approach in this area. They needed to be able to create a sense of presence, to feel it was OK to interact with others outside the organization even if not immediately connected to their business, to feel comfortable when they were noticed in terms of their more public role.

6. **The emotional reason** that explained the organization's reactions and the apparent difficulty in adjusting to the new set of cirumstances was that it felt normal and 'required' to be self-effacing and hidden, and it felt strange to them to be out-front in the public arena.

7. **One factor that needed to be dealt with was** that getting used to such activities takes time and cannot occur instantly as if the organization is a machine. The key emotional factor was that they had been penalized in the past whenever they had been high-profile so they needed a deeper level of acceptance that this would no longer occur. They needed help in understanding for themselves the psychological meaning of what was happening.

8. **The specific options to enhance this psychological nature** were to be high-class and artful in their promotions, interact somewhat more in well-chosen interactions rather than in terms of blanket coverage, and to hire a Connoisseur PR organization and people rather than people who pressured them to be Populists.

9. **The other two areas of experience** were affected in turn by the above changes. The control purpose of achieving results and expressing competence could be fulfilled more easily again and the company's affection purpose could start to be genuinely fulfilled for the first time

is much easier to find the answer to why the organization is doing something that seems nonsensical.

In the pharmaceutical company, the kind of individual this example resembled was someone who was uncomfortable when required to interact with others and uncomfortable projecting themselves and receiving attention from others. This discomfort can arise in an individual in two ways. The first is when a person has always performed well and obtained good results, but is comfortable being seen in a conspicuous, out-front way only in the context of their achievements or when in a work role. This is similar to the dynamic that existed in the pharmaceutical company and its subsidiary. Such a person is uncomfortable simply being themselves when with others. With such an individual the underlying assumption is that promoting themselves is 'not quite right'. Such individuals are quite commonly seen in people who assume that, if they do their job well, they will be promoted and succeed, but who realize later in their careers that it matters also that you can be yourself when interacting with others, can establish a sense of presence in a room full of others, and can interact without having to talk about work all the time. In an individual this pattern almost always arises because, when they were younger, their existence was only acknowledged when they were doing something 'useful' or performing a task. If they achieved results, they were acknowledged and given time and attention. Otherwise, they were not supposed to take up a great deal of other people's time.

The same dynamic can arise from another source, however. If an individual has, for one reason or another, been alone or isolated a great deal then they will also experience discomfort when required to interact with others. Such an individual, faced with a sudden need to interact with others a great deal more than they are used to, or with a need to project themselves more distinctively and clearly, will have to go through a learning process similar to that which applied to the pharmaceutical company. They will need to learn the skills of doing these things, and to take time to discover for themselves what their natural interaction approach is, as well as how to claim their own space when with many more people than they are used to being with. This resembles the pharmaceutical company in so far as part of that company's difficulty in making the adjustment to the new requirements in the market was that they were simply unused to having to claim space and project who they were in relation to the many other new companies in their market. They needed time to learn how to do so in a sophisticated and refined way.

In order for any such individual to make these quite fundamental changes they need, just as the pharmaceutical company did, to go the extra emotional step and not just perform these other activities as an obligation or a set of action steps. They need to change inside rather than just in their outer behaviour or appearance, or they will never make the transition required of them and they will start to become defensive. Without this inner reorientation they will go through all the motions of change, just as the pharmaceutical company did, but it will never really work or bear fruit. Such individuals almost always need to work out what they want to do differently only after they have established a clearer awareness of who they are, and who they want to be. This requires that the individual develop a much greater comfort with their innate right to exist as themselves in the world, alongside others. They need to accept, at quite a deep level, that it is perfectly all right for others to pay attention to them for their own sake and not just when they are doing things or performing well. They need to know how to claim space naturally alongside others in the same way that they know how to do so when more alone.

For some people, using this metaphor of the organization as a human being helps them get a perspective on the whole situation. It provides a 'way in' to figure out the organization as a whole. There are always people within the organization who will resemble a particular dynamic in their own behaviour, and you can figure them out to help you figure the organization out. As with the organization, individuals have their own internal reality. The other advantage of using the metaphor is that it makes the process of change applied to the organization a more intelligent one. This is because it works with the organization, not against it. Doing the latter only creates frustration and wastes time. Working with the organization, however, requires that you take into account these subtle factors rather than think you can ignore them and just get on with the business.

This approach is far from being the only way to figure out the emotional reasons an organization is doing whatever it is doing, and you can use your own ways of understanding a human person to help you do so. Sooner or later, you will be drawing on your knowledge of human beings and how they function, which is the real purpose of thinking 'psychologically' and using your innate perception.

The meaning in the strategy

The pharmaceutical company found it quite hard to make the change required within the organization. We need to bear in mind that this only occurred because they needed support to figure out the deeper meaning of what was happening. Another context in which we can see the same principle displayed is in the strategic priorities themselves, and it is to these that we turn in the next chapter, where we see how you can decipher the meaning in the strategy itself, rather than the meaning in the events of the organization as we have done in this chapter. The common principle is the importance of identifying the link between the strategic or business realm and the internal and intangible realm in the organization. We have to use our own eyes and ears to do so, and to apply our ability to 'see through' appearances as well as to apply the psychological perspective to discover the hidden significance of an organization's aims.

Deciphering the meaning in a strategy statement

CHAPTER 4

Understanding the meaning in the strategy itself

In the previous chapter we looked at the way in which one company, a pharmaceutical company, struggled to make an internal adjustment that was required in order to meet a change in the external or market situation they were faced with. It was helpful to be able to decipher the meaning of the actions of that company in a slightly deeper way than we are accustomed to using when we try to help organizations make such strategic adjustments. By deciphering them in this deeper way, we could understand why that particular company was doing what seemed, on the surface, to be quite odd yet, from an emotional point of view, was far more comprehensible. We needed to apply all three of the components of the approach I am describing in this book in order to do this. We needed to be able to see through the external appearance of the situation, to use the conceptual framework in order to understand the psychological significance of the events that occurred, and we needed to approach the organization with some degree of sensitivity and subtlety. These three components we apply also in the context we explore in this chapter. Here, we move on one step from understanding the events that accompany a strategic reorientation to the strategic stance itself.

Reading between the lines of any statement of business aims

Everything an organization says or does has a meaning and impact that can be understood by looking at it with a perceptual and psychological lens. We can use this perspective to understand the meaning in a company's strategy and business priorities, as well as any statement made about the business, such as in a company's Annual Report or simply a vague description of what the business is about and where it is heading.

In this chapter, we adopt this approach to decipher a set of priorities described by the chairman of a major company that is aiming to become global. While the company's strategic intent is obvious and constitutes the subject of the statement, we use the conceptual framework to read between its lines and decipher its psychological meaning and implications for the organization.

While we take note only of the priorities and intentions specified rather than the organization itself these are worth examining in their own right because, if these are lacking in some way, it is so much harder for the actions the organization takes to be effective or for people to put what they are doing in their everyday work into perspective.

Any statement of business aims needs to make sense at an emotional level

Any statement of business priorities, whether official or informal, needs to make sense at an emotional level and not just in terms of a business analysis, otherwise it will never be implemented in the way that is intended. Human beings implement these intentions so they need to make sense in a human way. This is where the psychological perspective helps, as we can use it to decipher the meaning of any business statement and determine if it makes sense in this deeper way.

A statement about the business aims will create emotional sense to people if it gives them 'something to go on' in terms of how that organization, and the people within it, are supposed to be acting within each of the three areas of experience. The three psychological areas that I have described in the conceptual framework explain the way in which people make sense of their world and their lives. The organization needs, therefore, in any statement about its business or its priorities to provide some indication of how it, and its people, should perform and behave within each area of experience. If it does provide this, it will make emotional sense to people and they will have 'something to go on'. People will know what is expected of them in a subtle and emotional way within that organization rather than only in terms of what business and resource allocation decisions they need to make.

However, there is another reason why any statement of business aims needs to make sense in terms of all three areas of experience. As we have seen, these areas describe actions and aims that are not 'psychological' as such but encompass the normal aims and activities of running a business. Categorizing them in terms of the three areas of experience simply enables us to interpret those ordinary business aims and activities in terms of their implicit psychological significance. One of the key things to look for, then, when we try to decipher any statement of business aims is whether those aims provide some way of actually meeting the

THE PSYCHOLOGICAL MEANING OF STRATEGY

Table 4.1 Key ideas in deciphering the strategy

> you can decipher any business statement in terms of its psychological **significance and meaning**
>
> the strategy needs to make **emotional sense** to people or it will not be implemented properly or as intended
>
> you can decipher any business statement to decipher something about **who** the organization really is

purposes of the three areas of experience. If one of these areas is not implicit in a company's strategic priorities, then the purposes of that area will probably not be met. The organization may, then, fail to project a clear identity and be unable to easily claim its own territory in the market, it may be unable to exert influence or release talent to meet goals or it may be poor at creating genuine engagement with other people and tasks.

What we will be able to determine also, as we try to decipher a statement of business aims, is something about 'who' the organization is, what its nature is, behind the words describing the business orientation. It is possible to do this by reading between the lines and detecting the thinking process behind the explicit statements and specific 'headlines' priorities, because it is the thinking process that will reflect how that organization makes sense both of itself and its world.

Table 4.1 summarizes some of the key factors in the approach to reading between the lines of a strategy statement.

A statement by the chairman of Daimler-Benz

The statement we focus on in this chapter is one made by the chairman of Daimler-Benz, on the business stance and priorities that he believes are necessary in order for that company to be a successful global organization. The statement from the chairman, Jurgen Schrempp, was one published for general publication, rather than the official version within the company. This allows us to see a statement that is designed to communicate to a wide audience. It makes the statement itself more readable and allows us to decipher it more easily. You can, in fact, interpret almost any description of a company's business simply as a member of the public or a shareholder, without having to be part of that company or an insider. Using a generally available news feature, part of a *Financial Times* series on globalization, illustrates what you can decipher about an organization with only this kind of information and with only a small snippet of information. We need to bear in mind that this is only one person's statement, but the deciphering process can be illustrated even so and, in any event, it is usually the case that those at the top of any company do reflect the thinking going on in that organization at a strategic level. We cannot treat the statement as official policy but my purpose was to demonstrate that you can decipher almost any statement about the business in this way. I make no claim to be providing an in-depth view of Daimler-Benz in the analysis and description that follows but simply illustrate a process of reading between the lines.

One reason I use this particular example is that the priorities mentioned by the chairman of Daimler-Benz do reflect the aims of all three areas of experience. What is more, they receive a rather balanced treatment in this statement of business intentions. This is rather unusual, so it forms a good basis to see how a company can strategize in a way that is psychologically complete, yet also be focused in terms of its business aims. And it shows us how a group of seemingly simple words can give people 'something to go on'.

'Five things' to be globally successful

The statement from the chairman of Daimler-Benz (*Financial Times*, 31 October 1997) is set out in Table 4.2. My interpretation of this statement follows this.

Getting an overall impression

Looked at overall, the five priorities set out in the chairman's statement are quite broad and seem to cover many things. At first glance, the chairman appears to ramble a little and the statement lacks a precise set of bullet points, the kind favoured by professional PR groups and communication 'experts'. In this example, however, this is a good thing, as it allows you to 'see through' to what the statement really means. It allows you to conclude that they are quite balanced in their orientation rather than being too narrow. This does not mean that everything will be straightforward and according to plan. On the contrary, it is clear, even from this rather short statement, that they have as many market challenges to face and find answers to as any other company. But it is an example where 'seeing through' with a psychological lens reveals strengths in the strategic orientation that may not be immediately apparent. What we need to keep bearing in mind is that we are focusing only on the aims specified by the chairman and not on how well these

THE PSYCHOLOGICAL MEANING OF STRATEGY

Table 4.2 'Five things' for Daimler-Benz

... globalisation is not an optional strategy, it is the only strategy ... We want to double our turnover and be among the top quartile of global companies in performance. How will we achieve this? We have to do five things.

First, we have to be in the growth markets around the world. We have to have the right products in place. So we are building the M-class in Alabama and the A-class in Brazil, trucks and buses in many parts of the world and aircraft too, because we have to be near the markets we serve.

Second, we want to be a leader in innovation. Only companies which anticipate people's needs, translate great ideas into products and services, and get them into the market fast, will succeed. You only have to look at the transformation of the Mercedes-Benz car and truck ranges in recent years to see what I mean.

The third thing is that it must be exciting and rewarding for our people. We know that globalisation creates jobs both in other countries and in our home market. We have been able to show our unions that for every three jobs we create abroad, we create one in Germany.

But we also have to have the right corporate culture. To be a successful global company we have to find exceptional executives – people who have industrial skills, but can also adapt to local communities – and respond to their needs. So we have to be prepared to transfer people from one place to another and make sure nationality does not play any role. We are not there yet, but we are going in the right direction.

Somebody asked, what is the single most important thing about being a global company? I said being a good corporate citizen and that is the fourth thing. You have to put down roots and make a real contribution to the community – and that takes time.

Then, fifth, you have to have access to global capital. That means listing on the leading stock markets. And it means presenting your financial accounts to the standards of transparency demanded by investors ...

Financial Times, 31 October 1997

are put into practice. In this chapter we are interested only in the aims themselves.

Interpreting the aims by reading between the lines

In what follows, each of the 'five things' specified by the chairman as being necessary if this company is to be globally successful is interpreted in terms of the three areas of experience and the respective psychological natures. The sequence I take you through looks at each of the 'five things' in turn and we interpret each one. In this way, step by step, we build up an interpretation of the whole statement and, by so doing, also develop a picture of all of the psychological natures that are conveyed by the statement itself. One of the key things I draw out is which of the areas of experience seems to be the focus of attention in the organization. The chairman doesn't really spell this out in his statement, but that is precisely the point. What you will see is that you can figure this out anyway, even if they never tell you. In this company we have a positive example since they are clearly engaged with the aim of moving somewhere. With other company strategies or statements about their business, however, the same process of reading between the lines may sometimes tell you that they are not really aiming to move forward even if they say they are. Whichever is the case, the framework of different psychological areas and natures gives us a structure and a set of terms to make sense of what we read.

However, instead of reading the statement as if it told you about the company's business aims, we need to read exactly the same words but understand them in terms of their psychological meaning. We can do this because each one of the 'five things' will contain phrases that are identifiable in terms of their psychological nature. As you read through my own interpretation that follows, you will see which words I have picked up on to tell me about the meaning hidden within the statement and the language it has been expressed in.

The first thing: being in the growth markets around the world

The 'first thing' mentioned by the chairman specifies the importance of the company being 'in the growth markets around the world'. He also talks of having to 'have the right products in place'. How do we interpret such a priority? Primarily it reflects the stance, priorities and thinking process of the Populist. However, the underlying thinking process revealed in this 'first thing' is also that of the Connoisseur. Let me explain which words reveal this.

It is the assumption of the Populist that the way to establish space in the market and project its identity is to expand and, in general, they look at 'markets' first and foremost. That being 'in the growth markets' is the first thing mentioned in the chairman's list suggests that the Populist orientation and focus is important in this company. Another reflection of this nature is the reason he gives of 'needing to be near the markets we serve'. This is the Populist way of thinking because that nature assumes that you create a space and territory in the market by having access to it and by being actively present in it, rather than just by creating and sending wonderful products to sell in it. The fact that he says 'near the markets we serve', therefore, provides clear reinforcement of the business stance of the Populist. However, deciphering a set of strategic aims is more complicated or subtle than that and there will often be a mix of two or three psychological natures in any small section of a strategy. In this 'first thing', there is also quite a strong Connoisseur presence. This is identifiable because the chairman explains this priority with an emphasis on features of the products, not just the features of the markets. An organization that was a much stronger Populist may do exactly the same thing as the chairman is describing, that is, produce one thing in Alabama and another product somewhere else, but they would have explained it with a very different emphasis, that of the nature of the markets with perhaps no reference to products at all. A Populist might give as a rationale, instead, that the company is in Alabama because the market there is expanding rapidly, for example. The sign of the Connoisseur in this part of the statement, therefore, is that the aim, of being 'in the growth markets', is explained with numerous words that refer to different products and not just in terms of being 'near the markets we serve'. Connoisseurs are conscious of 'the market', but their instinctive voice is to talk in terms of products relatively more than markets, because that is how they think. It is their reference point. Populists are conscious of 'products' but their instinctive voice is to talk in terms of markets relatively more because that is their starting point. With the chairman's statement, therefore, we have an interesting reflection of both of the inclusion natures here, with the main explicit priority being the Populist but with a clear Connoisseur way of understanding of the world as well. A more interesting company in terms of these aims than its image might suggest.

  The balance in natures here is quite interesting because this particular company has qualities and an image that are surely more that of the Connoisseur. After all, it is those qualities of being stylish, innovative and reflective that most people would use to characterize this company more than those qualities of the Populist, such as being outgoing, exploring and active. The watchwords for a Connoisseur organization are quality and design rather than those of expansion and marketing which the Populist can be identified by, and the former is how most people would identify Daimler-Benz. So far, and we have interpreted only one of the chairman's five things, he is speaking as a rather different company than we might have expected. Is this priority just an expression of buzz words, then?

  One way you can determine whether this is so is from the unintentional signs and language used. And, in this statement, you can see a very active, get-on-with-it style of the Populist. Look at the way he says 'We have to do five things', for example. He doesn't say 'we have to think about doing . . .', or 'we have to aim for . . .', but simply 'we have to

Table 4.3 Understanding the 'first thing'

> How will we achieve this? **We have to do five things.**
> First, we have to be **in the growth markets** around the **world**. We have to have <u>the right products in place</u>. So we are <u>building the M-class</u> in Alabama and <u>the A-class</u> in Brazil, <u>trucks</u> and <u>buses</u> in **many parts of the world** and <u>aircraft</u> too, because we have to be **near the markets we serve.**
>
> <u>underlining</u> shows the business priorities and ways of thinking of the Connoisseur
> **bold face** shows the business priorities and ways of thinking of the Populist nature.

(get on and) do . . .'. Another clue is the fact that he says five 'things' rather than the more formal way of saying five 'priorities'. This is the more accessible, user-friendly style of the Populist. So, the subtle style here reveals that this is not just a Connoisseur pretending to be a market-oriented, exploring Populist. However, as we move on to explore the chairman's 'second thing' we can identify the Connoisseur nature in its own right, but we need to keep in mind that this builds on the interesting balance we have just seen. You can refer to Table 4.3, which distinguishes between those words that show the business priorities and language of the Populist and those of the Connoisseur in relation to this 'first thing'.

The second thing: a leader in innovation

The 'second thing' of the chairman's statement explaining what is necessary to be a successful global company is to be a 'leader in innovation', which is unmistakeably the province of the Connoisseur. Innovative products, or innovation in general, usually reflect that particular nature. It might seem that most companies would want innovative products or to be a 'leader in innovation'. That is probably true, but they have to choose and prioritize and it is in the trade-offs made that you can detect the implicit psychological nature in the words. If the chairman had conveyed a Populist priority here, he might have referred, instead, to getting widespread distribution channels everywhere, keeping up to date and modernizing or expanding the model range. However, in this 'second thing' the focus on innovation is the stance of the Connoisseur. We can see this Connoisseur style present also in the way the chairman describes with pride the 'transformation' of certain product ranges, which provides for us again the reference point of products. However, we have another interesting sign of the 'dual' inclusion nature in this statement in the idea of needing to 'translate great ideas into products and services'. This expresses the value the Connoisseur places on thought and considered ideas and also the value the Populist places on 'doing' not thinking. You have to 'translate', that is, get the products and services out into the market. On balance, then, we have a statement that suggests the company has aims that are more complicated than its image suggests because these words speak in a clear mix of both Connoisseur and Populist.

So far, all we have found in the chairman's statement are words that define the inclusion stance of the company. But there is something more that we can discern in this part of the statement, which gives us our first sight of an aspect of the control area. The chairman also conveys in this 'second thing' a belief in certain work practices that reflect the approach of a Juggler. This is shown, for example, in the idea of the company 'anticipating' customers' needs and getting to market 'fast'. The word 'anticipating' is a key Juggler one and reflects one of the main ways in which this nature establishes a sense of being in control. This nature also places great emphasis on speed and being fast, because that is how they ensure the successful attainment of goals. These two phrases describe the means of achieving the primary aim of being a leader in innovation, so they suggest that the chairman believes that the company needs to use the expertise and style of the Juggler in order to attain this main goal. Another small sign of the Juggler is the way the chairman says that we 'only have to look... to see what I mean'. This is the Juggler way of making sense of things and providing 'proof' to others, by immediate and qualitative information.

So, in this 'second thing' we can see clear evidence of the Connoisseur priorities and ways of thinking and a touch of the Populist. And, in this section, we have been able to get a view of one aspect of the control area, which was the Juggler. The words in the 'second thing' that reveal these two natures are shown in Table 4.4. As we proceed step by step through the 'five things' we will start to create a more complete picture of the meaning in the whole statement.

Table 4.4 Understanding the 'second thing'

... Second, we want to be a <u>leader in innovation</u>. Only companies which **anticipate** people's needs, *translate* <u>great ideas into products and services</u>, and *get them into the market* **fast**, will succeed. **You only have to look** at <u>the transformation of the Mercedes-Benz car and truck ranges</u> in recent years **to see what I mean**.

underlining shows the business priorities and ways of thinking of the Connoisseur
italics shows the business priorities and ways of thinking of the Populist
bold face shows the business priorities and ways of thinking of the Juggler nature

The third thing: 'exciting and rewarding for our people', 'creating jobs', 'exceptional executives' and 'the right corporate culture'

The 'third thing' in the chairman's statement is by far the longest and most complex. From it, however, we can start to develop a more complete sense of the overall meaning in the statement. We have, so far, been drawn primarily to an understanding of the stance within the inclusion area because the chairman has focused on aims that reflect, in psychological terms, the intended way for the company to claim space in the market, interact with the outside world and project a distinctive identity. These, of course, are the province of the inclusion area and so the psychological natures that have received our attention have been the Connoisseur and the Populist. In this 'third thing', however, the chairman shifts ground completely. While this is not at all apparent if you are interpreting the words only in terms of their business significance, it is clear if you look at their psychological significance because what he starts to describe are aims that describe how the organization should engage with others, how people should behave, the values that exist to assess people and how the organization should sustain itself for the long term. The chairman does not mention any of these particular 'aims' but we can decipher them nevertheless and they bring us to the affection area. In what follows, therefore, we can start to build up a picture of aims that reflect the affection area.

The Attractor nature is reflected in several places, such as in the reference to creating an organization that is 'exciting and rewarding for our people'. There are many other words that could have been used here in place of 'exciting', such as challenging, interesting, stretching or motivating, all of which would have suggested the Professional nature instead. The word 'exciting' conveys a sense of a higher level of intensity and emotion and is something an Attractor organization would be comfortable with, and need. The chairman also uses the word 'rewarding', which suggests the Professional since this nature wants an instrumental exchange with the organization, to know that they get something back for what they give. This is a very different 'relationship' with the organization than the Attractor employees have. However, the indication that this whole phrase still conveys the Attractor nature is that the phrase refers to what is needed 'for our people'. The Professional nature would have been revealed, on the other hand, by a phrase that said 'exciting and rewarding jobs'.

We can see this Attractor nature again in the reference to 'creating jobs', which is always a priority for this nature. Here, the chairman seems at pains to justify the practice of locating jobs abroad rather than at home. We hear nothing here about technology saving the organization, or the hard work and professionalism of managers, which would have reflected an explicit commitment to the Professional way of thinking.

The need to have the 'right corporate culture' is another Attractor concern, although this phrase has become one that is often used with little real meaning behind it. It is always necessary to decipher what it is that is considered 'right' in that culture, and in the explanation of what this corporate culture should consist of we can decipher two meanings, one reflecting the stance of the Professional and the other the Attractor. The Professional is evident in the need for 'exceptional executives' who are defined in terms of their 'industrial skills'. These are factors that a Professional, but not an Attractor, values in people within the organization because, to the Professional, what is important is technical skills, abilities, executive standing. However, the other necessary qualities in these exceptional executives is that they 'adapt to local communities' and 'respond to their needs', which takes us back to the Attractor nature. We see the Professional in another small way as well in the very straightforward and revealing way in which he says 'we are not there yet'. This is a sign of openness, an aspect of the affection area of experience, which describes the manner in which people engage with others, and the businesslike way in which he comes out with this shows you the Professional more than the Attractor.

However, there is one more feature to take account of in this rather complex 'third thing'. There is great emphasis here on the fact that the company moves people from one country to another, and the essential factor in doing so is that nationality does not play a role in the way such people behave. Transferring people from one place to another can be understood to reflect the Populist but the essential point here is the description of the way in which these transferred people should behave. This 'tells' you that he is describing something that has a significance for the way people should behave in the affection area. Such an approach reveals the way that a Professional thinks, that is, that people are supposed to get on with the task and engage with others in a way that is divorced from personal attributes. To ignore nationality implies that those particular personal attributes should be secondary to general attributes others have. The Attractor assumption, instead, would be that the appropriate way to engage is to include all personal attributes and that these are paramount to general characteristics, such as nationality.

On balance, therefore, we have in this 'third thing' a reasonably equal weighting given to both affection natures but possibly with the dominance given to the Attractor. This particular mix of natures is, however, a little more confused than the Connoisseur and Populist combination and, if you look at this whole section describing the 'third thing', it is constructed of opposites that are not easily contained in the

94 READING THE MIND OF THE ORGANIZATION

same whole. However, we have more to this statement which, as you will see, can shed light on its overall affection meaning.

The third thing: the style and language

What makes this section more believable than most strategic statements is that the chairman describes these priorities in quite a detailed way. It is in this area of the statement that he elaborates the most and describes some of the real-life complexity that goes into creating an organization that is 'exciting and rewarding for its people' and having the 'right corporate culture'. I find it interesting that the chairman rambles a bit at this point. This makes the statement sound like something more than just a 'bullet point' list of five things that the company thinks it ought to say for the purposes of giving the right presentation. Whenever a company or person is more open and revealing rather than seeming to be reciting from a prepared script, you will usually be able to detect the meaning of what is being said more readily. In the statement, the chairman is 'talking out loud' some of the issues and concerns involved in this area of experience.

Table 4.5 sets out the words illustrating these two affection natures implicit in the 'third thing'.

Table 4.5 Understanding the 'third thing'

... The third thing is that it must be **exciting and rewarding for our people**. We know that globalisation **creates jobs** both in other countries and in our home market. We have been able to show our unions that for every three jobs we create abroad, we create one in Germany.

But we also have to have the **right corporate culture**. To be a successful global company we have to find <u>exceptional executives</u> – people who have <u>industrial skills</u>, but can also **adapt to local communities** and **respond to their needs**. So we have to be prepared to transfer people from one place to another and <u>make sure nationality does not play any role</u>. <u>We are not there yet</u>, but we are going in the right direction.

bold face shows the business priorities and ways of thinking of the Attractor
underlining shows the business priorities and ways of thinking of the Professional

The fourth thing: being a good corporate citizen

The 'fourth thing' is the only part of the chairman's list that reveals only one psychological nature and that is the Attractor. This is apparent in several ways. Note that this is, in fact, his 'first priority', the one he thinks is the 'single most important thing'. And it is this that 'answers' the question implicit in the 'third thing', which is what, if anything, is the dominant affection nature in the statement, for it is clearly the Attractor. The Attractor nature is partly revealed in the simplicity of this 'fourth thing', where he needs to state only the essence of his idea. Further, his reference point is not an aspect of the business, or what he thinks they should achieve, but a personal conversation, 'Somebody asked', which shows the personal direct style of the Attractor. Further, the content of the priority itself is clearly the Attractor, and reflects the idea of this nature having a purpose that is more than just a business. 'Being a good corporate citizen' is a phrase that reflects that deeper assumption. However, it is a phrase that can easily be used by companies so we need to probe. One way you can tell that the aim reflects a real Attractor nature, apart from the points I have mentioned already, is the use of telling words like 'real', 'roots' and the reference to taking 'time'. Only the Attractor would draw attention to the latter, especially in a business statement. Overall, then, this most important and simple priority is nothing else but an Attractor.

Table 4.6 sets out the words that reveal the psychological nature apparent in this 'fourth thing'.

Table 4.6 Understanding the 'fourth thing'

> ... **Somebody asked**, what is the **single most important thing** about being a global company? **I said being a good corporate citizen** and that is the fourth thing. You have to **put down roots** and make a **real contribution** to the **community** – and that takes **time**.
>
> **bold face shows the business priorities and ways of thinking of the Attractor**

The fifth thing: access to global capital

We have, so far, been able to build up a picture that helps us clarify both the inclusion and affection stances implicit in the meaning of this statement. We have not received the same clarity or attention to the control area and it is not until this last and 'fifth thing' that we do so. We have seen already the presence of the Juggler. However, in this last section it is the Boss that is expressed very clearly and, on balance, we can see that this is the dominant control nature expressed in this statement overall. You can see this in several places. It is primarily evident in the main point, the need to have 'access to global capital' in the 'leading stock markets'. This reflects a view that it is very important to have leverage, provided by capital. The meaning here is that the company wants the means to attain power. Psychologically, that is why a company wants access to resources. The chairman could have specified priorities that reflected the Juggler approach instead. If he had, these would have appeared in terms such as wanting people in the company to be more resourceful or to use resources in a different way, or assertions that the company needed to make a priority out of 'taking advantage of opportunities that flash by' or being 'entrepreneurial', and so on. No doubt these are some of the things that the chairman would want to occur in the company anyway. But you can only have a few such aims and objectives, and the priorities the chairman actually chose reflect an emphasis on the Boss approach to resources and capital, instead. The Boss assumption is that power comes from resources, which give the organization the self-confidence that it can attain its own goals.

Seeing the Boss nature in the style of the statement

Another way in which you can read the Boss nature in what has been set out is in the style rather than the exact priorities themselves. Notice that the style is quite definitive. The chairman has a clear idea of exactly what he thinks is necessary. Jugglers would frame the whole thing as a set of options that will likely change. He starts with the idea that globalization is 'not an optional strategy, but the only one'. This is a Boss speaking, quite clear and sure of what they want and where they are heading. In speaking like this, they create a feeling of reassurance, which is one of the aims of this control nature. Another small feature that tells you that you are reading the statement of a Boss is that the chairman makes sense of things by making them quantitative. This is the kind of data a Boss organization needs in order to feel in control. For example, he refers to 'double our turnover', the 'top quartile' and 'five things'. A Juggler may sometimes rely on quantitative data to set the tone and make key points but on the whole is less likely to do so. They will refer, instead, to some qualitative data, to a customer who has just told them they need this rather than that.

The last word goes to the Attractor

However, we are not left with only the control area of experience in this 'fifth thing' because the chairman takes us on to describing how the

Table 4.7 Understanding the 'fifth thing'

... globalization is **not an optional strategy**, it is **the only strategy** ...
We want to **double** our turnover and be among the **top quartile** of global companies in performance. How will we achieve this? We have to do **five** things.
... Then, fifth, you have to have **access to global capital**. That means listing on the **leading stock markets**: And it means presenting your financial accounts to the <u>standards of transparency demanded by investors</u> ...

bold face shows the business priorities and ways of thinking of the Boss
<u>underlining shows the business priorities and ways of thinking of the Attractor</u>

organization should engage with others and meet their needs, which relates to the affection area. It may not seem like this is the case on the surface, but the phrase referring to presenting accounts in a way that is 'transparent' in order to meet the needs and 'standards of investors' is telling us how the company should reveal itself to others and why. The manner in which this engagement should occur is to be open, indeed, to be transparent. And the reason for this is in order to meet others' (investors) needs and expectations. One way or another, we can decipher the hidden significance of one of the affection natures here. Which is the Attractor even though the superficial context is the businesslike domain of the Professional. This is so because the emphasis is on complete openness in order to meet others' needs whereas the Professional is always slightly less open than an Attractor and is certainly uncomfortable with 'transparency'.

So we return to the same nature which explained the chairman's 'single most important thing', which is the Attractor. Now, if you were like myself when you started to read the words of a statement from Daimler-Benz, you would never have expected to see hidden within such an innocent group of words such a dominant Attractor nature. But, if you read between the lines rather than take them at face value, that is indeed the primary nature signified within this whole statement.

Table 4.7 sets out the aspects of the statement which show the Boss priorities, ways of thinking and style as well as the phrases that reflect the Attractor. With this table we have built up, step by step, a picture of the significance hidden in the whole.

People have been given 'something to go on'

The statement we have just explored illustrates how you can translate the psychological meaning implicit in an organization's strategy. We can tell little from such a short statement about how good the company actually is within each area of experience. However, the statement does provide an example where the priorities do reflect all three. People inside and outside the organization are given a signal by any statement like this. In this particular case, they have a signal about which is the appropriate way to fulfil the inclusion purpose of the organization and the kind of interactions and identity the company wants, which is the balance between the Connoisseur and Populist natures that we saw at the start. People have also been given a sense of what is considered the appropriate way of attaining a sense of control and effectiveness, in this instance through a Boss approach primarily but with some of the Juggler specified as well. Finally, people in the organization have been given a signal about what the appropriate manner of relationships is in the organization, as well as what stance is considered necessary to sustain the organization for the long term. Here, the preference is for the Attractor nature more than the Professional.

Since the statement is felt, if not literally read, in this way, since these meanings are all implicit not explicit, it is a much more effective set of 'five things' than it may seem at first glance. It needs, of course, to be translated into activities that reflect the same mix and balance but, as it is, it provides the clarity and meaning to make emotional sense as well as intellectual sense. People inside and outside the organization have been given 'something to go on'. Figure 4.1 shows the meaning implicit in the statement, expressed in terms of the psychological natures that we could discern.

Development in the organization

It is possible to determine as well, from reading between the lines of the statement, what some of the areas of development might be in the company. In terms of the three areas of experience, these would primarily be the inclusion and affection areas because of the complexity we could identify in the mix or balance of the natures that characterize those areas. What this means is that the decisions and priorities that were relevant to those two areas would be the ones the organization is likely to be spending most time on. They are likely to be the focus of change and of debates. Note that it is possible that it is the control area which should receive most attention in the organization but there was no sign

THE PSYCHOLOGICAL MEANING OF STRATEGY 99

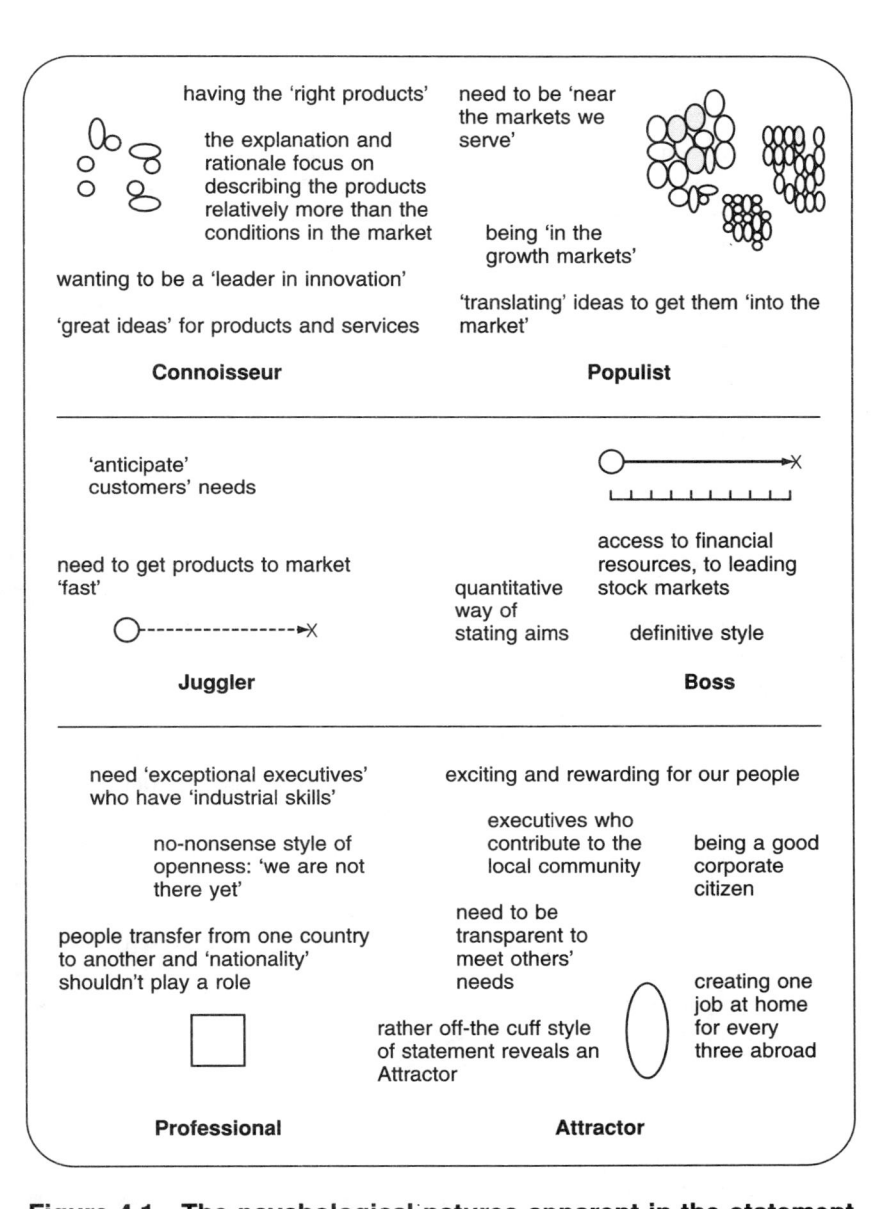

having the 'right products' the explanation and rationale focus on describing the products relatively more than the conditions in the market wanting to be a 'leader in innovation' 'great ideas' for products and services **Connoisseur**	need to be 'near the markets we serve' being 'in the growth markets' 'translating' ideas to get them 'into the market' **Populist**
'anticipate' customers' needs need to get products to market 'fast' **Juggler**	quantitative way of stating aims access to financial resources, to leading stock markets definitive style **Boss**
need 'exceptional executives' who have 'industrial skills' no-nonsense style of openness: 'we are not there yet' people transfer from one country to another and 'nationality' shouldn't play a role **Professional**	exciting and rewarding for our people executives who contribute to the local community need to be transparent to meet others' needs rather off-the cuff style of statement reveals an Attractor being a good corporate citizen creating one job at home for every three abroad **Attractor**

Figure 4.1 The psychological natures apparent in the statement

in the chairman's statement (assuming this has some relevance to the company itself) that the control area is actually undergoing real change.

One thing a psychological perspective can add to our understanding is the insight that many seemingly disparate business activities and aims are linked by the attempt at meeting exactly the same underlying goal. Another benefit is that the perspective tells you what is needed at a deeper level than the organization often assumes is necessary in order to genuinely address the strategic situation and opportunities it is faced with. In what follows, therefore, I explain what the issues might be that would be, or should be, the focus of attention and probable development in the company.

Beyond an exclusive reliance on their Connoisseur nature

One of the main things that we could discern was that there was a clear Populist nature as well as a clear Connoisseur nature in the strategic aims. This means that the way in which this organization should be claiming space *vis-à-vis* others in the market and creating a distinctive identity for itself would reflect the features and qualities of both natures. You can predict, however, that the Connoisseur is probably a more long-standing one for this company. It is possible, however, that the strategic priorities expressed by the chairman, reflecting a balanced mix of the two natures, are still reflected in the company's intentions more than the reality. Either way, the fact that both natures can be identified in this statement is not a bad thing. It is, in fact, a key sign of health if a company shows flexibility and development and that they are not rigidly stuck in a mould in terms of their aims.

However, the image and reputation of the company probably come as much from the Connoisseur nature as from any other and so one of the tasks that you might expect to exist in this company is to establish in the minds of others that such a change, psychological and business wise, has taken place or is taking place. Within the organization, the task would be to ensure that this dual nature is reflected in the various work practices, types of people and overall stance as well as in the aims. You need to bear in mind also, however, that, at heart, this is almost certainly still a Connoisseur organization relatively more than a Populist one. The task, therefore, would be to develop the stance of the Populist while at the same time keeping the Connoisseur as the psychological asset that it already is and has been. Remember that an organization does not have to be either, it can be both, so long as it knows what it is doing.

A lot of the dynamic and debates are probably engaged in determining how to function in terms of these two natures. That is, how to adopt the Populist business approach without losing the Connoisseur. Specifically, this would emerge in questions such as how to interact more widely and have more open boundaries and have more mass-market products, without losing the company's class, their high-quality production or their focused marketing approach, and so on. Their classy products need to make use of the Populist ways of getting access to markets, for example.

The real focus of time and energy seems to be the affection area

The definitiveness with which the relative balance between the Connoisseur and Populist natures was articulated in the priorities specified in the chairman's statement, as well as the clarity with which they were described, suggests that, while this may be an ongoing source of management attention within Daimler-Benz in terms of specific business decisions, it would not actually be the main focus of energy in the company. The clarity probably reflects the fact that they have long ago 'bitten the bullet' on this one and instead of being focused on deciding whether to make a shift to a more Populist approach, the questions and debates in the organization are about how to do so. Usually, you can predict what the main focus of attention is in an organization by detecting the area of experience, or the kind of issues, where the organization 'spends most time' or where it describes issues in most depth or detail. In the list of 'five things' itemized in the chairman's statement, this was clearly the affection area, so you can predict that this is the area in the organization that really draws people's energy and attention and is interesting to them. There is nothing wrong with this. Indeed, if you cannot read something like this implicit in a statement or description of a company's business, then they have either ceased to actively engage with the natural ongoing development of the business and are just going though the motions, or the statement, whatever it is, has been so wordsmithed by the experts that all the real interest has been taken out of it. The danger, when you see this kind of extensive wordsmithing, is that this same approach may be pervasive, and will have taken the life out of the organization as well.

The kind of issue that would receive attention and be a focus for action as well as debate would revolve around how to express their affection nature either in a better way or in new ways. They would be focused on what is appropriate to sustain the organization for the long term. Time and attention would be drawn to things like ensuring loyalty, real commitment and trust. Another key focus might be how generous to be within the organization itself, because maintaining sources of comfort are often seen as necessary in order to get commitment and productive work out of people. You can see this focus of attention on the affection area quite clearly in the chairman's statement, especially in relation to the 'third thing'. The deeper question implicit in such a focus, and which the organization would be trying to answer, is what their real purpose is, especially over the long term. The answer to this question is the essence of the affection area and any organization that has a strong focus on this area of experience will be continually trying to provide answers and solutions that meet this need for a sense of the company's real purpose. The reason why this becomes a concern is because it leads directly to benefits such as great commitment, belief in the organization and feelings of trust.

Seeing the connection in various debates

Where the expression of any psychological area is trying to be updated or improved in an organization, the different issues that surface are often seen as distinct, separate issues. However, they stem from the same source, the fact that the organization is attempting to better fulfil that particular purpose of the organization, or is adjusting its ways of doing so. A psychological interpretation tells you why debates and attempts at change are occurring and what they are really trying to answer for the organization. This will be not be resolved by a single decision or action, and until the organization has settled within its own mind a new way to fulfil whatever that particular purpose of the organization is, the debates and attempts to try new things will not go away. However, when there is a resolution at this fundamental level, where the organization forges a new answer or way for itself that makes psychological sense, it is very apparent. There is a quite distinct sense of the organization breathing a sigh of relief, of letting go of the questioning and moving on, typically to the next round of concerns. Usually, these will relate to another one of the three areas of experience. The conceptual framework helps you detect what the organization is trying to resolve in its various debates at any particular time.

Comparing this statement with that made by other companies

One thing to bear in mind is that most companies do not 'speak' in the voice of all three of the psychological areas and they can often specify the business aims of the control area only. When this occurs, the implications are that the organization will have been given a set of guidelines that, in themselves, miss both the inclusion and affection areas of experience. In other words, the organization will have a set of aims that show

THE PSYCHOLOGICAL MEANING OF STRATEGY

no way of projecting the identity of the organization and claiming a kind of innate space or territory in the market, and nor will the organization have been shown some way of achieving the aims of the affection area such as establishing loyalty, honesty and creating genuine engagement with people and tasks.

Such organizations may well think that they have provided priorities and business goals that will lead to such aims being met, but they are belied by this process of reading between the lines to determine the psychological significance and meaning of what is said or written. When the above scenario occurs, the organization as a whole either responds faithfully to the strategic guidance that has been given and so fails to meet the aims we can associate with the inclusion and affection areas, partly because the systems, resourcing decisions and work practices fail to reflect such aims as well. Alternatively, it is left to the troops down below to 'make up' for this deficit in the strategic aims but, when this is the case, people in the organization have to buck the system and are always having to break the mould set in train by their incomplete strategic objectives. You can see, therefore, how the process of reading between the lines is not done for the purposes of seeing what has been left out but to help an organization (or senior group) understand the deeper and follow-on implications of its strategy and business aims. Most organizations do not wilfully intend to ignore such aims as can be described by the inclusion and affection areas so they merely need to be shown a way to 'translate' their business words into their implicit meaning. Showing you how to do so has been the purpose of this chapter and in the next we move on to a context that allows you to figure out these things about the organization yourself.

Some questions to help you work with the organization

CHAPTER 5

Taking stock of the organization

Our usual means of assessing organizations is with a financial or strategic perspective. While this serves a valid business purpose, it is inadequate at providing the kind of measurement or assessment that allows you to figure out 'who' the organization is, whether it has the innate presence needed to claim space easily in the market, whether it truly exerts influence and power in a healthy, natural way or is secretly ill at ease with power, and whether the organization is genuinely engaging with its tasks and with people or just going through the motions and appearance of doing so. These are aims that, as we have seen in the preceding chapters, can be identified with the three areas of experience of the organization and, while these are part of a psychological approach, they clearly represent objectives that form part of many organizations' implicit but not expressed aims for the organization. In this chapter, we 'take a break' and take stock of the organization using a series of questions that allow you to figure out for yourself whether any organization is meeting these aims, how well it does so and which psychological natures it uses to do so.

Using the three components: seeing through, the psychological perspective and taking account of subtle connections

You can use the series of questions to think about the organization, both in terms of evaluating it in terms of the three psychological purposes, and describing 'who' it is in terms of the different psychological natures. The questions are aimed at getting people to stop and think, to take psychological stock of what they are doing to the organization and what they should be doing to it if it is to function well in terms both of its business aims as well as its internal health. We take stock in this way at this point in the book because, so far, our focus has been on explaining the organization in terms of these three purposes and the corresponding natures but, from this chapter, the tone of the book changes fundamentally. In the second half we focus on the more subtle aspects of organizations like feelings and perceptions, as well as reading the signs of change that help you move the organization forward. So it makes sense to pause at this point, to stand back and consider the organization as a whole. However, you can, of course, also make use of the questions once you have finished the whole book.

The purpose of the questions

In what follows, you will be able to calculate various 'scores', to work out whether an organization is a Connoisseur or a Populist in the way it projects itself, a Juggler or a Boss in the way it exerts control and a Professional or an Attractor in the way it engages in relationships. However, doing this is only a means to an end. The goal is not to categorize organizations into 'types'. Every organization is too complex to be described with a few names. The 'scores', and the names, help only because they give some shape to, and make sense of, the complexity and so that you can think about the whole. But, the overall purpose of doing this is to help you figure out how best to meet the organization's business and psychological aims, not to put a 'label' on the organization.

Uses to put the questions to

The questions can be used in a wide range of ways. You might, for example, want to understand what the differences and similarities are between different parts of one organization, or between different organizations who need to work together. Often, separate organizations, or parts of one organization, take too little account of how they work together. They focus only on the business decisions and goals, and avoid constructive discussion about how they are doing things, about the subtle differences in assumptions and approach that different units have. You can use the questions to put words to such things, and gain some objectivity. The effects of many of the decisions and actions we take in organizations can also be monitored in terms of their psychological meaning and impact. The questions can help you think through what those effects and implications are.

The series of questions can be used to help you figure out your own organization, individual parts of it that you want to understand in more depth or to figure out another organization entirely. You can use them on customers, on competitors, on a company that your own organization is thinking of having a strategic alliance with, acquiring or supplying, and so on. They help you stand back and take a longer view, to see the organization as if you were seeing it for the first time.

Keeping the organization in one piece during change

One constructive way to take stock of the organization is in situations where we need to understand the deeper and more hidden impact that another organization, a team of consultants or a change process has on the organization. We could see the need for this clearly in the example which I started with in Chapter 1, the financial insurance company. One of the themes was that some of the uniqueness of that company was lost during a process re-engineering project. Part of the reason was that different psychological natures existed between the consulting team called in to advise on, and run, the project and the company itself. Another was the arrogance of the group in the company as well as the project team that had greater corporate power over the rest of the organization. This is a problem in any organization where there is an assumption that one of the ways of achieving each of the three psychological purposes is superior to the other. One of the main benefits of using the questions, and the conceptual framework, is that they help to stop this kind of imposition of another 'way' on to either the whole organization, or on to one smaller part of an organization by another part.

It is clear that, if one organization or team of consultants tries to make the other the 'same nature' as itself, rather than working productively with the organization or part of it that is different, it will lead to an inevitable degree of disruption. The implication is that, instead of focusing on whether or not one party or organization is fulfilling its aims, the analysis is, instead, focused only on whether each party is the same as the other. The group with more power may attempt to impose its own 'way' on the other part of the organization irrespective of how well the latter is actually performing. What will arise will be a survival reaction, since it is the case that the 'way' of one organization (or business area) is being annihilated or eradicated. If an organization is having to become a Populist when it used to be a Connoisseur, for example, it is experienced as the death of an identity. The same will be true if an organization that functions with all the style and business stance of a Populist is 'forced' to behave in a Connoisseur way, even though it is fulfilling the aims of the inclusion area perfectly adequately. The reaction that arises in such organizations is confusion and fierce resistance, and so it should. The feeling of annihilation is the psychological meaning of attempts to change the nature of an organization, or a part of it, for no other reason than an innate bias on the part of a group, or a team of consultants who have not understood that their way is just one means to achieve an end. Understanding such situations in terms of their psychological meaning explains why some organizations experience great resistance to changing. The reaction can be understood more easily as an attempt to retain their way of being.

Of course, sometimes organizations need to make this degree of change in fundamental nature however, in order to survive or remain successful in a changing market. What is helpful is to be able to determine how much change is actually necessary, or whether the attempt to create such change is dictated by this kind of bias on the part of one business area, group, or team of consultants or advisers in the company. Usually, some change in any organization is always necessary, but we need to fine tune our judgement about the need for it and the extent of it more accurately than we do. Working out the psychological meaning and implications of what is happening within and to the organization can be one use of the series of questions that follow. Resistance in an organization rarely occurs in a serious way when people know that a fundamental change in nature is necessary for business reasons. When they sense that this is the case, they often just get on and do it, that is, change. Change is much easier if the implications of what the organization is doing are identified and understood which is one of the uses of the series of questions.

Working it out for yourself

Working these things out for yourself allows you to predict, or think through, the implications that any actions and decisions will have for the organization. At base, the questions are a means of making more conscious and deliberate what we are doing in organizations, so that we can predict the consequences.

The first stage: assessing how well the organization is fulfilling the aims of the three areas of experience

There is a separate set of questions for each of the three areas of experience and purposes. The first set focuses on how successful the organization is in creating an identity, establishing presence, claiming space and interacting across the boundaries of the organization. This assesses the organization in relation to the aims of the inclusion area. The second set focuses on the organization in terms of its effectiveness at achieving goals, releasing talent and expressing its power. This assesses the organization in relation to the aims of the control area. The third set is aimed at assessing whether the organization engages genuinely with others and sustains relationships, as well as itself, for the long term and whether it causes others to believe in it, trust it and remain committed to it. This assesses the organization in relation to the aims of the affection area.

The second stage: describing 'who' the organization is

The second stage in this overall process of taking stock of the organization is to get an idea of 'who' the organization is, its psychological natures. These describe the way in which the organization is trying to fulfil the purposes of each of the three areas. When you work through these questions, you will end up with scores that suggest the organization is relatively more of a Connoisseur or a Populist, or somewhere in between, in the way it functions in the inclusion area. You will do the same to determine your view of whether the organization is relatively more of a Juggler or a Boss, or somewhere in between, in the way it functions in the control area. You will also get scores that reflect your view of whether it is more of a Professional or an Attractor, or somewhere in between, in terms of the way it engages with others and sustains relationships.

Remembering the purpose

One of the key factors to keep bearing in mind is that the different psychological natures exist for a purpose. They should never be thought of as only a kind of personality or 'type'. When people think like that they end up thinking only of six different kinds of organizations, so start your analysis of any of the three areas of experience with the overriding question of whether or how well the organization is achieving the purpose of that particular area. This is the context with which to figure out what the organization is doing, how well it is doing it and what the psychological natures of the organization turn out to be.

For example, when looking at the inclusion aims, instead of thinking just of whether the organization is a Connoisseur or a Populist, focus on the purpose of this area and whether this is being met. Within that context, you can figure out whether the particular psychological nature is helping or getting in the way of meeting that purpose. Your evaluation of an organization should only ever be linked with this underlying purpose or reason for being, rather than just in terms of the organization being a Connoisseur or Populist. Out of context this kind of analysis is meaningless. Remember also that, in any case, there is a continuum implicit between the Connoisseur and Populist natures. Consequently, you need not feel constrained to interpret the organization as being exclusively one or the other. Using these terms simply helps you put the organization into perspective.

You might decide that the organization needs more of the Populist approach, for example, in order to meet the aims more easily or successfully, or you may decide that it is fine as it is. All these kinds of questions are more easily thought about if they have some kind of container or structure, which is the purpose of this chapter.

None of the answers to this part of the process have any relevance to working out the implications of whether and how well the organization is meeting the aims of the control area of experience. Once you have decided how well the organization is doing so, you can figure out whether its nature, or means of fulfilling this aim, is a Juggler or Boss. They can be analysed in terms of how appropriate that particular nature is for the organization, whether that style of control is changing, how real it is or whether it is intended but not realized in the organization. You can also explore how well the approach works in terms of establishing the kind of influence the organization needs in its market-place, whether some of the Juggler needs to be added to some of the Boss, or the other way around.

Remember also that, just as with the Connoisseur and Populist, there is a continuum implicit between the Juggler and Boss. Again, you need not feel constrained to interpret the organization as being exclusively one or the other, but, if there is a mix of natures, you need to assess whether that is a positive mix with both styles of control working well together or whether the mix is just a confused muddle that does not help the organization to better meet the aims of the control area.

The same approach applies to the affection area and its aims. Here, the purpose is entirely different. It is neither to ensure control nor establish presence, but to establish a manner of engaging with people and tasks that is genuine so that people believe in the organization, trust it and relationships are positive. These two natures here, the Professional and the Attractor, are the ways the organization meets the aims of this area of experience. You may decide that the organization needs more of the Professional nature, with its businesslike professionalism. Or, you may decide that more of the Attractor approach is needed in order to foster more creativity and deep commitment. You may, of course, decide that the organization is just fine as it is and that its 'ways' need to be cultivated, nourished and given time and attention.

Once you have figured out what the nature is, or where the organization sits along the continuum between the Professional and Attractor, you can figure out whether that is what the organization should be doing, whether there are misfits with what it thought it was doing, or whether it is exactly what is needed for the organization at that time.

QUESTIONS TO UNDERSTAND THE ORGANIZATION

The first series of questions: evaluating how well the organization is fulfilling the three purposes

The first stage in the process is to determine how well the organization is meeting the aims of the three areas of experience, and the questions that will help you consider this are set out in Questionnaire 5.1 (the inclusion aims), Questionnaire 5.2 (the control aims) and Questionnaire 5.3 (the affection aims).

However, before considering these questions, let me give you some other guidelines, which I call 'golden rules'. The range of questions you can ask to evaluate the organization in this way are immense. You can be creative yourself and add whatever other questions you think are appropriate when you evaluate it in terms of the three areas. Often people want to know what is 'the right way to be'. Needless to say, there is no such thing. Every organization has its own unique needs and ways. So, determining how 'good' the organization is can only ever make sense in context.

Five golden rules

There are, however, a number of golden rules I use. These come from seeing what works best in practice, and they are summarized in Table 5.1. I have included them here only because they help people get started. Even if you want to use other criteria to evaluate the organization, these five will usually help you think up which ones you want to use instead.

Table 5.1 Five golden rules

One	the organization needs to **know who** it is, be aware of what it is doing
Two	the organization needs to have a **clear** way of functioning in each area of experience
Three	the organization needs to be **flexible**, able to change its way of functioning in each area
Four	the organization needs to have finesse and **fine-tune** its approach in each area
Five	the organization needs to have **true**, genuine solutions to the requirements of each area

The need for an organization to know what it is doing, to be aware of itself

The first golden rule I have is that the organization needs to be aware of what it is like, what it is actually doing, to be conscious of itself and its ways. This can be referred to in other terms, of course, but one golden rule for a successful and smoothly functioning organization is that it sees through itself, and is conscious both of who it is and what it (really) does. This implies that the organization knows what its psychological or intangible assets are and keeps them as a vital functioning part of the company.

The need for a way to function within each of the three areas of experience

The second golden rule is that the organization should have the means to function well within each of the three areas of experience. This means that you should be able to identify some activities, aims, priorities and a style that can be characterized as part of the inclusion, control and affection areas. Otherwise there will be a weak spot in the organization. These ways of functioning need not be, for example, exclusively 'Connoisseur' or 'Populist'. You can have a definite mix of the two but you need to think about whether any such mix is simply a confused muddle or a productive integration of the best of both worlds. You will, in any event, be able to figure out which is the case by the guidelines within the tables that tell you if the organization is meeting or failing to meet the aims within each area.

The need for the organization to be flexible not rigid in its approach

The third golden rule follows from this second one. The organization needs to be able to change. Sometimes the market dictates this as a business necessity, and when this is the case, the organization needs to have the flexibility to do so. In any of the three areas of experience, if the organization fails to add some of the opposite nature to its existing nature when it needs to, it remains rigid. This rule requires that the organization has the psychological capacity to alter what it does and the way it does things.

The need for the organization to be able to fine-tune and show finesse

This flexibility needs to be monitored, however, and we need to bear in mind that organizations often try wholesale change when it is unnecessary. This brings us to the fourth golden rule, which is that the organization can discriminate and fine-tune what it does. The organization needs to have some psychological finesse and to be clever in what it changes and how it does so. We can think of discrimination and fine-tuning in another way too, that the organization needs to use the right means for the right ends. This means that an organization needs to avoid adopting a solution or taking action that can be associated with one area of experience when it should be using a solution or action that belongs to another area. If it does adopt such a wrong solution, it will be unable to meet the aims of that area of experience.

The organization needs to be genuine and not just give the appearance of acting and deciding

The fifth golden rule is almost a summary of all five. It is that the organization should function well in each area of experience in a real, true way rather than superficially. It is easy to evaluate an organization in broad terms. The important thing, however, is to be absolutely clear and penetrating in your assessment of whether the organization is really achieving the aims of each area or just going through the motions. Does the organization really deal with the requirements of each area or does it just appear to do so by doing all the right things on the surface?

These five golden rules are merely my own conclusions. You can use them if they are of assistance to you, or you can feel free to create any other golden rules that help you make sense of your own organization and help it function better.

The second series of questions: describing 'who' the organization is

Five sections to describe the organization's nature

The three areas of experience of the organization include a wide range of aspects of the business. The number of aspects that we could analyse in this way is endless. However, in order to ensure that the process is comprehensible and easy to grasp, I limit myself to five aspects of the organization in the questions that follow. These provide the best mix to enable you to get a view of the organization. There is a separate section to think about the key qualities that most define the organization, its business stance and philosophy including the beliefs held about what will really make the organization successful, intangible and subtle features that most people assume don't matter but do matter, beliefs and values about what counts in the approach to work, and assumptions about customers and what they want from the organization.

Determining the organization's psychological nature

You can fill out a separate set of questions for each of the three areas. In other words, you will be assessing whether the organization's inclusion nature is a Connoisseur or Populist or somewhere in between first, in terms of each of the five sections I have outlined above. You can then determine whether the organization's control nature is a Juggler or Boss or somewhere in between and finally you can determine whether the organization's affection nature is a Professional or Attractor or somewhere in between, also in terms of each of the same five sections I have described above.

The questions ask for a rating from 1 to 7 that best describes where you would put the organization. One thing to be careful of is that the score can introduce an air of pretence. It suggests that, if you have an exact number, then the results are more 'accurate'. I think this disguises the fact that it is more important that you have accurate perception than that you can calculate a numerical score. People's energy can be drawn to whether they should put a '2' or a '3' and what the exact definition is of the difference between a '2' or a '3' rather than focusing on getting a good view of the organization. This kind of diversion of attention is nonsense.

Determining the psychological nature of an organization will never be 'scientific' in the way we normally think of the term. However, neither will a set of questions asking people their level of satisfaction, or their view of the customer service provided. Having to use numbers helps you think more clearly but they should be interpreted with common sense. It is more important that you have the following approach in your mind when answering the questions. Then you will have an automatic orientation to be accurate and fair, one which comes from a psychological calibration as well as a mathematical one.

The approach that seems to help most is that you treat the organization with respect, and answer the questions with as much thought and care as you would want someone to apply if they were answering similar questions about you. In that way, it becomes easier to be objective, to put aside your own likes or preferences and to really try and describe the company as it is. Often, the questions will make you really think. They should do this if you approach the organization with the respect, care and attention you would want applied to yourself if someone were describing you. The results will be a guide, rather than a precise calculation, but they should be the best guide you can create for that particular organization. You should feel free to make up any questions

QUESTIONS TO UNDERSTAND THE ORGANIZATION 115

you like. Whatever will help you make sense of the organization and help you manage it more productively.

The sets of questions follow (Questionnaires 5.4–5.6) and at the end there is a summary sheet (Table 5.2) which you can use to get a view of the organization as a whole. Put a cross at the place on the continuum which best reflects the organization (or part of it) on that particular item. Each section can then be rated on the scale from 1 to 7 to reflect the relative balance of the Connoisseur or the Populist. When filling out each questionnaire, for each item put a cross or mark on the line at the place that best reflects the organization, or part or it, that you are assessing. After you have marked all seven items in each subsection, this subsection can then be given an overall rating on the scale from 1 to 7 to reflect the relative balance of the Connoisseur or Populist, Juggler or Boss, Professional or Attractor for the organization.

Questionnaire 5.1   Looking at how well the organization meets its inclusion aims

Evaluating how well the organization (or part of it) is fulfilling the inclusion aims and how well it functions within the inclusion area of experience

The aspects listed below represent some of the indications that an organization is fulfilling the inclusion aims well. You can use these to evaluate any organization (or part of it) as they indicate that the organization is functioning well within the inclusion area of experience. You can either rate the organization on a quantitative scale of 1–7 (low to high), or you may prefer to simply obtain a qualitative assessment about the organization's performance on each aspect. The items listed can be used as the basis of discussion or individual thought.

The organization has a clear identity to others. Other people such as customers have a sense of what the organization is like rather than just knowing what it does, or recognizing its 'name'.

The organization has a sense of presence, it can easily claim attention when it wants to without having to grab attention. It has a certain 'flair'.

The organization finds it easy to claim territorial space in the market. It easily creates a sense that it, and its products, have a 'place' in their chosen market. This makes it harder for competitors to move them out of 'their' place or to make inroads into that market space which seems to be 'theirs'.

The organization is at ease in interacting with other organizations and the environment generally, without being excessively outgoing, or too withdrawn. It can network, create alliances, work with the media in a comfortable way without either needing these contacts excessively or avoiding them.

The organization is able to go its own way and make up its own mind without following the current fads in the industry or the practices that other companies adopt. It can adopt strategies or work practices, create products or customer approaches that are unique or which lead the way, without feeling it is wrong or out of step when doing so.

The organization is good at creating products that are both innovative and easy to use at the same time. It can balance the priorities of both design and R&D with marketing.

The organization is able to let people have their own distinctive ways of doing things in terms of work practices, systems, style and yet at the same time it can create a sense that everyone belongs to the same organization.

Overall   How well, overall, do you think the organization is functioning within the inclusion area of experience? What, if anything, needs to be done to improve the way it functions within this area?

QUESTIONS TO UNDERSTAND THE ORGANIZATION 117

Questionnaire 5.2 Looking at how well the organization meets its control aims

Evaluating how well the organization (or part of it) is fulfilling the control aims and how well it functions within the control area of experience

The aspects listed below represent some of the indications that an organization is fulfilling the control aims well. You can use these to evaluate any organization (or part of it) as they indicate that the organization is functioning well within the control area of experience. You can either rate the organization on a quantitative scale of 1–7 (low to high), or you may prefer to simply obtain a qualitative assessment about the organization's performance on each aspect. The items listed can be used as the basis of discussion or individual thought.

The organization is effective at achieving the goals it sets itself. It has a sense of efficacy, that is, that what it aims for it will achieve.

The organization is comfortable with power without either avoiding its expression and therefore abdicating, or without abusing power and being unnecessarily forceful and alienating others. The organization finds it easy to exert influence as well as to be influenced, whether with customers, suppliers, its own people or alliance partners.

The organization has self-confidence, without being macho and boastful. This confidence is deep-rooted and is not based only on competence that comes from education or professional qualifications. It is based on the general feeling that, whatever the organization is faced with, it will be dealt with without excuses. As a result, the organization never blames the environment or competitors for its own results or failure to achieve a goal but takes responsibility for the consequences of its actions as well as its actions.

The organization is able to easily and naturally release the talent in the organization without having to go to great lengths to do so. It does not have to struggle to get others to use their skills or ideas because it manages people in a way that combines giving clear direction with the latitude to take risks at the same time.

The organization can both plan well and change plan instantly and comfortably. It can be steady and flexible at the same time, creating resilience in the organization as a whole.

The organization is good at creating products that provide customers with reliability and certainty as well as flexibility and choice at the same time.

The organization is able to gain the resources, leverage and power which it needs in order to meet its goals, but is able also to be genuinely resourceful and clever with whatever resources it has. It does not, therefore, engage in alliances only as a means to gain leverage, unless doing so also activates the innate resourcefulness within the company at the same time.

Overall How well, overall, do you think the organization is functioning within the control area of experience? What, if anything, needs to be done to improve the way it functions within this area?

Questionnaire 5.3 Looking at how well the organization meets its affection aims

Evaluating how well the organization (or part of it) is fulfilling the affection aims and how well it functions within the affection area of experience

The aspects listed below represent some of the indications that an organization is fulfilling the affection aims well. You can use these to evaluate any organization (or part of it) as they indicate that the organization is functioning well within the affection area of experience. You can either rate the organization on a quantitative scale of 1–7 (low to high), or you may prefer to simply obtain a qualitative assessment about the organization's performance on each aspect. The items listed can be used as the basis of discussion or individual thought.

The organization is effective at creating genuine, good relationships with others, whether customers, alliances or other organizations. It is also effective at creating genuine, good relationships within the organization.

The organization is good at sustaining relationships over the long term not only creating or initiating them. To achieve this, the organization needs to be capable of creating loyalty both outside and inside the organization.

Customers as well as alliance partners tend to be long-term and stay with the organization out of choice rather than because they are obliged to or contractually required to.

The organization is easily able to get others to believe in it and in what it is doing. It communicates a passion or enthusiasm for what it does, although this may be done quietly rather than in an outward or volatile way. It may be that other people believe in the organization's products rather than the organization itself but this pattern will be a prominent and noted feature of the organization.

The organization engages genuinely with its tasks. People truly fix problems rather than just appearing to. They resolve deeper issues rather than papering over them. The organization adopts the same attitude with customers, who receive genuinely good service that delivers what they want rather than just a well-trained response aimed at superficial 'relationship management'.

The organization evokes a personal response from others and may create a kind of 'affectionate' response, albeit that this may be unspoken. This happens because the organization will have made a genuine contact with them, even in advertisements, as well as seeming generally to be quite human, real or full of 'character'.

The organization manages people in a way that evokes real commitment without them having to be 'bought' or incentivized. People within the organization want it to do well for its own sake and take account of the agenda of the organization as a whole.

Overall How well, overall, do you think the organization is functioning within the affection area of experience? What, if anything, needs to be done to improve the way it functions within this area?

QUESTIONS TO UNDERSTAND THE ORGANIZATION

Questionnaire 5.4 Connoisseur or Populist

key qualities that define the organization

reflective..participative
individualistic...group-oriented
distinctive..diverse
dignified...jovial
interesting..entertaining
innovative..modernizing
stylish..current

Connoisseur 1 .... 2 .... 3 .... 4 .... 5 .... 6 .... 7 Populist

business stance and philosophy; the key success factors and tradeoffs made

focus on design, product.......................focus on marketing, image
believe in being innovative....................believe in being up-to-date
aim to do a few things well....................like diversity; try new things
quality, uniqueness are key...................quantity, variety are key
focus in distribution channels.................multiple distribution channels
aim for clear market territory..................want many different markets
few carefully chosen alliances................actively seek many alliances

Connoisseur 1 .... 2 .... 3 .... 4 .... 5 .... 6 .... 7 Populist

intangible, physical and subtle features of the organization

like unusual colours – aqua, lilac..............like common colours – red, blue
logo is elegant, stylish, discreet...............logo is easily noticed, bold
atmosphere tranquil, quiet......................atmosphere noisy, active
advertise their quality, selectivity..............advertise their mass popularity
language is refined, restrained.................use words that are current, 'in'
windows have barrier or curtain................windows left open for all to see
like individuality, style in clothing..............like clothes that get attention

Connoisseur 1 .... 2 .... 3 .... 4 .... 5 .... 6 .... 7 Populist

values and assumptions about people and their work practices

value people who can work alone..............value people who interact a lot
value specialists, expertise.....................value generalists, all-rounders
you 'should' have your own view...............you 'should' find a group view
it is OK to be different............................it is OK to be popular
it is best to consider, reflect first................it is best to act, talk, explore first
need separate offices, space..................need open-planning, mingling
originality and flair rewarded...................energy and impact rewarded

Connoisseur 1 .... 2 .... 3 .... 4 .... 5 .... 6 .... 7 Populist

assumptions held about customers by the organization

customers:

want to feel singled out.......................like to 'belong' to a group
want quiet, peace..............................want an upbeat atmosphere
focus on product quality......................focus on product accessibility
want to feel different...........................want to feel like everyone else
are all individual................................are all the same underneath
should not be intruded on....................should not be ignored
need time to think, reflect....................need immediate responses

Connoisseur 1 .... 2 .... 3 .... 4 .... 5 .... 6 .... 7 Populist

Questionnaire 5.5 Juggler or Boss

key qualities that define the organization

adventurous..careful
free..powerful
agile...strategic
streetwise...informed
experimental...directed
challenging...assured
resourceful...prepared

Juggler 1 .... 2 .... 3 .... 4 .... 5 .... 6 .... 7 Boss

business stance and philosophy; the key success factors and tradeoffs made

aim is to be resourceful......................aim for leverage, resources
must be able to change plan....................must plan far ahead
priority is creating flexibility..................priority is creating strategy
delegation is key to success....................management is the key
alliances are like partnerships...................alliances need one boss
ignore or challenge 'rules'.....................need clear industry rules
aim for the cleverest strategy....................aim for the right strategy

Juggler 1 .... 2 .... 3 .... 4 .... 5 .... 6 .... 7 Boss

intangible, physical and subtle features of the organization

like interesting colours – green......................like strong colours – black
use small letters in name, logo......................capital letters in name, logo
atmosphere lively, playful......................atmosphere steady, serious
advertising theme is freedom......................advertising theme is strength
own rules for grammar, words......................'correct' usage in language
like free access in company......................control access in company
wear low-key informal clothes......................wear formal serious clothes

Juggler 1 .... 2 .... 3 .... 4 .... 5 .... 6 .... 7 Boss

values and assumptions about people and their work practices

it is OK to change routine often......................a regular work routine is best
start before clarifying the aim......................clarify aim before starting
should find out for yourself......................people need clear direction
should experiment automatically......................people plan automatically
you should always be flexible......................you should always be in control
reward initiative, independence......................reward assurance, reliability
procedures ignored easily......................procedures should be used

Juggler 1 .... 2 .... 3 .... 4 .... 5 .... 6 .... 7 Boss

assumptions held about customers by the organization

customers:
prefer to think for themselves......................need advice and guidance
priority is maximum choice......................priority is predictability
often change their mind......................know own needs in advance
like a sense of fun, adventure......................like to feel all is under control
like to try before buying......................make clear final decisions
need to be able to influence us......................need to be taken care of
want flexibility in products......................want reliability in products

Juggler 1 .... 2 .... 3 .... 4 .... 5 .... 6 .... 7 Boss

QUESTIONS TO UNDERSTAND THE ORGANIZATION 121

Questionnaire 5.6 Professional or Attractor

key qualities that define the organization

    serious..generous
    well-presented..natural
    professional..spontaneous
    calm..expressive
    private..personal
    cautious..revealing
    honest...kind

Professional 1 ....2 .... 3............ 4............ 5............ 6............ 7 Attractor

business stance and philosophy; the key success factors and tradeoffs made

    aim for dedication, hard work.......................aim for commitment, loyalty
    focus on maximizing returns........................priority is the long-term goal
    aim to streamline, rationalize.......................aim to build the organization
    assess/measure efficiency.........................assess/measure contribution
    need to win in short term.........................it is OK to win in long term
    use technology to be efficient......................technology improves service
    alliances are business deals........................alliances are relationships

Professional 1 ....2 .... 3............ 4............ 5............ 6............ 7 Attractor

intangible, physical and subtle features of the organization

    colours are serious – grey, blue......................colours are warm – peach
    logo/name is impersonal......................logo/name sounds personal
    atmosphere serious, dedicated......................atmosphere committed, warm
    advertisements feel professional....................advertisements feel creative
    language focuses on business......................words focus on life, people
    like neat, 'professional' offices.....................like offices to look lived in
    people prefer to wear suits.......................personal element in clothing

Professional 1 ....2 .... 3............ 4............ 5............ 6............ 7 Attractor

values and assumptions about people and their work practices

    should stay serious, 'on task'.......................should be able to get off task
    work should be streamlined.......................work should be enjoyable
    should look well-turned out.......................should be real, human
    prioritize efficiency in work....................prioritize friendliness in work
    rely on e-mail, phone, reports......................rely on face-to-face talk
    it is best to be professional.......................it is best to be genuine, warm
    prioritize ability, presentation......................prioritize personality, integrity

Professional 1 ....2 .... 3............ 4............ 5............ 6............ 7 Attractor

assumptions held about customers by the organization

customers:
    place a priority on speed.......................put a priority on friendliness
    want a professional approach......................want a spontaneous approach
    like technology......................dislike technology
    want efficiency most of all.......................want a good relationship first
    like an impersonal atmosphere......................want a personal atmosphere
    expect us to be very polite......................expect us to be friendly, real
    focus on the purchase, product......................focus on how we treat them

Professional 1 ....2 .... 3............ 4............ 5............ 6............ 7 Attractor

122 READING THE MIND OF THE ORGANIZATION

Table 5.2 Summary

Overall balance in psychological natures of the organization (or part of it)

You can use the following diagrams to illustrate the psychological natures of the organization overall. You can use your responses in the three preceding questionnaires and transfer the global assessment in each of those to this table in order to create a summary of the organization. The overall balance between the two psychological natures in each area can be shown with a cross at the appropriate place on the continuum for each section.

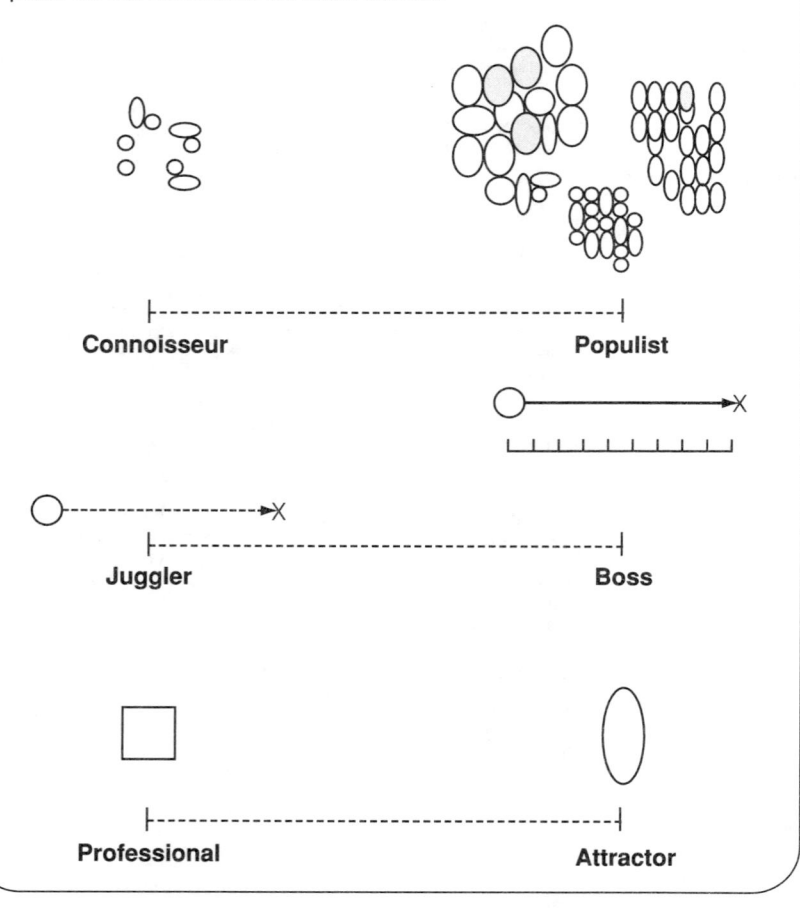

Connoisseur	Populist

Juggler	Boss

Professional	Attractor

Understanding the feelings and atmosphere in the organization

CHAPTER 6

Coming to land

Many years ago, my father used to pilot the beautiful flying boats on the Imperial Airways routes around Africa through Alexandria and Khartoum, down from Southampton to Athens, Basra, and through to Karachi and Singapore, and then across the Tasman and the Pacific with Teal. In that era, there was tremendous affection for the 'boats', as he used to call them. They flew, yet they were 'boats', they knew the sea as well as the sky. They have the same magical significance even today. When you mention flying boats to most people, it conjures up an air of romance, of adventure, elegance and pleasure, that 'ordinary' planes have never matched. People refer to the land planes as 'ordinary' planes to distinguish them from these seabirds. When the time came for the transition from sea to land, there were quite a few battles between the pilots and aircrew, and their management. The public loved the seabirds but it was clear to most of the pilots and crew that they had to be replaced by land planes, which had pressurized cabins and could escape the weather and fly above any storms or squalls.

In the company where my father was, there raged many such arguments. One incident emerged when, after the top managers had decided to continue using flying boats after political pressure from the government, a new fleet had to be grounded because of continued faults, and the airline was virtually brought to its knees. With the staff hanging around doing nothing for many weeks, the General Manager at the time decided that the answer was to rally the troops and get them in the right mood and spirit. They were all called to a big gathering in a local hall for a talk. The backdrop of the stage where he was to speak consisted of a tropical scene with palm trees, golden sand and, above, a brilliant sun perched just on the horizon with its rays flooding the sky. Against this backdrop he attempted to use his words and this scene to send a message that would get everyone feeling positive.

One of the other pilots at the time wrote about it many years later. The General Manager stood at the front of the stage behind a lectern and 'speaking words of hope and cheer told of the great days that were ahead. When the new day dawned the rising sun would shine on our dramatic future. The wag who was sitting beside me whispered with an eye on the dramatic tropical scene across the stage, "Is the sun rising or is it setting?" The staff was somewhat bemused by the whole performance for we all knew how serious and almost insurmountable were the problems that affected [the planes]'.[1]

This is a personal story and it concerns a company of many years ago. But the human reality in it remains identical to that which occurs in organizations today. The call to the troops, when handled like this, can make the situation worse. The result in this particular situation was that people were bemused and cynical, and they remembered it in this way for years. When organizations try to raise morale or give a 'pep talk' to galvanize people today the effect is often the same. The people at the top of the organization, or those in the position of trying to turn such situations around, are trying their best, yet people stand by as onlookers instead of joining in with the attempt at generating enthusiasm, if the situation is not handled correctly.

The importance of knowing what people are feeling

What situation are we dealing with here? The planes being grounded? The business losses being made? What we are dealing with here is the way people view, and feel about, what is going on. The situation being dealt with in such events is an emotional one, rather than the business predicament itself. In this chapter, we focus on determining what those strange things called feelings are, so that we know what we are dealing with and why certain feelings and atmospheres arise in an organization.

Our focus in the book so far has been on understanding the events and business aims of the organization as a whole from a perceptual and psychological perspective, and in the previous chapter we paused to take stock of the organization seen in this new way. However, from this chapter on the tone and focus change as we start to understand more about the internal state in the organization itself. Our foundation for all the themes we explore in this second half of the book is the world of feelings and subtleties that we need to take account of in organizations. In what follows I show you how much easier and simpler it is to run an organization well if you take feelings into account before you start.

---

[1] *A Noble Chance: One Pilot's Life*, Maurice McGreal, 1994. Published by Maurice McGreal, 19 Woburn Road, Northland, Wellington, New Zealand.

A set of terms to link the business world and the emotional world

Knowing what people feel, whether we are talking about employees, customers or the people an organization is engaged with in an alliance, is critical to creating a successful organization. The skills an organization has in working with feelings and knowing how to create a positive ambience and mood are vital, but at present we have few ways of figuring these things out. We may know that people are 'reacting' to something in some way, but we have few words or terms to describe these emotional facts of the organization, in contrast to the business facts. One benefit of a psychological approach is that it gives us a set of words to make sense of these things.

Creating a positive atmosphere, an esprit de corps, and dealing with any emotional dynamic requires that you can identify feelings in a more finely tuned way than by simply making distinctions such as 'positive' and 'negative'. For example, we could take the story of the flying boats and determine what the feelings were in that situation. At present, we only have words like 'cynicism' or 'disbelief' to describe what people were feeling, but there are a whole range of identifiable feelings and emotional needs that exist in human beings. The descriptions I provide in what follows are only one set of such terms, and most people would assert that they experience a wide array of different feelings. However, if we are to work with the feelings in the organization we need a way of bringing order into this vast complexity, which is one benefit of the framework I outline. Moreover, the particular terms I describe are useful because they relate directly to the terms already used to describe the business aspects of an organization. The three areas of experience of the organization relate to an identifiable emotional world, in exactly the same way as they relate to an identifiable set of business features. This means that you can make sense of the business, its aims and its events, using terms that relate directly to the emotional reality of the organization.

A framework of feelings

Each of the three psychological areas of inclusion, control and affection is associated with very specific feelings. The original specification of these formed a key component of Will Schutz's interpersonal theory which inspired my own conceptual framework of organizations (see Chapter 2), and it is his pioneering work that deserves the credit for identifying and labelling these feelings. The terms I use follow those used for the areas of experience themselves, whereas Will used quite different labels for the feelings associated with each area of experience.[2] The description of these different feelings is set out in Table 6.1.

Notice that the differences between the psychological natures are irrelevant here, since everyone to varying degrees wants the same kind of inclusion feelings, control feelings and affection feelings. There is no difference, at this level, in the nature of the feelings associated with each of the psychological areas. People may need different solutions or approaches in the surface world of the business in order to generate those feelings, and the chapters we have explored so far have set out what some of those business features are. The essential starting point in this chapter, however, is to realize that, underneath, the same set of feelings potentially apply to everyone and these feelings may be present even if we can never see or hear them. Furthermore, the same kind of feelings arise in people today as they did in the days of the flying boats. I use the example of the latter in what follows simply to provide the context with which to identify in more precise words what people might be feeling in any situation.

Facing up to the feelings that may be present rather than avoiding them

Let's look at the scene with the flying boats. The people in that organization, sitting in the audience listening to the General Manager, fail to respond with the feelings of hope and cheer with which they are expected to respond. Just being 'told' that great days lie ahead will never make people who are miserable about a situation feel better. What the people in that organization were probably feeling was a range of the negative feelings specified in Table 6.1, and a show of sun in the visual backdrop will do little to lift them. People are allowed to feel miserable, they are allowed to be annoyed. Denying that negative feelings are present simply means you will be unable to do anything about them. It does little to

---

[2] In the framework of feelings as originally described by Will Schutz in his pioneering theory, each of the three areas of experience is associated with a corresponding set of feelings. The specific term he uses to refer to the feelings associated with the inclusion area is 'significance'; that used to refer to the feelings associated with the control area is 'competence'; and the term used to refer to the feelings associated with the affection or openness area of experience is 'liking'. In the framework I have developed to apply to organizations I simply refer to 'inclusion feelings', 'control feelings' and 'affection feelings' because I am trying to create a set of ideas that are easily used in business by people who are often impatient with too many psychological terms. My description of these different sets of feelings, however, tries to retain the same meaning as Will's significance, competence and liking.

Table 6.1 The feelings in the organization

inclusion	control	affection
people want to feel **included**, that their existence is acknowledged, that they are **recognized** in the sense of being seen and heard in their own right not just when they achieve or perform, want to feel accounted for, as well as recognized as being **unique and distinctive**, that they stand out in some way, want to **feel that they exist**, want to feel they can include others in a way that retains their integrity and boundaries, want to feel they **belong** to some larger grouping	people want to feel a sense of **efficacy**, meaning that when they do something they will have the desired effects or results, want to feel a **sense of control** over their world as well as themselves so it means feeling **self-control**, they want to feel **competent, admired, proud**, successful, a winner and that they are seen as competent and successful by others, to feel coordinated in themselves, that **they function well**, to feel that they use themselves fully	people want to feel that they are **accepted** when they relate to others, to feel real and genuine so they believe in themselves, to feel **engaged** by others and their work, to feel they take **care** of themselves, that others care, to feel depth, commitment, purposeful, to feel that they **can engage** with others without being rejected, to feel they can remain private when it suits them, to feel closeness, to feel they can discriminate between who to **trust** and who to distrust

people want to **avoid** the corresponding feelings of

feeling **excluded, ignored**, that they are **invisible** or that they count only to perform, that they are noticed only when they do a good job but otherwise are barely acknowledged, **feeling invaded** and intruded on by others, to avoid feeling overly included	feeling **humiliated**, ridiculed, shamed, **incompetent**, feeling out of control, that they are unable to cope, feeling that they are **overly responsible**, blamed when it is not their responsibility, burdened, feeling chaotic or uncoordinated	feeling **unappreciated** or rejected, **unprofessional**, feeling naive, as if they have been **taken for a ride** or too trusting, feeling used, feeling **unlikeable**, feeling hollow and superficial, without purpose, depressed, betrayed, empty, uncaring

deal with a situation that you are, by virtue of staging such an event in the first place, acknowledging you need to do something about.

Creating 'enough' positive feelings in each of the three areas

What people in such a situation need, specifically, is to feel included or recognized, the inclusion feelings. What they need, specifically, is to feel effective, competent or a sense of control, the control feelings. Finally, what they need, specifically, is to feel trusted, loved, accepted or appreciated, some of the affection feelings. If those specific feelings are created, or enough in each particular area, you will have a situation where there is buoyancy, a positive esprit de corps. Then, the troops will well and truly be behind you. Generating some mix, and some level, of the positive feelings in all three areas is the aim. Creating a positive spirit in a situation like that of the flying boats might be quite hard, and you may have as an objective simply removing the negative feelings so that the organization is in 'neutral'.

Whatever the intention, it helps managers to get a handle on what is going on and what they can aim for if they have this framework of feelings to provide some perspective. If they can label what is going on, they feel able to do something about the way people feel. It helps to make the invisible 'visible' and the unspoken 'heard', which are some of the components of dealing effectively with the emotional world of the organization. The approach is quite simple. The first stage is to specify the psychological reality in the situation. We use the terms of the framework to understand in a little more detail what might have been going on in the situation with the flying boats.

Understanding the feelings that would have been present with the flying boats

The feelings present in the situation with the flying boats would have had a complex nature, and we can identify them, even though we are unable to see them, using the terms set out in Table 6.1.

Needing to make people feel included instead of irrelevant and excluded

Some people will respond to a situation like this with the feeling that, because they are unable to be at work, they miss the sense of identity, the recognition they normally get from carrying out their day-to-day activities. They would feel *irrelevant*. That would be one of the key feelings that you would need to try to change if you wanted to address the inclusion feelings in the airline at that point. It may be that feelings of being left out, excluded, are uppermost in the audience. These will only be made worse if people feel excluded from being told the full story about what is going on. By leaving out vital information and talking only of positive hope and cheer, the General Manager can only worsen those feelings he is trying to improve. He is trying to make them feel included but is more probably leaving them feeling excluded.

Needing to make people feel competent and on top of things instead of helpless and inadequate

What of the feelings in the control area? Here, people's feelings may be those of inadequacy. Some people will feel *humiliated*, especially if they were involved in making the original decision to stay with the 'seabirds'. Any kind of mistake can evoke feelings of humiliation or incompetence. Others may feel a sense of incompetence simply because they aren't working. They may be accustomed to generating the feelings of competence they need from their work, but this is now impossible. It may not be the General Manager's fault that people are lacking feelings of competence, but that is nevertheless the emotional reality he faces as he stands up in front of the people there. And that is the kind of feeling he needs to know exists, if he wants to turn the situation around. People may also feel a lack of power in such a situation, and a feeling that matters have been taken out of their hands. If so, they would feel *helpless*. All of these are key feelings that might arise in any difficult situation, and ones that you would identify as being control feelings.

Needing to make people feel engaged and caring instead of betrayed and not trusted

The feelings that might arise in relation to the affection area would be the following. Some people may feel *betrayed*. They may feel let down by the senior managers involved, or no longer liked by them. They may feel a lack of trust in those people or that they themselves are far from being trusted. These would be the affection feelings generated by the lack of openness on the part of the General Manager, because he avoided referring to the real situation they were faced with, which might suggest to some people a lack of genuine engagement. They may cease to care, or feel that no one cares about them. They may simply feel depressed or miserable. These are the kind of feelings that are likely to exist in such a situation, and which we could define as affection feelings.

Figuring out the sensitive area in the organization

Most of the feelings human beings experience can be understood as being one of these three kinds of feelings: inclusion, control or affection. The framework is simple in appearance but allows for great complexity in reality. However, in this book all I am aiming to do is outline the basic framework. Being able to name and identify what feelings are likely to exist, and understanding why they might exist, is one step. However, there is another key aspect to understanding the emotional world of the organization. While we now have a way to name and identify feelings more precisely than just with words like 'positive' and 'negative', or 'satisfied' and 'dissatisfied', we can fine-tune our understanding even more precisely than this. It is this next level of discrimination that gives you the means to both understand what is going on and to change whatever is going on. This involves taking account of what is special and most definable about a company. The latter is almost always related to what I refer to as the sensitive area of the organization. Let me explain what this means.

Some people 'respond' to one of the psychological areas more than to the other two, and so are sensitive to certain feelings more than others. Organizations do exactly the same. For example, some people will respond to any difficulty or negative situation primarily with feelings of being excluded or ignored (inclusion feeling). Others may respond to exactly the same situation primarily by feeling incompetent (control feeling). And others will primarily feel rejected or disliked, in exactly the same situation (affection feeling). Some feelings are triggered more easily than others because people have a different degree of sensitivity to each area of experience. This is a critical fact to take into account when working with the feelings of the organization.

When an organization has a particular sensitivity to feeling included and recognized, not ignored

Sometimes whole organizations will have a similar sensitivity. It may be their 'way' to feel the inclusion area more deeply than the control or affection areas. What does this mean? It means that, throughout the organization, any signs that people are excluded, ignored, left out or unrecognized are especially powerful in their impact. What this also means is that these people will need more attention given to anything that will boost those positive feelings associated with that same area. They will have a greater positive response to anything that fulfils those specific feelings. If the sensitivity is with the inclusion area, people will have the greatest response to anything that 'tells' them that they are recognized, acknowledged, drawn into an inner circle or that they stand out. With such groups or organizations, the positive feelings related to their sensitive area need to be fulfilled more than those feelings that correspond to any of the others. This is their favourite emotional 'food' so you must feed them that kind of food.

When an organization has a particular sensitivity to feeling competent and strong, not powerless

When an organization has a particular sensitivity in the control area they may respond to situations primarily with feelings related to a sense of competence. A downturn in business, for instance, will create worries about their competence. They may feel humiliated and helpless yet have no feelings that they are irrelevant or ignored, which we could identify as inclusion feelings. Instead, they are more likely to feel out of control. This will be their particular sensitivity. However, you can turn this situation around by an active cultivation of anything that will make them feel competent, able to cope and functional. Then they are 'all right' and they can get on with the business. If you have a group or organization with this particular sensitivity but you instead create aims and activities or communicate in a way that makes them feel recognized, acknowledged or included, the feelings associated with the inclusion area, you will be unable to have the same effect. They will want those feelings too, of course, because people need a minimum of the positive feelings from all three areas, but when the organization has control as its sensitive area it is from activities that fulfil control feelings that the most benefit comes.

When an organization has a particular sensitivity to feeling appreciated and trusted, not disliked

We can explore the last area of sensitivity, the affection area, in the same way. When this psychological area is uppermost, often the feelings are deeper, more hidden. In business, people rarely admit that they need these feelings. That is, that they need to feel appreciated or even liked. People, groups or organizations with this particular sensitivity often try to perform well so that you appreciate them rather than because they want you to see them as competent. They will rarely tell you this, and may never themselves know that they need these feelings as much as they do. However, many of my clients at senior levels have this particular need uppermost. They really want the troops to like them. Or they want people to appreciate their concern to do what is 'right' for the organization and that they are taking care of it for the long term. In an organization as a whole, if affection is the sensitive area rather than inclusion or control, people will tend to respond to a business impasse or a difficult situation with feelings of being depressed or of feeling that they are no longer trusted, rather than with feelings of lack of recognition (inclusion) or helplessness (control). On the other hand, if you cultivate the positive feelings here you will benefit from people caring about the organization itself. Really committed organizations have affection as their most sensitive area. If you try to deal with people in such organizations in a way that rewards their competence, or pay them extra, it will rarely have the effect you think. They may even distrust you if you do this, because it will seem like manipulation to any group with affection as their sensitive area. They need to know that you know that they care about, and are committed to, the organization.

Taking an organization's particular sensitive area into account

So far, we have explored the need to take into account two key things when considering the feelings within an organization. One is that each organization, group or individual will want some of the positive feelings of all three psychological areas present in their work and life. These were set out in Table 6.1. This is a helpful tool because it makes people stop and think about feelings in a more precise way. By making use of it, people's reactions are more comprehensible, and creating a positive esprit de corps seems more achievable.

The second aspect to take into account is the particular area of experience where there is most sensitivity for an organization, group or individual. This is different from a 'problem' area, and represents an aspect of their character that you need to acknowledge. It creates the strength in any person or organization just as much as it represents where they get hurt most easily. It is their particular gift, if you want to think of it in such a way. It helps to think of the sensitive area as a very positive thing, something to pay attention to and nourish especially well, precisely because it is so defining of that organization or person. It is the sensitive area of an organization or person in one sense, and their 'special' area in another sense. It tells you what kind of 'food' they need and like most and, therefore, what you must feed them. It is identifying, understanding, appreciating, nourishing and working with this that will give you the most benefit in understanding the organization as well as understanding the flux and flow in its events. We will make further use of this idea in the chapters that follow, but for the moment we will use it to focus on the emotional world of the organization.

Table 6.2 summarizes the characteristics of the sensitive area of an organization.

FEELINGS IN THE ORGANIZATION

Table 6.2 Characteristics of the most sensitive area of the organization

	The sensitive or special area of the organization
inclusion	Feelings of recognition, feeling distinctive, that they count in their own right are especially important. These need the most attention, get dissatisfied most easily. As a strength, having this as the sensitive area creates characteristics of being unique, having utterly their own style, a one-off company that is interested in others and the world around them. Aims and activities that create these feelings need to be emphasized in order to satisfy this sensitive area.
control	Feelings of competence, feeling admired, successful, able to cope, a winner are especially important. These need the most attention, get dissatisfied most easily. As a strength, having this as the sensitive area creates characteristics of being resilient, having influence way beyond what their financial performance might suggest, a brave company. Aims and activities that create these feelings need to be emphasized in order to satisfy this sensitive area.
affection	Feelings of fulfilment, feeling appreciated, real, engaged, liked and loved are especially important. These need the most attention, get dissatisfied most easily. As a strength, having this as the sensitive area creates characteristics of being attractive in a deep way, an icon in some way, a company to believe in and trust, one that is liked and creates a feeling of affection in, and cooperation from, others. Aims and activities that create these feelings need to be emphasized in order to satisfy this sensitive area.

Keeping it in perspective; making sure all three sets of feelings are attended to 'enough'

Over the long term, it will be the feelings associated with the organization's special area of sensitivity that you will need to focus on, and fulfil, the most. However, you need to keep this in perspective since, no matter how sensitive one psychological area is, people always need to feel enough of all three of the different kinds of feelings for a really positive atmosphere to exist. The aim is to have 'enough' of these various feelings rather than to aim for perfection, and we have a great advantage in being able to achieve this because of the fact that the three psychological areas relate both to the emotional world of the organization and to its business world of strategies and work practices. This means that you can relate one world to the other, and you can understand both specific incidents and the implications of the longer-term business stance of the organization.

Applying your knowledge of feelings to the business world

In what follows I try to illustrate that you can work productively and harmoniously with the feelings of the organization quite easily. I explore a specific incident, where the emotions in an organization 'blew up' and they needed to figure out what feelings were involved. I use it to illustrate a process you can adopt to understand what is going on in such situations. Most managers feel at sea when faced with anything 'emotional'. Describing this example, and this process, tries to fill in this gap which many managers feel. We then look at how you can detect a positive atmosphere in your organization, and interpret what different atmospheres mean and the effects they create.

Understanding the emotional explosion in the communications company

One client company of mine was very good at setting goals, and was quite successful in its industry, related to communications and the media. They seldom met these goals, but this was disguised by the fact that they worked so hard. The company was in a very fast-paced market, and people were used to setting goals for each year, as well as broad goals for the next three years. They were quite creative and innovative in their products, and found it easy to generate new products and new ideas. Working with them tended to be a lot of fun and very entertaining. There was an esprit de corps there that many other companies would have envied, and their people were dedicated. The company was also highly professional, and, as I have indicated, people worked extremely hard and intensely, as many companies involved with communications and the media do. Their business was reasonably profitable, and there were no dramatic market threats on the horizon at the time of this story, although their market was, in general, always highly competitive.

The company was run by a managing director with six direct reports, each of whom looked after a 'customer' segment. The bulk of people in the company were grouped into teams who took 'team responsibility' for a group of customers or for a particular product. What the senior group, and their direct reports, had decided at their annual strategic away-day was that the company needed to be run more 'efficiently'. They saw that there was some overlap between the teams, for example, and that sometimes the same customers would have to deal with two or three different teams within the organization. They thought also that they should, as a long-term measure, produce more products that could be sold *en masse*, rather than meeting particular requests from a customer. This was another way in which they had defined the desire to be more efficient.

The senior people come back from their away-day and spark off an emotional explosion

The group came back from their annual away-day to inform the employees in various ways what they had decided, and to communicate the main overall aim, to be more efficient. Each of them had worked out some ways in which this need for increased efficiency might be met, but since it was quite a participative company many of the group, as was their usual practice, decided to get 'their' teams to figure out exactly how their respective areas would become 'more efficient'.

I had been involved with the company on and off for some time, as it is generally the case that my clients are quite long term. However, at this particular time I had just returned from being in the US for nine months and had had no contact with anyone in the company over that period, so the reaction of the employees to the 'news reports' from the away-day was as much a surprise to me as it was to the senior group. The employees were furious. There was what could only be described as a kind of emotional explosion in the organization. There was no one troublesome group or person behind it but, all of a sudden, this active, full-of-life company with dedicated employees became a churning, angry pit. What, for goodness sake, was going on, the senior managers asked me. 'All we did was the same as we do every year,' they said. Each year they had come back from their away-day full of ideas to improve the company. Each year they had communicated them, with great openness, to their respective reports and their teams. Each year they had worked out ways in which they could all work towards whatever the goals were. It was a complete mystery to the senior group what had 'got into' their people.

The managing director asks me to see if I can find out 'who is behind it'

I was asked by the managing director to see if I could find out what was going on and 'who was behind it', since he was unimpressed by my explanations that this kind of situation can arise simply as a collective dynamic without there being any group or individual behind it at all. So, I went off to try to get some clues. I had worked at one time or another with many of the people in the company and had good relationships with a lot of them. I was known and trusted by people and they were used to discussing all manner of things that arose, including political clashes, as well as the normal concerns of the business.

I promised the managing director I would get back to him after a week with my soundings. I had some time that day before my next meeting, outside the company, so I used the time to wander around and see if there was anyone to tell me what the 'problem' was. Why so many of the employees had suddenly become so angry with such an innocuous event as their managers arriving back from their away-day with news of their attempts to improve efficiency.

Finding out what was going on in the company

I spent an hour in the company. Each person I spoke to was very cagey with me, even though they usually talked to me about anything. They had never dealt with me like that before. One person snapped at me: 'It's all their fault,' he said. Since I had been away for nine months, I wondered what he meant 'What do you mean?' I asked. He glanced away and said, 'You know, I just don't care about this company any more.' 'Why?' 'Oh, nothing.' I got nothing much more out of him. This kind of non-response continued with others. I was hitting a brick wall. One other piece of data I picked up when I was wandering around was that people's doors were often closed. This was unusual, and I was used to just popping my head around into offices and saying hello quickly, but this time I was prevented even from doing this.

Making sense of the 'data' I had gathered even though it seems that I had no data

Now, let's stop and work out from this what was going on, and why people were reacting in the way they were. For the truth is that, by now, I had all the data I needed to be able to tell the managing director what was going on. My role was to report back what the emotional situation was, and we could work out from there what practical steps were needed. First, however, we had to understand what was going on, which meant identifying which particular feelings had erupted in the company. Otherwise, all the senior group had to go on was that an 'emotional' situation existed.

There is, in the description I have given you, enough data to enable you to figure out that the area of experience that was the source of the eruption was the affection area. The area of experience involved is the first thing to determine. It may be that the feelings of two or even all three areas are 'active' but, even then, there is usually one set of feelings that is a domino factor which sets off the others. In this situation, I had several pieces of data that led me to the conclusion that the affection feelings were yelping. After my experience in the company that day, as I have outlined, I did go back to talk with several people to see if my figuring out was correct, which it was. However, I want to stay with only the pieces of data I have given you, to prove a point. That is, that you can decipher what is going on from the surface level of appearances, without getting anyone to bare their soul to you. And, more importantly, that almost everything and anything constitutes useful data. Let me tell you what that was in this situation.

Everything pointed to the affection feelings needing attention

First, I had discovered that people didn't want to talk with me, yet this was unusual and they usually liked to talk about anything, or even just gossip. The fact that this occurred didn't mean I had no data. On the contrary, this *was* the data I was looking for. Secondly, I had discovered that doors were closed, when they were normally open. This also didn't mean I was blocked from getting data. People had, in fact, been very obliging in showing me so openly what the emotional reality was by shutting their doors. Thirdly, I had had a conversation with someone who couldn't really be bothered telling me anything. That, also, was data, a clue that led me to the right psychological set of feelings that were affected at that time. The fact that this person blamed others for the situation was another piece of good usable data. His comment that he didn't 'care' about anything any more was a pretty obvious clue, and this feeling of his was the key sentiment repeated in my other, later conversations with others. By now, it is probably clear that the precise feelings that were involved in this emotional dynamic related to the affection area.

You can decipher this in all the pieces of data I have given you, even though at first glance there probably seemed to be little data at all. The affection area is about being open and trusting, about caring for what you are doing and for the organization as a whole. It relates to being direct and honest, about saying what you think. The feelings that lead to people closing doors, on the other hand, are those of lack of trust, an avoidance of engagement, not wanting to be open. The doors being closed and people's lack of willingness to talk could, in themselves, have been a function of negative feelings in the inclusion area, shutting me out, excluding me. However, I discounted this because of the wealth of other data that told me that it was their feelings of lack of trust, disengaging, that were uppermost. The atmosphere was one of feeling hurt, rather than of people feeling excluded or ignored.

Eliminating the inclusion and control feelings as being the source of the explosion

If the inclusion feelings are particularly active or needing attention, you can almost always tell because people will have some way of trying to get attention from you. It might even be by staring at you, for instance. Whatever occurs, their behaviour will have an undercurrent of wanting some attention from you and you will feel a kind of demand being made on you. Sometimes, this need will be disguised in other ways. It may be that people ignore you so that you have to 'go towards them'. The feeling this is aimed at generating is that of recognition, one of the key feelings identified with the inclusion area.

However, there was no behaviour that I witnessed in this client that had this character to it. Nor, for that matter, was there any sign that the area of feelings involved was the control area. If it had been the control feelings that were yelping, I would have seen or felt some sign that people felt humiliated, incompetent. They would have revealed this by needing to prove their competence and they would have done something that served to 'prove themselves', either to me or to themselves. But nothing like this occurred.

Definitely feelings of hurt and distrust (affection), not lack of recognition (inclusion) or incompetence (control)

Instead, all the feelings I had detected or deciphered pointed in the direction of the affection area being the area of feelings that was affected in this incident. The feelings related to being closed, untrusting, feeling betrayed and cautious. When people 'switch off', and if you hear a phrase like 'not being bothered', then it is the affection area that is involved, since that area is about engaging. Blaming others was another sign that it was people's affection feelings that were involved since that area relates to people being personal.

Table 6.3 summarizes the key pieces of data that indicated the relevant area of feelings in the communications company.

Table 6.3 Detecting what was going on in the company

key pieces of data

people did not want to talk with me and they usually did

doors were closed

people blamed others, snapped

comment of 'not caring' about the company

I felt like I was hitting a brick wall

general level of non-response even when they did talk to me

feeling that they 'couldn't be bothered'

all these pieces of data, the lack of engagement, lack of trust, lack of openness, not caring or being bothered tell you it is the affection feelings that needed something, that were hurt

Understanding why these particular feelings had exploded

These clues only told me *what* was going on in relation to the feelings within the company. The next question was *why* those feelings existed. Many people stop their figuring out process once they have determined what the feelings are in a situation, and are reluctant to delve into the deeper question of why these feelings are present. Sometimes it is unnecessary to delve further because the conceptual framework relates not just to the level of feelings in the organization but to the level of business activities as well. It is occasionally possible to get people to feel good by sorting out what needs to be done in terms of getting on with the activities of the business. However, it is far more likely that avoiding the task of discovering why people are feeling as they are is the equivalent of hiding your head in the sand. You usually have to go the next step and understand the source of the feelings.

In this particular company, it certainly was necessary to understand why this reaction occurred, or it might happen again. The managers needed to understand how the emotional reality of their organization functioned if they truly wanted to manage their company well and honestly. They wanted to get their business back on track but there was a much bigger agenda than this. In the long term they needed to understand their organization in its entirety and that includes its emotional world. Getting everyone to 'put their head down' and get on with their work would simply have buried the problem. People might well have put their head down, but they would never have had the same level of engagement as they had before. Since such engagement and commitment was the secret of this company's success, it was necessary to understand what was making their people react in this way. The managers knew this, so they wanted to find out what had caused the eruption.

Working out the emotional context of the company

The reason *why* the people in the communications company exploded in the way that they did can be understood from some of the details I have already given. As I have traced out, the key feelings included a lack of trust, and they had indicated a lack of openness or willingness to engage. We can decipher that other feelings that these people might also be experiencing would be feeling unappreciated, or that the senior managers didn't care about them. You can predict this because, even though there is no immediate data or comment referring directly to such feelings, they are associated with the affection area.

Another step in trying to figure out these kinds of incidents is to work out the area of experience that is the most sensitive one in the organization. This may be different from the area where the feelings are affected in any one instance, but the area of sensitivity characterizes any organization so much it is always worth figuring out. So, even if the sensitive area is different from the one being affected at any one moment in time, you may still need to attend to it in conjunction with any other area involved.

Figuring out the long-term sensitive area of the communications company

They don't care if they don't meet their set goals: control is not their most sensitive area

We can decipher some of the business events, or features, that might be relevant to discovering what the sensitive area was in the communications company. For example, the company set specific goals every year, but these particular goals were seldom met. This means that the control area is unlikely to be the sensitive area of the organization. If it were, the fact that those goals were seldom met would have provoked some kind of discussion, some attempt at fixing what would have been seen as a 'problem'. But it wasn't a 'problem' in this company and there was no real need for it to be. They made good profit figures, and often exceeded their own expectations. Goals are important and act as a kind of 'truth' only if an organization has the control area, and its purpose, uppermost. In this company, the fact that they set goals tells you that they used these control tools as a tool only. The control area was a secondary area to them.

Intense and dedicated, with a wonderful esprit de corps, suggesting affection is their main area

Another detail was that, although they seldom achieved their goals, this was disguised by the fact that they worked so hard. They worked intensely. They were dedicated. They had an enviable esprit de corps. They were highly professional and creative. All these pieces of information tell you that the affection area of the business was very important to them. It suggests that this was their area of sensitivity in general, not just the source of the feelings involved in that immediate incident. If they were the same, it would explain why the emotional reaction had been so strong, almost extreme. This would be their soft spot, even if it was also the source of strength and specialness in the company.

They are innovative, so their inclusion area is a strength

What of the inclusion area? This seemed to be a strong area of experience for the company, since they were innovative and found it easy to create new products, signs that you would identify with an organization's fulfilling its inclusion purpose well. The inclusion area was therefore something the company could 'rely' on. The industry they were in is often one where companies have the inclusion area as the main or most sensitive area, since communications and the media are focused on interacting, on projecting, on going into others' worlds, all activities that are associated with the inclusion area of experience of people and organizations. However, in this company, the inclusion area was not their main area, their area of sensitivity, even though it was a source of strength for them.

The decisive factor is the internal condition and atmosphere of the organization

You can distinguish the key, or sensitive, area by the approach, the internal condition and the atmosphere in a company more than you can from its products or the general industry it is in. A company can be atypical in its industry, for example. What goes on inside any company tells you 'who' it is and what it is like more than anything else. In the case of this client it was the atmosphere of dedication and their deep engagement with what they did, the intensity with which they approached their work, that told you that the real kernel of this company, what really made it tick, was the affection area. This area 'explained' the company more than either of the other two areas of experience did. It was how you would characterize what was special about it.

You could, then, 'order' the three areas of experience in terms of importance. With this particular organization, the first area of experience was the affection area, which most defined them. The second, which was a source of strength, was the inclusion area. The third, which was used as a tool but which had less importance than the other two, was the control area.

Using this emotional analysis to understand what 'set their people off'

This analysis tells us about the emotional context of the company, in the same way that we would perform an analysis of the market as the context to understand the strategic needs of a company or its strengths and weaknesses in terms of business criteria. It suggests that, since the feelings involved here are those of the affection area, and since this is also the company's area of sensitivity, something has triggered these highly sensitive feelings. That is how an individual behaves. They react like live wires because of a small thing that sets them off.

Telling them to be 'more efficient' when they have been so dedicated: what they 'heard'

We can trace out what set off the emotional reaction. Why would people who were so dedicated suddenly get so angry when asked to be 'more efficient'? Imagine that the feelings in your organization revolved around people really trying, caring about what they were doing, being dedicated. Imagine what would happen if you came back every year with great ideas about what to improve. What would this mean or say to the people there? When the senior group came back with ideas on what to do 'better', the people in this organization 'heard' it as saying that all their hard effort up until then had failed to be *appreciated*. They felt as though the senior managers had been unaware of how much they had contributed. Otherwise, why would they be telling them they needed to be 'more efficient'? They felt as though they had been taken for granted.

This may sound trivial, so long as you are not one of those people who have been dedicated, who have cared a great deal and who have worked very hard. If you are one of those people, then being told that you need to be 'more efficient' seems to say that what you have been doing has been a waste of time. Can't they see that I care, how hard I have worked? It is a small thing, to tell your people that you have some great ideas on how to be 'more efficient'. But it feels enormous if you have forgotten to let them know, one way or another, that you did appreciate, and notice, that they had been working themselves to the bone because they care about the company and what they are doing.

It is a waste of time thinking that 'they shouldn't feel that, they get paid don't they?'

You may think that these people 'shouldn't' feel like this, that they get paid enough so why should they need to feel appreciated on top of that? But the problem with such a response is that we employ human beings rather than numbskulls, and human beings do feel like this. 'Should' is a word that has little usefulness when you are working out what needs to be done in the world of feelings. The only thing that matters then is what you have in front of you. What is, rather than what you think should be. What has to be dealt with in this kind of situation is what others are feeling for their own reasons. Therefore, if you want to get the business back on track, that is what you deal with, rather than thinking about what people 'should' feel.

Taking into account any past emotional history

In the communications company, the problem, or explosion, arose over a period of time. Such an explosion in any company would never arise from only one incident. One of the features of having the affection area as the most sensitive area is that it has a long fuse. It is deeper than the other two areas of experience. If this is the sensitive area in a person or organization, you may go for a long time thinking everything is fine when, in fact, everything is being bottled up. That is the nature of the affection area. If it is the inclusion area that is affected, or which is the long-term sensitive area, tempers and emotional outbursts are quick to erupt and quick to go. And if it is the control area that is involved, there will be aggression, lashing out or whining. But the affection area is a different matter altogether.

They had started to feel taken for granted, yet these are their most sensitive feelings

In this company, people had started to feel taken for granted. The senior group had become used to the high level of caring and dedication that their people felt. It was because this was the background emotional context that, when the senior group did something that, in their eyes, seemed trivial, it had an effect that was disproportionate. That does not mean it was irrational. The reaction was emotional and entirely rational, if you understand feelings. And since the senior managers wanted their nice, dedicated, caring company back, they were the ones who had to do something about it. Which they did.

Being precise in knowing which feelings to address or you will escalate the problem

Once the managers had figured out what was going on and why, they were in a position to address the exact feelings that were causing the reaction. Different managers did different things, all of which could now be aimed at ensuring that their people were aware of the fact that they *were* appreciated, and that the managers had noticed their dedication. Some managers talked about the situation very openly, and got it out of people's systems in that way. Others made little direct mention of it, but made absolutely sure that they communicated in other ways the sense of appreciation that needed 'filling up'. People can let go of an emotional reaction quite quickly if the feelings that are yelping are attended to directly and met. They can be met by future actions and words, without ever having to refer to the specific incident that set them off in the first place. But what is vital is that it is the right feelings, and no others, that get attention.

What the deciphering of the emotional explosion helped these managers do was to determine which feelings to focus on and which to ignore. One of the easiest ways to make any emotional situation worse is to aim for the 'wrong' set of feelings. Wrong, in this context, means the feelings of a different area from the ones yelping. You will escalate the situation instantly if you do this.

Trying to make their people feel competent would have escalated the emotional situation

For example, if the managers in this company had interpreted the reaction as arising from people feeling that their performance was failing or lacking, they might have said or done things to try to make their people feel competent and successful. But this kind of solution would have been irrelevant. People would have become even more depressed, even less caring. It would merely have proved to them how 'stupid' the managers were.

Trying to make their people feel included or recognized would have been a waste of time too

On the other hand, the managers could have interpreted the reaction as meaning that people felt left out or unrecognized. They might have decided that the real problem was that their people felt left out from participating in events like the away-day. They might have concluded that the solution was to involve them more, to get them to have their own away-day. Such a solution would have provided merely a temporary boost. It would have made people feel recognized, that they had been paid attention to, both of which are inclusion feelings. But these people needed something deeper.

The only thing that will work is to focus only on their affection feelings, not the other two areas

They wanted to know that their dedication was appreciated, and that the fact that they cared so much was valued. This is an entirely different psychological need, associated with the affection area, and can never be answered by either including or recognizing people, or by telling them they are competent and successful. Figuring out what the relevant area of feeling is, then, is vital in order to know what to avoid doing, as well as to know what to do.

General signs you can use to 'read' the feelings

We have explored one company in detail to get across the general process and approach you can adopt to help you understand what is going on in the feelings of others. In Table 6.4 I have set out some of the signs you can pay attention to in general. On the left are the signs you may notice in the world around you. These are things that people might say or do. The things listed here are the equivalent to those that were described to help you understand the communications company. On the right of Table 6.4 are some things you can pay attention to in your own reactions. These also can give you the data you need to let you know what is going on in the emotional reality of an organization. The table gives you another tool to make the mysterious comprehensible, and the emotional world of the organization both more interesting and manageable.

Table 6.4 Signs to pay attention to to understand the feelings in the organization

signs of an area of feeling needing attention

	what they may do, that you can observe	what you may do, that you can pay attention to
inclusion	people will try to **get your attention** in some way, even if it is by excluding you or shutting you out, or by 'performing' or dressing in a way that attracts attention or comment. People can make mistakes as a way to get attention if their inclusion needs for recognition and being noticed override their needs to be seen as competent. They may also become invisible and retreat, wanting to **'disappear'**. These are all signs that the inclusion feelings are the ones affected.	you will be very aware of the **energy** in the organization, whether it is hyped up or becomes boring. Either will alert you to the inclusion area. Being **hyped** occurs when people need attention and 'reach' out for it, losing their boundaries. Being **boring** occurs when people want to disappear, become invisible and not stand out. You may start to feel 'hyped' yourself, find yourself staring too hard, for example, or you feel 'burnt out' by them very quickly. Or you may start to feel jaded and bored yourself.
control	people will try to **prove their competence** in some way, and strain to do so. They will want to prove they are successful and so may boast. They may start to be extremely organized, or irritable with disorder as they feel out of control. Or they may become far more disorganized, chaotic. People say they are **'confused'** as a way to avoid responsibility, and resist new things to avoid facing a test of their skill. All these are signs that control feelings are the ones affected.	you will be aware of the **smoothness** with which the organization functions, whether it becomes stuck and seems **tense**, or **chaotic**. Either will alert you to the control area. You may start to feel tense yourself, holding yourself back, as this reflects the concern in the organization to perform, to be perfect, yet also be afraid to test themselves. Or you may start to feel chaotic, dropping or losing things, being uncoordinated, as this reflects the confusion and lack of control that exists in the organization itself.
affection	people will **disengage** and say they 'can't be bothered', they no longer 'care'. They become too personal in assessments, may attack or blame. They may avoid openness or do the opposite and spill everything out excessively and inappropriately. Some act in a way that gets closeness from others, whether by being upset or from physical illness, not to get attention but to get a feeling of 'engagement'. All these are signs that the affection feelings are the ones affected.	you will be aware of extremes in **emotion** when it is the affection area involved. This may be **deadness**, numbness, as if the organization has been flattened. Or you may be aware of **depths** of simmering anger or deep depression. You may start to feel rage that is out of proportion, reflecting the emotion in the organization itself. Or you may feel as if life is meaningless, feel like 'nothing', which reflects an organization where the reaction has been deadness, numbness.

The sum total of the way people feel creates that organization's atmosphere

The feelings that exist in an organization are felt, in aggregate, as the atmosphere or tone of that organization. We are familiar with such terms as 'atmosphere' more than we are with using such terms as 'feelings'. But the atmosphere in an organization is simply the sum total of the way individual people feel. When the feelings of the organization are satisfied 'enough', you will know because of the generally positive tone that exists. This is palpable, quite noticeable, and can be deciphered in exactly the same way as an emotional situation can.

Often, it is only when you need to address the feelings of people in an organization in some direct way that you start to think with words like 'emotions' or 'feelings'. If the overall tone or atmosphere that exists is positive, you can be sure that the feelings of people are being taken care of, even if you didn't realize you were taking care of them. Most of the time, organizations function with a quite straightforward atmosphere, where they can make progress without having to stop in their tracks and figure out what is going on in people's feelings. While it is essential to know what to do when the atmosphere has become charged, or negative, most of the time we can be satisfied if people's feelings are reasonably fulfilled.

Creating an esprit de corps in your own unique way so long as you are real

We can satisfy people's feelings simply by conducting the process of the business well, by creating the conditions and systems of the business in a way that meets those needs, without ever having to talk directly about 'feelings' at all. Some managers create a wonderful esprit de corps yet can be extremely uncomfortable and awkward with open talk of feelings. It is a myth that you need to be able to bare your soul or share what you are feeling with your people in order to be good at generating positive long-term commitment. People's feelings are rarely duped and they pay far more attention to what other people do than to what they say. The aim is for people to feel positive and to create an esprit de corps that is real, genuine and well-meaning. You can achieve this in many ways, and it is important to do so in your own unique, believable way, even if you are clumsy in doing so.

Figuring out that all is well from the atmosphere that exists

However you create an esprit de corps, it helps to have a way to assess what the atmosphere and tone of an organization is like. I use the qualities that characterize a particular atmosphere to let me know that all is well in the internal state of an organization. If it is, you leave it alone. We can discriminate among the three psychological areas to identify this atmosphere, in exactly the same way that we could use the framework to discriminate among the feelings within an organization in a more precise way than merely describing them as positive or negative.

Assessing the atmosphere of an organization in this direct way will tell you whether each area is functioning as it should be. In the list set out in Table 6.5 (page 150), you can easily figure this out by the qualities that best describe the atmosphere in the place. You should use the descriptions to assess the atmosphere associated with all three psychological areas as well as the most sensitive one. As with deciphering the feelings of the organization, you need to place particular attention on the sensitive area but also ensure that all three areas of experience are functioning well at any one time.

Identifying the atmosphere or tone of the organization by the effect it has on you

We can easily get an assessment of an organization's real internal state by the effect that its atmosphere has on us personally.

If the organization leaves you feeling alert, awake, lighter and interested

For example, when I am in an organization where the inclusion feelings are satisfied, and this particular area of experience is a positive aspect of the organization, I will leave feeling lifted up. I will be more aware of the light and of the details in the world around me, all of which will seem more positive. I will feel more alert and awake, without feeling hyped up or straining. This is the effect that a positive inclusion area of the organization has on others, and on the people within that organization. They are aware of what is possible, and are interested in the world around them and in each other. They actively seek out others' ideas because they are genuinely, innately interested, rather than because it is part of their job to do so. They can't help themselves. They love it, get a kick out of it. As a result, they make others feel good about themselves. You can see how this atmosphere and tone, this instinctive behaviour, generates exactly those positive feelings we can identify with the inclusion area. People within such an organization feel recognized. They have really been attended to, listened to and they know that others have been interested in them.

If the organization leaves you feeling capable of doing anything and willing to try things

When the qualities of an organization have the positive tone of the control area, you will be more aware of an air of confidence. After I have been in organizations like this, I will feel capable of doing anything I put my mind to. I feel as though I am gliding along, coordinated, rather than walking. People within an organization where this is the main tone feel as though they are embarking on a heroic adventure wherever they come up against a challenge. They think of 'work' in terms of having great fun testing themselves against some new aim. There is an unmistakable can-do spirit that pervades such an organization that needs to be distinguished from macho bravado. It is accompanied by an innate confidence, and people in such an organization should have little need to boast. They are too busy with their next achievements. When this is the tone in an organization, it encourages everyone to test themselves quite naturally, and they can accept change because they want to find out what more they are capable of. If they make a mistake, they pick themselves up and set off again. You can see how easy it is in such an organization for the control feelings, feeling competent and effective, to be fulfilled. There are many times each day when such feelings can be met. They can be self-fuelling, without anyone having to deliberately or actively satisfy them. The tone and atmosphere of the place generate activities and behaviours where this happens naturally. They can't help themselves. You can conclude from all these signs that this control area is a positively functioning area of that company.

If the organization leaves you feeling still inside, with a sense of purpose

We can also decipher the affection area in terms of the tone that will arise when this is a positive aspect of the organization. After I have been in an organization like this, I feel quiet inside, centred, deeper, more fulfilled, as if I have been reminded of why I am doing whatever I am trying to do. The effects such organizations have can be quite deep, and sometimes you will notice a feeling of timelessness as people get so involved in what they are doing that they lose track of time. In such organizations, people can find it hard to articulate what really motivates them to do what they do, since it often has deep roots. These organizations have a set of principles that guide them, even though they can be quite pragmatic. Within such an organization, it is easy for affection feelings to be fulfilled. The needs people have to feel worthwhile, to care about what they are doing for its own sake and believe in it can be easily met without having to deliberately do so. They can't help themselves. Such organizations can be just as successful in their financial results as any other company. They have a different motivation, however, and can be characterized by a belief in what they are doing that can seem funny to other people, since they can believe devoutly in some product that seems, to others, to be nothing special. But the secret of such companies is precisely the fact that their products are so special to them. This faith communicates itself to others and creates the loyalty that is the hallmark of any company which has the positive tone and atmosphere that arise from an affection area that has been well looked after.

Table 6.5 sets out the key signs, qualities and reactions that tell you that all is well.

Table 6.5 Signs that all is well

	qualities and atmosphere that tell you all is 'well'
inclusion	people pay attention to others, are interested in what they say, seek out their ideas, atmosphere is alert, sparkly, alive, people walk with a spring in their step, you feel energized, atmosphere is positive, people are very aware of possibilities, what to hope for, look forward to, atmosphere is light, 'up'
control	general atmosphere of everything working smoothly, atmosphere is of confidence without boasting; people are embarking on tests they look forward to rather than hard work, you will feel as if you glide rather than walk, feel as if you can do anything you put your mind to, feel as if everything will 'work', a can-do atmosphere
affection	general atmosphere of being fulfilled, purposeful, because people feel that what they are doing matters, a quality of depth pervades the atmosphere, and that it is all right to be yourself, there may be a sense of stillness within, even if busy, at times a sense of timelessness and at others a feeling of inner peace and comfort

Starting with a knowledge of the feelings of the organization

We have focused in this chapter on understanding what people in an organization feel, and how you can determine what feelings are present in a particular incident. We have also touched briefly on the atmosphere that reflects the overall internal state of an organization. Neither the feelings nor the atmosphere in an organization are 'separate' from the everyday events, the business decisions or the more apparent aspects of running a company. I have singled these things out in this chapter only to provide a focus and language with which we can take these things more seriously, and give them far more attention than we usually do.

Now that we have this foundation we explore various ways in which this knowledge can help us design jobs and help move the organization forward. These are key aspects of running an organization successfully and well but we usually understand them from a purely business perspective. The intention is to show you how to work in a way that pays respect to these feelings we have explored, as well as meeting the business aims. The virtue of using the conceptual framework is that, since it relates to both the feeling world and the business world, we can devise solutions that 'marry' the two up. This provides one way to meet the aims of individual people, as well as the aims of the business, at the same time. In the next chapter, I try to show you how that can be done.

Designing work so that it fulfils feelings and business aims at the same time

CHAPTER 7

Creating the effects you want rather than just working practices that 'look' right

One of the main themes of this chapter, and indeed the book, is the importance, and possibility, of relating the emotional world of the organization with its business aims. Most companies focus on their business needs first and foremost and pay too little attention to generating the right mental orientation or getting the emotional commitment that will meet those business aims. However, this may create an organization where everything looks right, since it has well-defined jobs, clearly specified career structures and paths, and formal appraisal systems, yet these are not nearly enough, and in themselves may create effects that are very different from those you want or the organization needs.

We need to design work in a way that meets the aims of the business and the aims of individuals at the same time and the purpose of this chapter is to describe some basic principles that will help you do so. One of the main reasons that work design and practices may look right but still not create the approach that the organization needs is that they do not make psychological sense to people. It is because of this that people often try to get around the system or don't play by the rules in terms of the way they approach their work. When they do so, they are simply trying to get their own individual psychological aims met, even if at the expense of the aims of the larger organization. It makes sense, therefore, to try to organize and design work that fits with the way people are and with the way human beings function.

Creating virtuous cycles in the organization

All the organization's working practices will have an impact both on how people feel and on how well the organization carries out its business tasks. You can integrate the two so that a kind of *virtuous cycle* can arise. If you can construct these virtuous cycles then you are well and truly managing the organization to best advantage. It will glide to success rather than struggle to success. If we construct them we are not restricted to thinking that there is an inevitable trade-off that has to be made between meeting the feeling needs of individuals, and meeting the needs of the business.

Two contexts to explore: job design and performance and reward criteria

We first explore these principles in relation to designing jobs. At the end of the chapter I describe briefly specific performance and reward criteria that also illustrate how you can achieve this same integration of the emotional aims and the business aims.

I set the scene with a tale of two Treasuries and my experience in working in both, which forms the context for elaborating how these virtuous cycles can be created when you design work.

Same job title but a different world

Working in the NZ and UK Treasuries

I once worked for several years in the New Zealand Treasury, my first career being that of an economist. This seeming bureaucracy had the kind of responsibilities you would expect a Treasury to have. It was the key government department, with delegated powers of approval and recommendation that meant it affected almost every other avenue of government. However, it also had an influence that went beyond these formal powers and was, and still is, the source of very original and creative ideas and policies, some of which have been transported elsewhere around the globe. Later, when I went to London, my first job was at the UK Treasury, also as an economist. Perhaps it was because I could only bear to stay for a very short time in what was an actual bureaucracy that I never discovered their creativity and originality. I expect, though, that I would never have found it wandering around their long corridors, no matter how long I had stayed.

The two Treasuries have, of course, quite similar roles within their respective governments. The Treasury in New Zealand had far fewer people, partly because they had responsibility in a much smaller country, with a far smaller total government budget, but also because they made more out of every person who worked there. Another difference was that they had an influence and a degree of persuasion over other government departments that went way beyond their delegated powers. Yet, it was not because they relied on their formal authority that they had such an influence. On the contrary, the situation in the NZ Treasury arose because people within that seeming bureaucracy had a very different understanding of what their responsibility was.

NZ Treasury: a Juggler control nature even in government

They were, in fact, a Juggler organization, the kind we think can exist only in small companies or those companies with some independent ownership. They ran a very tight ship and there was no room for anyone 'extra' nor anyone in a kind of duplicate role. I cannot recall a single person without a 'real' job. Most people assume that it is inevitable that organizations become a high-control Boss once they reach a certain size, and that anywhere within government must inevitably function as an ossified Boss. However, this particular government organization had managed to establish the equivalent of 'independent ownership' in the minds of the people employed there. They took genuine responsibility for a very wide remit, as well as for the wider effects of their actions and decisions, and it was this which served to create the greatest differences between the NZ Treasury and the UK Treasury that I experienced at that time. The latter has since had quite a few changes as has the NZ Treasury, but I describe what I saw at the time I was there in what follows, because it was the comparison between these two government organizations that formed the basis of the ideas I have since put into practice in my work, and which I outline here. The basic ideas and principles I describe apply to many companies, however, not just to these two Treasuries, and relate to the way in which we design work and our ability to use people in the organization well. If a government department can use talent well, create a tightly run, original organization where everybody takes a great deal of responsibility for the effects of what they do, and create a great deal of enjoyment at the same time, then any organization can.

Never really being able to 'do' anything in the UK Treasury

I handed my notice in at the UK Treasury after I had realized several things. All of these related to the fact that I knew I would never be able to actually 'do' anything there. I would be busy. We were all busy doing things, but this was mostly because the people there worked longer hours instead of being efficient. I knew, also, that I would never be able to really have an effect, to personally have an impact on anything, other than creating pieces of paper and reports and attending meetings. In fact, the whole point of the way they organized things was to prevent any one individual from having such an effect. This meant that people rarely engaged head-on with tasks in a way that I was used to seeing, which was the main cause of their frustrating inefficiency. As an individual, I would certainly feel responsible for a report I had written or the comments I made at a meeting, but that was far short of feeling that what I personally did would, and could, make a difference, which is what I had experienced in the NZ Treasury. There, it was up to us to ensure that the system within which we worked actually 'worked'. If the system got in the way of our working effectively, it was up to us to find a way around it, or attempt to change it. We didn't have to be told to do this or to have this fact written into our job descriptions. In fact, there were no job descriptions. They had something vaguely resembling an 'appraisal system' I think, but it was pretty irrelevant and unnecessary.

If you have to try too hard to use talent then you are miles away from being a good Juggler or Boss

A good Juggler, one that functions as such in reality, has an automatic inclination to be efficient, and uses talent with a kind of ease, as if it is natural to do so, without having to perfect the structures and systems that other organizations need in order to artificially induce the talent in their people to be well used. If you have to try too hard, or keep redrawing the organization chart in order to achieve these aims, you are a million miles away from the operating assumptions and practices that make a good Juggler or, indeed, a good Boss. In what follows I describe these assumptions and practices within a good Juggler because that was the nature of this particular organization. In a good Boss, the same end goal applies, since they too have an automatic inclination to be efficient, to use talent naturally and well, without having to struggle or strain to do so. This, indeed, is one of the signs that an organization is achieving the control purpose, irrespective of how it does so, or what its nature is.

Having my own territory, or having a job

Having territory

There were three key work design features that really made a difference to the way the two Treasuries operated and what they achieved. The first was that, in the NZ Treasury, while I had no job description, I did have my own job territory. In the UK Treasury, on the other hand, I had a job rather than 'territory'. The two things are entirely different. In New Zealand I might, for example, 'look after' the Labour and Education departments. That meant that these departments were 'yours' and nobody else could do any kind of work in those areas except via you. This held true also for your boss, who consulted you about the departments which you looked after and made an input into these areas only through you. Similarly, no other work, whether policy appraisal or budget review, that related to your departments would be done anywhere else in that organization, by anyone else, because it was 'yours'. Even as a new recruit, you had 'your' departments, and anything that affected those departments came to you. That was one key design feature of the way work was organized. It meant that a person had some experience of boundaries or territory, which is different from just having responsibility for that area. You need both, and I explain the kind of responsibility that existed in each organization in more detail below.

Having a perfectly well-defined job but needing my own territory

In the UK Treasury, by way of contrast, I had a specific job. It was very well defined, and it was clear what the remit was. But I had no territory that was 'mine' and no sense of overall integrity to my job remit at all. One reason this was so was that almost every role was duplicated. At the time I worked there, my brief as an economist was paralleled by someone elsewhere called an administrator. I was in the specialist 'expert' role and they were in a role that, essentially, was what we might think of in business as being more a management stream. This duplication seemed quite necessary to the people there. Most reports I wrote, or policy documents I was studying and commenting on, had someone else somewhere doing virtually the same thing. While the separate tasks each had a different intent and papers might be written from a slightly different perspective, in the mind of anyone in the private sector this would have been called duplication. The department prevented mistakes this way, and they could 'make sure' of whatever was recommended or decided. These two roles each had clearly differentiated job descriptions, separate career structures and reporting lines, but they established no clear differentiation of territory and, therefore, created no sense of ownership. They made sense at a formal level, but none of these 'correct' things helped in getting work done as it could be done, in creating an active engagement with tasks or in establishing any felt responsibility for the overall way the system operated.

The concept of immediacy

Real rather than formal responsibility

The second key design feature that was critical in the two organizations relates to *really* taking responsibility, rather than just assuming formal, narrow responsibility. The term I use to define this is 'immediate responsibility'. In the NZ Treasury, responsibility really did stop with you. You had to answer for what you recommended and wrote rather than anyone else doing so on your behalf. In the UK Treasury, actual responsibility was taken and felt by those at the senior levels, or those you reported to. You, personally, were never really on the line, because of the checks and balances that were in place to 'protect' the whole system. There was always a boss to assume the real responsibility at some stage. Someone senior to you, for example, would explain and justify whatever was in a report or policy that originated from your area. Even if they knew less about what they were talking about than you, the assumption was that the process of government was so complicated that you needed to gradually amass wisdom and experience before you could hope to understand its arcane ways.

The other way to design work, which still achieves the same end result, is to ensure that people have a very real interest in taking responsibility for what they do and the effects they create. This can be achieved in many ways, but I will try to illustrate what is quite a subtle process in creating this particular sense of responsibility (see below).

Responsibility really did rest with you rather than being transferred to your boss

In the NZ Treasury, you reported to a section head, who functioned as a kind of 'back stop' and watched what was going on, asked a few questions about your ideas or recommendations, discussed policy ideas with you, but rarely managed either you or your work particularly closely. I cannot recall any time when a recommendation or decision I had made was overruled by a 'boss' and, like everyone else, I was involved in creating policy with other departments with no interference from my boss. The word 'interference' probably sums up both the nature of the relationship you had with those above you, and the nature of the responsibility that you took on, since any intrusion by your boss into your deliberations on a policy area had to be made as a colleague. That is a sign of a Juggler in operation, and it applied to every official from the minute they first walked in, another aspect you will see in a Juggler organization. Such organizations assume that you should actively make use of people right from the beginning, in real jobs, rather than putting them into jobs where they are slowly trained up, or kept from doing much harm.

Above the section head was a divisional director, who gave formal approvals and signed reports to be sent up to the Minister, or to one of the Cabinet committees. All this probably sounds pretty bureaucratic, since on paper it looks as if there were two levels of management above me and I had to get approvals all the time for what I was doing. In reality, however, the organization was very unbureaucratic in practice and experience, and I have never had a job that has given me so much latitude. It is the way a system operates in practice and in terms of daily experience that determines whether it is bureaucratic or otherwise, not what it looks like on paper.

For a start, you were the one responsible for what you did rather than your boss. They put their signature on the report, but that report was your responsibility. If it meant explaining the Treasury line to a Cabinet committee, you went yourself, even if you had been in the organization for only three months, or even three weeks. In the UK Treasury, in contrast, the person who had signed the report would usually have gone, assuming responsibility for it and, therefore, taking away the feeling of immediate responsibility from whoever was doing the actual work. Secondly, the operating assumption in New Zealand was that, if the person with all the information – that is, the particular Treasury officer concerned – had decided or recommended a particular 'line', then they were the experts on that particular decision so their recommendation must be the best one for the Treasury. Only once while I was there was a 'lowly' Treasury official's opinion overturned by one of the most senior people. That is the essence of the Juggler way of operating. The decision is made where the information and knowledge is. This emphasis on giving you responsibility right from the start also meant that your contacts in other government departments were far senior than you. Our main contacts were with the financial secretaries or people one level down from the heads of departments. Did it matter? No, why should it? We were doing tasks instead of filling 'roles'.

Such practices meant that everyone took a very real responsibility for doing their jobs well. If you had to answer personally for your expenditure analysis of 'your' department, in front of a Cabinet Expenditure Committee, then you had all the incentive you could possibly need to do it as well as you humanly could. Your boss didn't go on your behalf. Why should they? They weren't responsible. You were.

Why I had 'no responsibility for anything'

In the UK Treasury, the idea that, as a single individual, you could enjoy the same degree of responsibility as I had experienced in the NZ Treasury was a very odd notion. For a start, when I asked them why I had no responsibility for anything, they assured me that it was 'dangerous' to give one individual the kind of responsibility that I was already used to and which I had seen exercised very well without any such 'dangerous' effects. I was talking a foreign language to them. One of the basic differences in interpretation was that, to them, to talk of giving people 'responsibility' meant giving a greater degree of delegated authority and, as they assured me in some general discussions about what the purpose of the Treasury was, they had enough trouble with various government departments resenting their 'authority' as it was, without asking for even wider powers. However, I was referring to responsibility rather than authority, and I was unsurprised that other departments resented their formal authority, because they did not exercise it in a way that seemed, to me, to be responsible.

Taking responsibility for your effects, not just what you do

Thinking forward to the effects you create

The third key design feature that was apparent in the two organizations relates to the manner in which people take account of the wider or longer-term effects they create. Taking into account the effects you create is different from taking responsibility for what you do. Essentially, it means thinking in terms of how, and how well, any decision or policy will be implemented, and what effect it will have when it is implemented. These stages, implementation and the end effect, are part of your thinking, even if they will have ceased to be part of your defined territory. A good decision, for example, is one that has good effects when it is implemented, even if it is someone else's job to do that. It can never be a good decision if others have to 'sort it out' after you and, because of various factors, when it is put into practice it fails to work properly. This means that any decision, recommendation or idea requires that people have 'thought forward', and that they know about factors that will affect whether that decision or recommendation will work in reality rather than just seem an excellent decision in the confines of the organization's walls.

Actively engaging with your remit and the world outside

The only way this can happen is if people actively engage with their remit. Let me give you one example of how this occurred in the NZ Treasury. My brief, at one stage, was the Labour Department. It was assumed, partly because I was still finishing off a thesis on an industrial dispute, that I would have some knowledge about the labour market, real-world knowledge instead of theoretical knowledge, since they had relatively little interest in the latter. It was also thought desirable that anyone looking after that department should know, or find out, a far wider brief than just labour market statistics, for example, or what was behind those statistics. It was assumed that I should know and meet people in the Employers Federation, as well as the Trade Union bodies. I was expected to use my own initiative in setting up any meetings or contacts like this or, indeed, in suggesting other ways of getting to know the real world outside that might make me better informed. In general, you were expected to keep a very wide watching brief, as well as to find out, from close up, how the real world operated, especially that part of it that you, as a Treasury officer, might have an effect on. You were supposed to be face to face with it rather than be at a distance. Otherwise, you could hardly fulfil your role properly, because a good policy idea, or a good recommendation, was one that would work and be implemented well in the real world. It was supposed to have the right effects, rather than just be right in itself.

The outside world might 'influence my judgement'

I should have known, just in the recruitment interview, how I would feel in the UK Treasury. Instead of finding out what independent thoughts I had about various real-world problems, I was quizzed for answers to theoretical economics questions. I was asked questions that reminded me of some of my economics exams at university. Consider the following conversation I subsequently had with my 'boss' there. I asked him if people ever went 'out and about'. I was interested in whether they had close contact with employers or unions, whether they went and talked to them a great deal so that they would be better informed of the tangible effects of their policy recommendations. His reaction was as if I had suggested some native ritual from the South Seas. I was assured that it was 'better' not to get too close to others outside. 'Why?' 'Because they might influence your judgement.' I started to ask other people at the Treasury why they were there, since it seemed incomprehensible that anyone would like to work in this way and I wondered if I was missing something in my analysis. I asked one person why he worked there, since 'It seems that you never have real responsibility for anything. You don't know what is going on out there.' He said, 'Of course! That is the whole point. That is why I like working here.' It was at this point that I resigned.

Putting the organization chart in its place

One of the reasons I use my tale of the two Treasuries is because it draws out the three design features that seem important in creating organizations that are naturally efficient and which use talent well, but which do not have to struggle and strain to do so. The general principles in these design features I explain in what follows, but there is a subtext to the tale which I want to mention first because it provides the perspective we need to make any design features, whatever they are, work well in the real world. This is that it is the mental structures you create in people's heads as well as the emotional commitment that you create that matter more than the right organizational structures.

Many companies have taken out layers of managers in order to create an organizational structure that is very flat, and would look in horror at the apparently bureaucratic system I have described in both these government departments. Yet most of those same companies which have delegated formal authority way down to the front line are still acting in their day-to-day work in ways that are bureaucratic, inefficient and overly controlling. Many attempts at lessening control fail to work because the ingredients that make it work in practice are different from those of simply redrawing the organization chart. Being more efficient can only ever happen when people actively engage with whatever they do and get their hands around it, and many companies fail to get anywhere near this even with the flattest of hierarchies.

Even delayered organizations can rarely let go, in practice

Few delayered organizations function in a way where a person is never overruled by a boss or where the operating assumption is that you should rarely be. Almost all assume that, of course, one of the whole points of having a boss in the first place is so they can overrule you. Few newly entrepreneurial organizations function in such a way that a boss would be seen as 'interfering' if they told you what a better policy or idea was, rather than bouncing all the ideas around with you, as a colleague. Very few managers have the psychological capacity to function in this way, or to let go of the idea that they know more than someone reporting into them.

Very few managers can resist taking responsibility from their people at some stage, especially if something goes 'wrong'. Yet, many clients also come to me to complain about their people 'refusing' to really take responsibility for their jobs. What, they ask me, can we do to redefine the roles and set clear levels of responsibility to make sure that 'they' know what they are responsible for. What your people need, I answer, is for you to leave responsibility with them, especially when things go wrong, and to know, at any time, that such responsibility will stay with them. When it does, they have to fix the mistakes, make good any errors and mend the fences that need mending. Redefining roles and specifying levels of responsibility for your people is a waste of time unless you can stop yourself from 'rescuing' them or speaking on their behalf, because doing so takes away their daily awareness that responsibility really does stop with them. When you can show me you have changed the way you think in your head, I tell these clients, I will help redefine the roles for you.

In truth, there are instances when the boss really does need to step in, but the operating principle should be that this is an exception rather than an expectation.

The point of an organizational structure is that it does not get in the way of the business

It is not the nature of the organization chart that makes a difference, it is what you do in the minutiae of every day. The principle that I follow is that the organizational structure and reporting lines should be altered or constructed so that they get 'out of the way', so that they cease to interfere with the workflow. Beyond that, to tinker relentlessly with either in the belief that the structure or organization chart causes very much to happen is usually a waste of time. However, sometimes it is the case that you have to change an aspect of the structure first. For example, in the UK Treasury (as it was when I worked there), there would have been little point in trying to change much unless you first stripped out the duplication of roles. Trying to alter work practices or trying to change the culture would have been a waste of time unless you had altered this aspect of its structure. In other companies, the same principle holds. If some aspect of the structure seriously gets in the way, you would be kidding yourself if you invested a lot of time on any other change before removing that blockage first. However, beyond this kind of situation, tinkering around with the organization chart is often a delusory activity.

What is important is to ensure that, whatever system you construct for your organization, it creates the right mental structures and emotional orientation inside people's heads and hearts, rather than creating the right-looking structure on a piece of paper. One of the reasons why the operating practices in the NZ Treasury worked well is because they fitted with the way people make sense of their work, and in the next few sections of this chapter I elaborate why the key job design features which I highlighted in my tale create this kind of fit.

Summarizing the key principles

The first design feature was that people should have their own territory, and this is different from a job. Territory has a connotation of space. When you have territory, you have some sense of boundaries and some say over who can go in or out of it. You have first sight of anything that comes within your territory. The second design feature was that

Table 7.1 Key design features

> having a defined **territory** rather than a job, a concept of *space*; you have boundary rights over that space
>
> **exercising responsibility**, which moves to your boss only as an exception, a concept of *immediacy*
>
> taking responsibility for the **effects** of what you do, not just what you do or achieve, a concept of *time*

people should have immediate responsibility. The concept of immediacy means the source of responsibility stays the same, and shifting it anywhere, such as to a more senior person, is an exception not an expectation. The third design feature was that people should take into account the subsequent effects of what they do, rather than just focus on what they do in their immediate work. This is a very different notion from simply being responsible for 'results'. It implies taking into account ahead of time what will happen as a result of what you do, or decide.

Table 7.1 sets out the key characteristics of the three job design features.

Understanding why the three design features make psychological sense

Some work structures create a pattern that is like a virtuous cycle. They encourage people to behave in certain ways, and those ways fulfil their needs or feelings, so that they have an in-built incentive to continue to function and do their work in this way. Yet those work structures are meeting the business aims of the organization as well. In what follows, I describe the way in which the three design features set up those virtuous cycles. If we design work in a way that goes with people's needs, they will want to use their talents, and you will have little need to actively exhort them to do so, all you will need to do is get out of their way. Designing work in this way creates an automatic desire to be efficient, because it seems as though there is no other way that 'makes sense'. Both the business and the individual get their needs met, which is why organizations that have managed to achieve this kind of mutuality seem to flow smoothly. It makes sense in both directions.

Understanding the psychological purposes of the individual

In order to understand how to create virtuous cycles and meet the aims of the individual, we need a way of describing what those aims are. We can use the same framework that we have used throughout the book to do this. Like every organization, every individual has their own 'inclusion purpose'. They need to establish their own identity, an awareness that they exist alongside others, and they need to establish a satisfactory way of interacting with others and remaining 'intact'. They will have their own control purpose, too, exerting influence and power to ensure they meet their goals and are effective in the world, in exactly the same way that an organization needs to in order to fulfil its control purpose. Finally, individuals will also have their own affection purpose, needing to engage with people and tasks in a way that feels real and that sustains them for the long term. Together, these individual psychological purposes form the context that allows us to explore the three design features and why they make sense to people. In what follows, I go through each one in turn, and you can see how the virtuous cycle that links these individual aims with the organization's aims is set up.

Territory creates an experience of intactness and identity: the inclusion purpose

Having a sense of territory provides the experience of intactness and integrity human beings need

Every person needs to function in a way that makes them feel they are a distinct unit, with intact boundaries as they exist in the world alongside others. One of the psychological aims of the inclusion area of experience, in terms of work, is that each person creates for themselves a unique identity, they are known, and can make a 'mark' on the world that is distinctively theirs and no one else's. These are all fundamental aims that fulfil the inclusion purpose of an individual.

The work design feature of having territory fulfils this purpose, whereas having only a job can never do so. Having something called a territory creates for that individual the emotional experience of being intact rather than being invaded. They experience some boundaries. To divide work up in this way, into a 'territory', therefore has some similarity with the fundamental experience everyone keeps seeking, namely that they are alive and well as a distinct person. It creates the deeper awareness that they exist as a unique, intact individual. If a person has a clear territory, it allows them also to be identified with what goes on in that territory, to get personal credit for it, and they can put their own stamp on it. Doing so fulfils some of the feelings that all individuals want. In relation to the inclusion area, this means that it is possible for them to feel recognized, that they count, that they can be seen, noticed or stand out. If they have a work role defined in such a way, they feel they 'exist'. When they have this experience of themselves, people feel they are fully alive at quite a deep level. People will feel this sense of territory in different ways, but it needs to exist at a psychological level for the benefits to be obtained.

If there is a threat of invasion it is impossible to fulfil the inclusion feelings

Without this sense of territory, people will have the emotional experience, or potential experience, of invasion, that their boundaries are permeable rather than intact. They can never feel that they 'exist' as a unique individual in the same way, and they will be unable to experience the fulfilment of such inclusion feelings as being recognized in their own right. When there is overlap, or duplication of roles in an organization, an individual has less opportunity to meet these needs, or feel the same experience of being an intact, distinct individual. This does not mean that people cannot work closely together, however, or join together on specific tasks. I am referring to the larger sense of their overall job, within which they need, for the time they are in it, to have some sense of psychological territory.

People become turf-like and counter-productive only because their feelings are unmet

This feeling of psychological territory is quite distinct from the idea of people being 'territorial' meant in the pejorative sense of being 'turf-like'. The latter means resisting cooperation with others and constructing departmental or 'feudal' boundaries. However, the reason why people often do this is precisely because they do not experience the feeling of intactness that human beings all need to experience at an emotional level if they are to cooperate and interact fully with others. When people do experience having their 'own territory' whose boundaries and integrity are respected, they invite others into that territory. They will not do so if they feel a threat of potential psychological invasion. Turf-like wars and barriers arise because people have invented counter-productive ways of getting their needs met, that is, their inclusion feelings fulfilled. In so doing, they meet their own needs even if it is at the expense of the organization's business needs.

The atmosphere created when there is a sense of territory and intactness

The net effect of this will be apparent in the general atmosphere that exists in the workplace. If people have their own territory and the feelings of intactness that come from having their own space, if they feel deeply 'alive', the sum total will be the positive atmosphere I described as existing in relation to the inclusion area in the chapter on the feelings and atmosphere that exist within the organization. In other words, the energy will be alert, people will seem alive and on the ball, and there will be a spring in their step. People will be interested in others, and there will be a lightness in the general tone within the organization. When these particular needs are unmet, the overall tone in the organization is either that of flatness or of boredom, a kind of jaded feeling where people are slightly tired all the time. Or they may react in the opposite way, and overreach themselves and become hyper instead. In terms of the conceptual framework, they are unable to meet their own inclusion purpose as individuals. One group has given up trying and the other is desperately still trying to meet that aim.

The benefit to the organization's business aims

The benefit to the organization when the individual's aims are met in this way is that those aims and activities of the business that we could also identify with the inclusion area are more easily met. It is in organizations where the atmosphere is like this that innovation is easier and people have novel and interesting ideas. Innovation always arises when people are interested in what is going on around them and explore others' ideas naturally, without needing to force themselves to do so. Innovation arises also only when people are themselves as individuals and create their own unique spark. Innovative ideas are never easy to generate until an organization has this kind of atmosphere. In such organizations, there is an overall spark and flair to what they produce. Sales and promotional activities are interesting and attract everyone's attention because there is a certain energy, a buzz to these things that has an 'edge' to it, without being garish or desperate in its attempt to get people's attention. The organization as a whole would find that it is known, that it has a distinctive identity to those outside. Claiming space for itself in the market is far more straightforward when the inside of the organization has people functioning like this, and when the atmosphere is positive in these ways. Table 7.2 summarizes the virtuous cycle that can arise with this design feature.

Table 7.2 Job territory as the first design feature

job design feature	making psychological sense and fulfilling feelings	general atmosphere in organization	advantages to organization
having clear territory or job space that is 'yours', a sense of private boundaries, so you have first rights over what goes on in that territory and others have to respect those boundaries	creates a sense of intactness and what people do within their territory has their stamp on it. This means they can be identified with it and no one else. This provides the possibility of feeling noticed, acknowledged, recognized. They can feel they are a unique distinctive individual. They feel intact as a person in their own right, with boundaries that are respected. It avoids creating feelings of being invaded or intruded on, or having their boundaries ignored. When positive, people are more aware in general. They really 'exist'.	the overall effect is an atmosphere of alertness without strain; the organization has a spark and aliveness, a lightness and energy about it. People have a spark to them, some life to them, walk with a spring in their step.	people are more innovative, have more interesting ideas and are naturally interested in others without having to strain to be so. They find out more about what is going on in the world. There is a flair to what the organization produces, an extra edge, promotions are talked about, taken notice of, without having to shout for attention. The organization can claim space and attention for itself in the market-place easily, and people are aware of who it is. It 'exists'.
	This helps to fulfil the inclusion purpose of that individual		This helps to fulfil the inclusion purpose of the organization

Immediacy in responsibility creates a sense of capability: the control purpose

The concept of immediacy

The second key design feature is that real responsibility exists for people in the organization. The most critical aspect of this is expressed by the word 'immediacy'. What this term brings to the somewhat vague idea of responsibility is the importance of keeping that responsibility in one place. If responsibility can shift, most commonly to an immediate boss, a person can never feel real responsibility in their work. The results of a person's acts and decisions must stay with that same individual. That is the concept of immediacy.

The reason this is so critical is that it provides the mental framework that 'tells' a person that they need to perform well. More importantly, it provides the emotional basis for them to *want* to perform well. If they experience this kind of responsibility, then and only then can they meet the fundamental needs people have to feel fully competent and able to deal with the world. It is this design feature that can fulfil the control purpose of an individual. If a job can be designed so that these needs are met by the individual's own actions, that person will have little need to be encouraged to do their job well. All you need to do is let them.

Wanting to perform well in order to fulfil their own control feelings

The control purpose of an individual requires that they exert power and influence, and express their capabilities in such a way that they meet their own goals. By doing so, they establish a sense of effectiveness, that is, a person is aware that what they do has the effect they want. What this also means is that they develop a sense that what they will do at any time is likely to have the effect they want it to have. This is the true meaning of efficacy, and provides a deeper concept of capability than we are accustomed to.

People tend to focus only on the skills and knowledge people have. A job description typically focuses on competence and capability expressed at this level. However, this superficial understanding of competence only partially generates the feeling of innate power and effectiveness that human beings really need if they are to use themselves well. Having knowledge and skills can still mean that a person feels inadequate at dealing with whatever they encounter in their work. They may resist change because they rely on fulfilling their need to feel competent from using specialized knowledge. If, instead, people have an innate sense that they can cope with anything, that they can have the effect on the world that they intend now and at any future time, they will be ready to face anything new and to try, because their sense of self-capability derives from something much deeper and profound.

Immediate responsibility is necessary to provide the deeper sense of capability people need

The way responsibility is defined and understood is one of the key factors that creates this awareness of deeper innate capability, or just of being highly skilled or highly educated. If people can shift responsibility at some later time, depending on the results of whatever they do, they can never generate that experience of full capability. Instead they will have short-circuited their experience of it. If, at the back of their minds, they know a boss can step in later on their behalf, the conditions within them to fully take on responsibility will never occur. They will, therefore, only feel a superficial level of competence and capability, and they will never really know if they have what it takes. That is why this second design feature is so critical to get right.

The atmosphere that is then created is a can-do one

When people in the organization feel this deeper sense of competence, the atmosphere is a can-do one. The general spirit within such an organization is that people get stuck in, they try. When faced with a challenge, they approach it as another way to see 'what they are capable of'. They have an innate sense that they will figure out how to make it work, because they carry within them this awareness that they can be effective, no matter what. Such organizations find change much easier than organizations where people's sense of competence has been only superficially experienced and is therefore shakier. The positive atmosphere leads to a virtuous cycle since everyone generates this same sense of confidence in others.

The business aims are then achieved more easily

The advantages for the business when this is the case relate to the easier fulfilment of the control purpose of the organization itself. One component of this is being able to respond and change, and such an organization will be able to face external challenges with the same sense that they will find the means to deal with whatever might arise. They are more likely to take risks, which leads them to develop new products and try new markets. Their aims become higher as people within the organization feel much more relaxed at stretching themselves, and those aims are more often achieved because people make sure they are, and find ways to be resourceful, determined and clever. Whatever the aims are, they have to be achieved with no excuses. The environment, the stock market or the actions of competitors are never used as excuses to 'explain' why the organization has failed to meet a goal. As with the people within, in such an organization the buck stops with them.

Table 7.3 summarizes the virtuous cycle that can arise with this design feature.

Table 7.3 Immediate responsibility as the second design feature

job design feature	making psychological sense and fulfilling feelings	general atmosphere in organization	advantages to organization
real responsibility which has the component of immediacy, the responsibility stays with the person and it can be shifted, for example to a boss, only as an exception not an expectation	creates an innate awareness of capability. A person feels truly effective if they operate in an environment where they are responsible for what they do and this responsibility can rarely be shifted. If it can, the sense within them that they are deeply competent can never be experienced. They will be unsure if they have what it takes to deal with whatever happens. When positive, people try things they have never done before. They stretch into new areas, out of specialized ones, because they feel the innate capacity to do what they set their minds to do, whatever happens.

This helps to fulfil the control purpose of that individual | there is a can-do atmosphere and a spirit of adventure in the place that comes from seeing work and any challenges as a new way to test or use themselves fully. The general tone is encouragement of others' attempts to do whatever they are trying to do. | the business aims are set high but realistically because people are used to stretching themselves. Their approach to challenges from the market is straightforward and immediate, as they are used to dealing with everything with a direct assumption of power and doing whatever is necessary to achieve new aims. The business is more likely to create new products and find new markets because they are unafraid of risks. They learn fast because they have little need to prove they already know everything.

This helps to fulfil the control purpose of the organization |

Taking into account the wider effects of what you do: the affection purpose

Feeling real and that life has a purpose rather than feeling superficial and hollow

Every person needs to function in a way that makes them feel they are actively engaged with others and with their work. This is the affection purpose of a person. By doing so, they establish the knowledge within themselves that they are capable of sustaining relationships with others which are real, rather than just a matter of form. By doing so, they also establish for themselves that they can genuinely engage with whatever they are doing rather than just going through the motions. By this direct contact, whether with work or with another person, they feel real rather than superficial or hollow, and that living is worthwhile. Life has a purpose to them. These are the psychological aims of the affection area of an individual.

Feeling they contribute to a wider agenda fulfils people's affection feelings

If people feel they contribute to a wider agenda, and if they are aware of the effects of what they do, they are more likely to satisfy their affection purpose. This is why the third design feature meets these psychological aims of the individual. Feeling useful, that you contribute something, are fundamental human needs. None of these needs can be met if people work with their heads buried in the sand because there is no purpose to what they do and they have no idea what effect they have on others. Many organizations prevent people from feeling these things, because they structure the work in such a way that the subsequent effects of what people do happen 'elsewhere' and it is up to those people 'elsewhere' to do their own narrowly defined bit in turn.

This third design feature contains an element of time. This is because the wider effects that an individual has often occur after a period of time. If a person takes those knock-on effects into account, at least to some degree, then that person will have 'thought forward'. This is a different notion from that of responsibility because it includes anticipating the effects of what you do ahead of time. A key factor is for people to know why they are doing what they are doing. Then they will have a sense of the larger purpose to what they do and it is this that is necessary for them to genuinely engage with others and with their tasks instead of merely going through the motions.

Structuring work so people think forward creates the virtuous cycle

If work is structured or performed so that these wider effects and deeper purpose are taken into account, it is easy for an individual to feel that what they do matters, and they will have little need to be told that it does. They will know it is true simply from carrying out their jobs. The evidence that what they do matters to others will be clearly apparent to them. This is the virtuous cycle that is set up in this design feature, since it meets the individual's needs automatically, as well as the needs of the business.

The atmosphere that is then created is one of purpose, timelessness

When this is the general case in an organization, the atmosphere is one of purpose. The general tone is of caring about what you are doing. This is the distinctive note to the atmosphere when people think and act in this way. As I have set out in the description of different atmospheres in Chapter 6, when these feelings and needs are generally met the net effect is often that of timelessness. People lose track of time quite easily as they are so immersed in what they are doing. Their work has such interest that it takes people 'out of themselves'. They are filled up with the feeling that what they do matters.

The benefit to the business that is then created is great commitment and loyalty

The benefit to the business is that there is a high level of commitment. People believe in what they are doing, and in the organization as a whole. In addition, if people 'think forward' and have an understanding of the larger purpose of what they do the organization functions with a much better degree of coordination. The knock-on effects of what one business area does will have already been thought through, and when mistakes happen it is far easier to sort them out because people have as part of their ongoing frame of mind the agenda of the organization as a whole rather than just that of their own area. One of the end effects, therefore, is a better cohesion and camaraderie in general in the organization.

It is often at the top of the organization that you see the effects of this, since it is at this level that there is such a great need for people to have the agenda of the whole organization in their minds, as well as the agenda of their own area. It is only when the people at the top feel a deep sense that they have a larger purpose, and that they are responsible for the effects of what they do, that you can hope to have the senior people act in the interests of the whole organization rather than just themselves or their own particular area. Arguments can still occur, of course, and will do so in any organization where people care about what they are doing. However, the benefit comes from the sense that they still share an agenda that is much bigger than that of any one person or that person's division.

When the organization functions in this way, it means that there is little need to manage people closely since they can be trusted to take the wider agenda of the organization into account. The organization has a very positive but subtle impact on those outside such as customers or the public, since it tends to be liked precisely because it has this palpable belief in what it is doing. It is often curious to see how such organizations get away with doing things that others would be criticized for, because it is so hard to dislike organizations that really care about what they are doing. Their enthusiasm and commitment communicate quite easily to people outside and they create great loyalty. People want such organizations to do well.

Table 7.4 summarizes the virtuous cycle that can arise with this design feature.

Meeting the needs of the individual as well as the organization

The three key work design features seem, to me, to be vital in order to create organizations that function effectively. Some organizations can perform successfully, in the sense of meeting goals, but only at great expense, and with an effort that belies their apparent effectiveness. If getting results takes too much struggle and strain, the organization can never be functioning as it should. It requires also that the organization's success is accompanied by some degree of internal well-being. True effectiveness implies that people within the organization are reasonably fulfilled, get a kick out of what they do and naturally want to use their skills. Sustained success is much easier if it occurs because people's mental and emotional orientation and the atmosphere in the organization are well looked after and invested in. It is for these reasons that we need to construct organizations with the needs of both individuals and the organization itself in mind. As you can see, if you decipher the psychological implications of the work design, it is possible to meet both needs and, by so doing, create an organization that functions with ease and grace.

Table 7.4 Taking into account the effects of what you do: the third design feature

job design feature	making psychological sense and fulfilling feelings	general atmosphere in organization	advantages to organization
taking into account the wider effects of what you do rather than just what you do, as well as the longer-term effects of what you do	people feel fully engaged with their work, and with the larger agenda of that work. They then feel that what they do contributes something, so they feel real, they feel good, that they stand for something. They are more likely to believe in the organization, and know what its overall agenda is. Otherwise, people go through the motions and are never fully engaged or they are too selfish. They ignore the long-term effect they have on others. When positive, you can trust people to do what is in the best interests of the organization. This helps to fulfil the affection purpose of that individual	the overall tone is of commitment and purpose, and the atmosphere can become timeless and still, even when very busy. The general feeling is that people can be themselves as there are few games. There is a deeper sense of trust and faith in others' intentions.	the business advantages stem from people knowing why the organization does what it does, so there is a level of loyalty within that typically communicates to the market-place. People outside the organization believe in it as well, or are loyal to it, and what the organization does or produces is usually well received. The market 'likes' them and trusts them so they can sometimes get away with things other companies find hard to. People want companies like this to succeed. This helps to fulfil the affection purpose of the organization

The general principle holds for any system or practice in the organization

We have explored the idea of integrating the aims of the individual and those of the business in one of the key aspects of organizations, that is, the way work is designed. 'Getting the work done' forms the daily reality of organizations so how that work is done is worth paying particular attention to. However, there are, of course, other aspects of the organization that are essential to 'get right' as well. In my work as a consultant there are several systems or aspects that I focus on that need to be in good working order if we want to get the organization running as it should do. Aside from the way work is designed, another fundamental factor is the various criteria used in appraising, evaluating, rewarding and promoting people, and it is to this that we turn our attention briefly as a way of rounding off this chapter.

Such criteria, and the systems that reflect them, can also meet the aims of the individual and the business at the same time. However, there is usually one missing ingredient to getting these criteria, and the systems which 'house' them, correct and that is that we choose criteria only on the basis of their performance-related impact and ignore the significance of the fact that it is human beings we are trying to affect. We need to take into account how people feel and know exactly what feelings we need to generate with those criteria. One way or another, we have to take into account that people feel things within organizations and don't just perform and do things. And, as you can see from the principles I have outlined with job design, it is possible to take those feelings into account in such a way that we can satisfy them and also meet the business aims at the same time. When this happens, people within organizations work with the grain of the system, since it meets their needs and aims, instead of trying to 'get around' the system.

In order to achieve this integration, we need to be able to identify the link between the various criteria that can be used to assess people's performance and reward them, and the feelings they fulfil. That is what we explore in the next section.

Understanding the emotional impact different performance criteria have

The criteria used to evaluate and reward people affect both business aims and individual aims

The general criteria by which people's performance or behaviour is appraised and rewarded tell people what kinds of behaviour are recognized, what qualities in people are valued and what kinds of activities should be performed rather than others. Many organizations spend a great deal of time sorting out what the basis for such evaluations should be. They may have slightly different criteria for reward systems compared with those used in promotion systems, and use slightly different criteria for appraisal compared with those used in reward systems. Nevertheless, such performance and reward criteria receive the attention they deserve because they represent key components of any organization. These same criteria also have a dramatic and immediate effect on how people feel.

The way they are appraised, promoted or rewarded fulfils or frustrates the feelings that all people in an organization want to experience.

Different performance criteria will fulfil very different feelings

We start by identifying the feelings that different performance and reward criteria will affect. In Table 7.5 I have listed skills, behaviours and qualities, many of which are quite typical of criteria used by my clients. However, I have categorized these in terms of which feelings they will affect and, by implication, which feelings will be unaffected by such criteria. If the specific skills, behaviours or qualities shown in one area are recognized and acknowledged, then the corresponding feelings will be fulfilled.

'Being innovative' as a criterion will fulfil feelings of recognition but not competence or appreciation

One of the reasons for using such a table is that it enables you to fine-tune and discriminate among the criteria you use. Some behaviours, such as 'generating ideas', 'being innovative' and 'having a spark', if acknowledged in performance criteria will generate the feelings we would identify as inclusion feelings, such as recognition, feeling that they exist, feeling alert and aware, feeling that they count. Notice, though, that such criteria do not, as is often assumed, create feelings of competence or capability, or a feeling of being on top of things. They do not create feelings of effectiveness or achievement, all of which are control feelings which can only be generated by criteria or rewards that have a control meaning or nature. If you acknowledge behaviours like 'being innovative' or 'having a spark', you will only affect that individual's inclusion area of experience so that they feel more aware of themselves as a unique individual and feel they have a distinct place in the world but they will not feel, any more than they do already, that they are in control or effective. The two effects are entirely different at an emotional level.

Other behaviours and qualities, such as being flexible or being able to plan, even if acknowledged and rewarded have no effect on feelings of recognition and will not create in people a deep sense of their own distinct identity or an awareness of their unique place in the world. Instead, such performance or reward criteria will fulfil feelings of competence, those feelings we would identify with the control area. Such criteria enable people to feel they are in control and on top of things. If we reward people for their achievement of objectives that, too, only generates feelings we would describe as control feelings. Such criteria can never generate feelings of either recognition (inclusion) or of appreciation or self-liking (affection).

On the other hand, criteria that reward or acknowledge such things as commitment or loyalty will never fulfil feelings of competence, but will fulfil feelings we would associate with the affection area, such as appreciation, caring or trust. The criteria that are required in order to generate these particular feelings are probably less common than those criteria that we can relate to the inclusion and control areas. Indeed, it is because this is often the case that it is also true that many organizations find it hard to meet the aims we would associate with the affection area, such as obtaining genuine commitment rather than an instrumental or selfish approach to the organization. One of the criteria that is effective in creating affection feelings, such as appreciation and trust, is that the person takes into account the agenda of the organization as a whole, even if that agenda contradicts their own personal agenda or interests, or if it contradicts those of their business area or division. It is, often, only when people are explicitly appraised, rewarded and promoted on the basis of such a criterion that the organization prevents too much political infighting. Yet, the benefits of having people work for the organization as a whole and not just themselves are almost always sought by organizations. If, however, organizations have no idea what the effect of such criteria are or, conversely, have no idea what the emotional requirements are to obtain those benefits, they will always be frustrated and disappointed in people's behaviour. Turf wars, political behaviour and selfishness will be described as 'just' human nature. But it isn't 'just' human nature that causes these negative phenomena to occur in organizations. It is also because those human beings we are trying to affect are being judged and rewarded with inappropriate criteria.

It is essential, then, that the criteria you apply are not 'mixed up', psychologically speaking, and also that the organization does not assume that feelings of appreciation, feeling accepted and liked are irrelevant compared with people's need to feel competent. Within organizations, people may not easily admit that they want such feelings fulfilled but the need to feel such things is part of human nature. And, as I keep mentioning, we employ human beings not numbskulls nor machines so we need to take all these various feelings into account when we decide on which criteria are to be used in any organization.

If you know the effect of the performance or reward criteria, therefore, you will understand the wider effects that they have. Notice that I use a mix of skills, behaviours and qualities in Table 7.5 because a focus on competences inevitably ends up with a bias towards the control area. As we know, it is more than control feelings that need fulfilment, and it

Table 7.5   Feelings associated with different talents, qualities and performance

significance, recognition, feeling you count in your own right irrespective of achieving, feeling seen and heard, distinctive, special, feeling you are alive, that you 'exist' in the world
innovative, has interesting ideas, stands out from others, focused on quality, creates a spark in a group, brings things alive, opens up possibilities, capable of reflection and thought without knee-jerk responses, good at networking and interacting, has contacts that knows how to use, keeps abreast with others inside and outside the company, has presence, easily gets others' attention, people really listen to them, able to 'sell' themselves and company easily and naturally without it being excessive, avoids blandness and avoids creating a sense of sameness or conventionality

inclusion feelings and the performance criteria that will create those feelings

competence, feeling admired, successful, proud, effective, feeling able, functional, on top, able to cope, able to achieve, feel capable, feel able to be relied on
has initiative, able to work independently, takes responsibility, able to think strategically, setting clear goals, meeting precise targets or goals, meeting deadlines, being persuasive, using influence well, competitive, adaptability, most conceptions of 'general management' such as following things through and implementing, good at organizing, able to take control, ability to plan, able to get others to achieve and perform, sets clear standards, can manage managers, able to stand back, flexible

control feelings and the performance criteria that will create those feelings

feel appreciated, trusted, fulfilled, liked, feelings of belief in organization and self, self-acceptance, feel fully engaged, feel that work and life is worthwhile, feel 'good'
has integrity, is honest, trustworthy, deeply-held values and principles, committed, understands wider objectives outside own immediate work role, takes organization's aims into account, thinks of effects of actions on others, creates loyalty and trust from others, sustains relationships over long term, deals genuinely with things rather than superficially, creates genuine commitment in others, acts as a sounding board to others, is wise, learns from experience, has empathy and is comfortable with people, emotions and feelings

affection feelings and the performance criteria that will create those feelings

is more than the control purpose of the business that needs to be met. However, most organizations tend to have an innate bias towards the control area. In other words, most organizations use criteria to monitor people's performance, to promote and reward people, that are associated with this area of experience at the expense of the other two areas, inclusion and affection. The implications of this bias are profound both for individuals as well as the business because neither can get their full range of needs met.

Table 7.5 sets out the kinds of behaviours and qualities performance systems use to evaluate and reward people, and the particular feelings they will create.

Seeing how the behaviours relate to the business aims

So far, I have only detailed the effects such criteria have on specific feelings. For some people, this is all they want to know because they use the knowledge to motivate their people and create the esprit de corps that they need. However, we can also trace through the effect these exact same criteria have on the way tasks are performed and the aims of the business met. The set of skills, behaviours and personal qualities identified in Table 7.5 also lead to people performing their work in particular ways because such criteria induce people to behave in one way rather than another. Indeed, that is one of the main purposes of such systems in the first place, that they shape the way people in organizations carry out their tasks. We can trace the way this occurs in such a fashion that the process of performance evaluation can be seen both to meet the business aims of the organization as well as to fulfil specific feelings. I illustrate the principle by exploring just the inclusion area of experience, but it is easy to apply the same process to the other two areas of experience simply from the previous chapters on the features and aims of the business that relate to each area.

A virtuous cycle between certain evaluation criteria, feeling recognized, and meeting business aims

If people are innovative, have a spark and generate interesting ideas, for example, they are likely to perform those activities that create the innovative products the company needs. They will be good ambassadors for the company and create the kind of distinctive identity, in others' eyes, that the organization needs. Both innovative products and having a distinctive identity are often key aims of most organizations, that can be described as 'inclusion aims' within the conceptual framework I have described in this book. Other aims of the business are also met by the

Table 7.6 Meeting the individual's purpose as well as the organization's

satisfies the inclusion purpose of the individual through fulfilling the feelings they need, as well as satisfying the inclusion purpose of the organization through generating the behaviours, skills and activities that meet those aims	innovative, has interesting ideas, stands out from others, focused on quality, creates a spark in a group, brings things alive, opens up possibilities, capable of reflection and thought without knee-jerk responses, good at networking and interacting, has contacts that knows how to use, keeps abreast with others inside and outside the company, has presence, easily gets others' attention, people really listen to them, able to 'sell' themselves and company easily and naturally without it being excessive, avoids blandness and avoids creating a sense of sameness or conventionality.
satisfies the control purpose of the individual through fulfilling the feelings they need, as well as satisfying the control purpose of the organization through generating the behaviours, skills and activities that meet those aims	has initiative, able to work independently, takes responsibility, able to think strategically, setting clear goals, meeting precise targets or goals, meeting deadlines, being persuasive, using influence well, competitive, adaptability, most conceptions of 'general management' such as following things through and implementing, good at organizing, able to take control, ability to plan, able to get others to achieve and perform, sets clear standards, can manage managers, able to stand back, flexible
satisfies the affection purpose of the individual through fulfilling the feelings they need, as well as satisfying the affection purpose of the organization through generating the behaviours, skills and activities that meet those aims	has integrity, is honest, trustworthy, deeply-held values and principles, committed, understands wider objectives outside own immediate work role, takes organization's aims into account, thinks of effects of actions on others, creates loyalty and trust from others, sustains relationships over long term, deals genuinely with things rather than superficially, creates genuine commitment in others, acts as a sounding board to others, is wise, learns from experience, has empathy and is comfortable with people, emotions and feelings

everyday acts of individuals which, hopefully, the reward and performance criteria are encouraging rather than discouraging. For example, being interested in others, and interacting well inside and outside the organization, both behaviours that relate to the inclusion area, lead naturally to the organization gathering the ideas and information it needs on customers or competitors. Getting this kind of information, as well as generating interesting ideas from it, occurs easily and naturally when these are the kind of individual behaviours or qualities that are rewarded and acknowledged in the organization's performance and reward criteria. These are the skills and activities the business uses to create novel products, and to keep abreast of changes in the market so that it can stay one step ahead of competitors.

In other words, the day-to-day activities that meet the inclusion aims of the business are generated by the same performance criteria that also satisfy the feelings of people that we would associate with the inclusion area. This is what I call a virtuous cycle, set up to meet both the personal aims of the individual and the business aims of the organization at the same time.

Table 7.6 sets out the same list of skills, behaviours and qualities as in Table 7.5, with both the feelings generated within people in the organization, as per Table 7.5, and the business aims these behaviours meet.

Moving on

In this chapter we have explored two ways in which you can 'marry up' the emotional world of the organization with its business world. Both illustrate exactly the same idea that, if you take into account the subtle and psychological meaning of what you construct in organizations, it is far easier to create the effects you want and it is much more likely that the organization will function with ease and grace rather than struggle and might. This same aim we explore in the next chapter, but within an entirely new context.

Helping the organization move forward in its own way

CHAPTER 8

Figuring out which area of experience is the most 'real' to the organization

So far, we have explored the implications of the areas of experience from the perspective that each organization needs to deal with the activities and aims of all three areas. In reality, however, many organizations, even if they focus their attention and time on the activities and requirements of all three areas of experience, nevertheless consider that one of them is, in truth, a bit more 'real' than the other two. I have never been sure why this is so, but it is something I have learnt from experience is usually the case. The consequences of this, and an explanation of how to decipher what that key psychological area is for any organization, are the themes of this chapter. One of the key implications is that most organizations have a particular bias, that we can identify using the conceptual framework, which predisposes it to place a higher priority on some aims more than others, to emphasize certain aspects of the internal organization more than others, to use a different 'psychological language' and it also characterizes any emotional dynamic that arises. Much of the complexity of running an organization arises from these innate biases or predispositions that we are often unaware of.

Noticing which area is most 'real' is easiest when the organization is embarked on change

It is often easiest to determine this main area of experience, the area that is most 'real' to the organization, in times of change and when the organization is trying to move forward. In these circumstances, many small as well as major incidents occur that can be interpreted well beyond their immediate significance. They need to be attended to for their own sake, of course, but they need to be attended to also because of what they tell us about the overall predisposition of that company. The context for illustrating the ideas in this chapter, therefore, is a series of events that occurred when I was trying to create change and forward movement in a consumer retail company.

Creating forward movement in the consumer retail company

One project which I ran for a client in the consumer retail industry was related to their attempts to create a great deal of change in the structure and processes of the company. The objectives of their company at that time were quite familiar: getting more decisions delegated down to those people in direct contact with customers; taking out layers of bureaucracy in the middle of the organization; getting the managing directors of the subsidiary companies to include the other members of their top team in more of the strategic decision-making; working out key strategic goals for the next three years; getting a generally higher level of initiative throughout, and so on. The environment within which such internal changes would be made was, given the industry, very fast and highly competitive. Working in organizations which are very aware of the need to be stretched in the way they use people is always refreshing as you have no need to convince them of the daily reality that everyone in the organization needs to be used well.

Working with one company in South Africa and another in Nigeria

However, in this company, there was one extra factor that I had to take into account. One of the autonomous subsidiary companies that I was working for was in South Africa, and the other in Nigeria. The events in South Africa were predictable in some ways and surprising in others.

The events in the South African company

For example, some of the top team in that company worked throughout with guns, loaded, in their pockets even though I was holding my sessions with them in one of those expensive retreat centres about an hour out of Cape Town. My client was the senior group in the company but, in order for them to realize the goals of the project, it was critical for them to work intensively with people lower down in their company. I had struggled for some time, from a distance in London, to arrange for some of the people two to three levels down from this top group in the organization to be on the same programme with the senior team for a certain number of hours, a method that is quite standard to me. Such a design is basic practice when the goals of the project include anything to do with change, or with getting the organization loosened up a little, but in the company in South Africa, where race was a major subtext, putting this into practice was not as simple and straightforward as it often is elsewhere. It was this level of people two to three levels down from the top team that also formed the invisible ceiling for the blacks in the company.

They try to redesign the programme

The political reality of the organization could hardly fail to impinge on the change process. What I was faced with when I arrived in the country was the fact that the group that had been singled out to work with the senior team consisted of a very different group from those that I had specified earlier, since they were people who worked directly to that team. This was a waste of time for the purposes of the programme, as people at this level are too close to the top team and so are never open about many things that concern that team and it defeats the whole purpose of the exercise anyway, which is that they find out information of a different sort, the kind that can only come from those closer to the front line and to customers in particular. Whether the people on that invited team were black or white was not the agenda, but whether they were two to three levels down from the top team was. Their particular choice of people to attend seemed to be a way for them to evade the issue of race, and having blacks present with the top group, working alongside discussing the strategic goals and the organizational issues in the company.

Their shifting explanations and shuffling in their chairs

The explanation I was given, that their decision to invite people at a level that was blatantly different from that spelt out on pieces of paper, faxes, and so forth as well as spelt out clearly and many times in conversations was simply a mistake, was absurd. Yet that was the explanation they gave. As I discussed the implications with them, the explanation kept shifting. It was because they were confused about what I wanted. It was because they couldn't find the kind of people I had asked for. I carried on. Why, if it was confusing, did they never check with me in our many exchanges of faxes, in the conversations I had had with them? That they had chosen a group of people who were direct reports rather than from further down in the company was a major problem just in terms of the effectiveness of their whole change process, as it was a key design principle to have those people that I had specified present with them.

Whatever occurs in front of you can be deciphered in terms of its larger purpose

However, while in one way this incident posed an immediate difficulty, the whole point of outlining what happened is to illustrate a key part of the process you need to use to understand an organization and what makes it 'tick'. As I will explain through the chapter, you can interpret every minor or major incident that occurs in terms of its larger purpose and meaning. In this little scenario, what was going on in front of my nose, apart from the shifting explanations, the shuffling in the chairs as they tried to convince me, and the increasingly nasal, high-pitched tone in their voices as they realized I was not going to give in was something that I could and did use to interpret what their company was like and what it needed to do in a larger sense to move forward. In the meantime, in order for the objectives of their programme to be fulfilled, the people participating in the retreat had to be changed. I had to play a game back myself. I gave them an ultimatum. Either they got people in that invited team who fitted my specification or their programme would not go ahead. So they did.

Interpreting beyond the superficial level

The situation I was watching involved far more than the business reality of the project, the explicit objectives such as I have mentioned above. Those objectives would have to be met within a world, a set of assumptions, that were vastly different from my own. Nevertheless, these events also helped to enlighten me about what it was that made this organization function in the way it did. I had been faced with some silly gameplaying on arrival and yet this had 'revealed' the organization to me in a way that helped me to know what they needed to do with their organization. Anything that occurs is actually revealing the organization to you, and you can decipher many aspects about it other than the immediate surface incidents. However, before exploring that process of revelation in relation to my experience in South Africa, let's see what happened in Nigeria.

A different scenario in Nigeria

The situation I worked with in the company in Nigeria brought out another angle to the organization. In this company, their explicit, genuinely felt goals were to create a more effective organization and one where the talent was well used. Here the political subtext was more subtle, but one that they also had to face if the company as a whole was to be run effectively.

The events that occur are quite different

The situation that occurred in Nigeria was very interesting. In this company, they had followed my instructions to the letter and there was no gamesmanship. The perceptual bias was, however, still very present. Here also, my client was the senior group that was running the company but here the group that they had chosen to work alongside that top team was exactly what I had specified. One of the explicit agendas for this part of the company, at least on the part of those at HQ in London, was that more blacks would be represented at senior levels. They were quite clear that this should happen, and that blacks should, ideally, be on the senior team. People in this organization actually got on quite well together, and the senior team were seen to be 'a good team'.

The agenda of the head office

In my prior discussions with the powers-that-be in London, who consisted of the senior people to whom the MDs of the companies reported, I was told that, while they wanted to promote more blacks in the Nigerian company, they were unable to do so because the talent was unavailable. They had no one they could promote even though they wanted to do so. It would 'take time' to find potential senior people and to train them. One of the tasks of my project was to identify something constructive they could do about this while I was down there.

I arrived in the country a few days early to meet the senior team, as well as the invited team, prior to our retreat. I always meet with the teams prior to an event, so it was standard practice to explain what I would be asking them to do and, in the case of the invited people, why they were involved in something that, typically, they had never been involved with before. Members of such teams are usually nervous about what the purpose is, and so I am quite open about why they are being invited and what will happen.

The obvious ability and intelligence of the invited team

I walked into the room where I was to meet the six people from the team two to three levels down, all of whom were black. I spent two hours in their company, with them briefing me about what was going on in the organization, as they saw it, and me briefing them about what their role was and why I wanted them to be there. It was unquestionably one of the brightest, most switched on, alert, fast and aware teams I have ever had such a discussion with. I work in this way frequently and am accustomed to sussing out very quickly the level of competence of people in the teams I will be working with. It should have taken anyone who was half-awake about five minutes to realize that this group was extremely bright, and underused. Far brighter than people at that level typically are, and far less used.

I talked with them about their ideas for the strategy of the company, what it should be, and they had far clearer ideas about this than some of the senior managers I had spoken to individually. I discovered that several of them were doing part-time MBAs at university, and another was studying part-time to establish a higher technical qualification. I asked if their managers knew that they were doing these things, especially since none of the managers themselves had an MBA or business qualification. Most of their managers had no idea that they were involved in these extra studies but, even so, you didn't need to be aware of these small facts to know that this was one very bright and astute group. It took only minutes to register their intelligence simply from the speed of their response to my questions, the incisive questions they asked me in return, the fact that they were so articulate and that they were so piercing in their logic. You should never even have had to know that they were studying for an MBA to put two and two together and figure out there was real talent in that organization at that level.

The same people who were convinced there was 'no talent' had met them many times

Yet the same people from HQ in London who had assured me that there was no such talent in the blacks in this company had visited them many times, spoken to these same people and, indeed, were walking around the corridors outside as I was in the meeting room talking and listening to what was unfolding in front of me.

This kind of situation, in which people at this level are unable to put most of their talent and brainpower to work in the company, is relatively common in organizations, whether there is a racial subtext or otherwise. These people, however, were limited to an extreme degree, unable to make even the most minute, trivial decisions that you should, if you were running an organization properly, have let almost anyone make. This was far from being an issue of race, or of treating people equally. It was a question of running a company sensibly, intelligently and well. It was an issue of making use of resources and talent in order to meet the objectives of the business. The ethical issue was one of responsibility to shareholders as much as anything else.

The contrast between their intentions and their inability to notice the evidence in front of them

But it was the contrast between the intentions of the senior team to make the organization more effective and the fact that they were so obviously ignoring the evidence of their own eyes and ears that was so stunning. They had hired an expensive consultant to help them make more productive use of the talent in the organization, or to find it, yet it should have been completely unnecessary to spend their money on me. All they needed to do was to listen to the same blacks that the people in head office and the senior managers had assured me were unable to take up higher positions in the company because the talent was, apparently, 'unavailable'.

Taking stock of the organization

In my tale of the two companies, there seems to be a common theme. In both, their inability to see, let alone use, the talent in the organization was clearly limiting their ability to meet their own business aims. The explicit objectives of both companies were to be more successful in terms of getting market share, meeting revenue projections and achieving cash flow forecasts. In order to meet their own objectives, they needed to operate and structure themselves in a flexible way so that they could make maximum use of any talent and resources they had. These were their own aims. Yet, these companies were not acknowledging the extent of the talent available to them.

Deciphering the two organizations with a perceptual and psychological mind-set

In what follows, I set out a process which you can use to understand how such situations as well as incidents like those I described earlier can tell you about the organization in a quite fundamental way. I use these two companies as examples to illustrate how to 'read' the organization. With this mind-set, anything that occurs in an organization can be deciphered. If you understand the events that occur in any organization from a perceptual and psychological viewpoint, you will learn what it is that the organization needs in order for it to change and move forward. The organization will be able to change in a way that goes with its own grain. Let me explain how you could do this in the case of the two companies in South Africa and Nigeria.

The same business analysis but a million miles apart psychologically

The two companies seemed to be faced with a broadly similar business situation. They were in a similar kind of market and were selling the same products and services. When they each conducted individual strategic/marketing reviews, they came up with far more similarities than differences in terms of what they were faced with, and what they needed to do to address those challenges. In terms of an organizational analysis, focused on their own structure, systems and style of management, as well as a separate human resources analysis in each company, they also came up with aims and issues that were very similar. There were, of course, many differences in the detail of the two companies. The one in South Africa was more tightly run and their managing director was notorious for his apparently top-down style, whereas the company in Nigeria had a team approach. These were some of the differences between the two companies but, overall, their strategic and organizational analyses described very similar broad objectives and challenges to be met in each company.

The two companies could not have the same managing director be equally successful in both

However, if we look at the two companies with a psychological lens, there is hardly any similarity whatsoever between them. The factors that would help them change, and those which would not, are as different as chalk and cheese. It would be absolutely impossible for them to apply the same formula for change and for that formula to work equally successfully in both. It would be impossible for the same managing director to be equally successful in both. Looked at psychologically, these are two radically different companies.

Predicting this simply from the events that occurred when I arrived there

You could predict this purely from the events that surrounded the way each company dealt with me and how they responded to my requirements for an invited team to attend the retreats. You could use these incidents to tell you what was making each of these companies function in the way that they were. With this knowledge you could then figure out what different things made sense in each company, what things each would respond to and what they would never respond to.

Using the conceptual framework to help you decipher the meaning of the events

The conceptual framework helps us decipher the meaning of these incidents and, therefore, what makes most sense to the organization. The way to do this is to determine which one of the three psychological areas is the most important to each company. Once you have figured that out you will know which parts of the internal organization are the most real to it and the nature of any dynamic that arises. In what follows I illustrate how you can determine which of the three psychological areas was the most important in the two companies in South Africa and Nigeria.

The company in South Africa and that in Nigeria had a different psychological area dominant

The events that surrounded the two retreats and my meetings with the people in each country told me that, in South Africa, I was dealing with a company that operated with one of the three psychological areas 'uppermost', while in Nigeria I was dealing with a company that made sense of the world in another way entirely. Because they each had their own completely different way of making sense of the world, not because of their different national culture but because of their dissimilar psychological orientation, the way they operated in each company, and what each believed to be a priority, were completely different. Each company responded to different words, different pacing even. They each had a completely different 'main' area of experience. For each company, one of these areas was more real than the other two.

Knowing the different psychological orientations is one of the secrets of the organization it helps to find out about. It can be detected quite readily, however, even from such a series of incidents as greeted me when I landed in each of the two countries in my earlier story, and I will outline how you can figure this out so that you can apply the same kind of diagnosis to other situations.

Deciphering the South African Company

In my earlier account of the South African company I described a situation where the people there had initially 'refused' to obtain the invited people that were clearly necessary. The group they had drawn together were people who were 'direct reports' instead of from two to three levels down in the company. In addition, I mentioned that the MD was notorious for being a top-down manager and that one of the prime objectives of HQ in London was that his behaviour change as part of the overall change process. How I was supposed to instantly transform such a dominant character is anybody's guess, but clients often assume that you carry a magic wand in your pocket to help you achieve such things. Figuring out how this company should move forward meant deciphering these and other pieces of data.

Making sense of the organization in terms of which area determines its sense of purpose

We need to be able to make sense of the organization in a way that tells us whether it is the inclusion area of the organization that is uppermost and creates the main sense of purpose in the organization, or whether it is the control area that is doing so, or the affection area. This parallels the process we used in Chapter 6 to help us decipher the main area of feelings in the organization, what I call its sensitive area.

Deciphering what the underlying purpose is

What you need to be alert to, and decipher, is the underlying purpose of whatever people in an organization decide, say or do. Is that purpose to gain a sense of identity and ownership, an emotional sense of being an intact unit that cannot be invaded by outsiders? Is it to enhance their presence as a company? Is this the underlying motivation behind their decisions on which market to go into, or which niche to stay in? Is this the underlying psychological purpose behind their decisions on the kind of distribution channels they want? If so, the main rationale for what they are doing and deciding will be that of satisfying the purpose of their dominant psychological area, in this instance the inclusion area. This particular psychological area will characterize the dominant actions, ways of thinking and events in the organization. It will also characterize the words people use and need for things to 'make sense'.

If the purpose that seems to underlie most of the organization's decisions and behaviours is to ensure a sense of control, a confidence that they can have the effect on the world that they intend, then you know that it is the control area that is dominant and makes sense to the organization the most.

If the underlying purpose behind whatever they do, decide or say seems to be to enable them to feel a sense of active engagement and that they are 'real', then you will have found an organization, or part of it, in which it is the affection area that is the most important.

Sometimes the psychological area that is the most real to the organization may not be a strength

One key factor you need to consider is that the psychological area that is most important or real to an organization may be fulfilled well, in which case it will be that organization's main source of strength and create those characteristics that most define it as an organization. However, no matter how important such a psychological area and its associated purpose may be to the organization, it can be poorly fulfilled. Even so, it will still be the key area to that organization, in the sense that that is how the people in the organization make sense of their world. It may be a weakness in terms of business reality, yet it can still represent the main psychological area of the organization none the less.

Seeing beyond the obvious in the South African company

Interpreting the events as a control battle would have been a superficial analysis

From what I described in the South African company, it sounds a little like the organization was engaged in a control battle with HQ in London. Their behaviour could have been a way to say 'we are not going to obey London'. However, their behaviour told me something quite different. It was not the control area of experience that was dominant in the organization and so to see their reaction as a control battle would be wrong. It was, in fact, the inclusion area that was uppermost in this company and, if it had not been for the events that occurred when I first arrived in that company, I doubt if I would have figured this out so clearly or deciphered what mattered and made most sense to this company so early. Instead of their reactions being an obstacle, they had in fact provided me with the most marvellous insight.

In the South African company their main area was inclusion with its aims of establishing their own territory and boundaries

The underlying reason why the people in that company had played the games they had was a reflection of their need to have their own private territory, and a reflection of their assumption that their HQ had to be 'told' repeatedly, in various ways, that they were not at liberty to invade them. That company was 'their' territory, and they felt as if they had private ownership rights over it. Consequently, when they were asked to do something by myself, at the time I was in London prior to travelling there, they simply responded in the same way. When HQ did treat them as if they had their own psychological territory they received wonderful performance from the company and had good relationships with them. The South African company had to feel this sense of their 'own space' or otherwise the organization simply couldn't function properly and certainly couldn't perform at their best. The inclusion area was their dominant area and had to be respected.

The 'incident' that had occurred was over an issue of who was 'in or out'; an inclusion concern

One of the key pieces of data that tells you that it was the inclusion area of the organization rather than, say, the control area, that was behind their actions is that the conflict occurred over a decision about who was 'in or out', who was going to be in the invited team and who was not. It was over a matter that was quintessentially an inclusion type of decision. If you can characterize the nature of key incidents like this you will have found the area of the organization that is primary. You will need more than one piece of data or incident to tell you this but, if several point in one definite direction, you will know which area of experience is most meaningful for that organization.

The 'fierce' MD was aiming to keep their organization psychologically intact

In the South African company, the reason why the MD had such a fierce reputation in the eyes of London HQ was because he was defending his patch and ensuring that they remained psychologically intact. He was not defending his ability to control and be the boss, but his ability to preserve the integrity of 'his' company and its boundaries. That was the psychological meaning that made sense to this organization. His reputation was far less fierce in the company itself or, indeed, justified by anything that occurred in front of my own eyes. In fact, 'fierce' was a word that was never used about the MD by anyone in the company itself, even behind his back, and they had a great deal of respect and affection for him. This was a different person by far from the one I had been told about.

What people will most want to find out

Inclusion: they can identify with you so you can be 'let in'

I confirmed my hunch that the primary psychological objective was to have their 'own' company with inviolable borders by asking the person I was dealing with directly whether the reason they 'had been such a pain' was because of the 'colonialists in HQ'. Since I had been brought up in New Zealand, I had a very good knowledge of what it felt like to be told what to do 'in your own country' by other countries. He burst out laughing when I asked him this and, from that time on, became my invaluable ally for the rest of the time I was there. I had been 'let in' to the group, and this is the first task or aim if you are dealing with any organization, or part of it, where it is the inclusion area of experience that is most real to them.

Control: that you are competent, able to engage in debate and can 'win'

If it is the control area that is uppermost for an organization, you will have to prove yourself in some way and what they will want to know most about you is that you are competent, can debate with them and that you can 'win'. When this happens, it is their way of 'telling' you what psychological area makes sense to them, which is the control area.

Affection: that you are 'real' and fully engaged rather than just putting on an appearance

If it is the affection area that is uppermost, you will have to prove that you are fully engaged and real in some way. What they will want to know most about you in this kind of organization is that you mean what you say and that you can be trusted with 'their organization'. You need to prove you care about them, or about what you do, to a high degree. That is the way people in that kind of organization make sense of things.

In South Africa, however, the key area was undoubtedly the inclusion area. The areas of the business they focused on, therefore, also had to deal primarily with priorities that related to this inclusion area of the business. The dynamic that you could detect in the Nigerian company, however, showed an entirely different company.

Deciphering the Nigerian company, in contrast

You can predict that the inclusion area is not the main area

In this company, the most important area of experience was the affection area. You could predict, by the clarity and straightforwardness with which they dealt with my requests to choose an invited group, that the inclusion area, focused on issues of being 'in or out', was unlikely to be the key area of this organization. What was apparent, though, in my earlier description was the contrast between their well-meant objectives of creating a more effective organization and the obvious waste of talent within the company. The other piece of data I gave you was that people 'got on' quite well with each other and the relationships in this company were relatively good. The senior team was praised for being 'a good team'. Another key piece of data was that the people I had spoken to in the group two to three levels down had not informed their own managers that they were doing MBAs or higher technical qualifications. All these things, even the lack of openness, point to different facets of the affection area.

The real issue is that their control purpose is being overridden by their need for relationships

The real issue this organization had to deal with was that their control purpose, achieving results and being effective, was being superseded by their affection aims. They wanted to be liked, to have good relationships, to be 'good friends together', and this overrode the necessity to make the most out of their business. Their fulfilment of the request for an invited team was not quite as desirable as it seemed. It actually reflected a stance of too much obedience towards London. They should, in fact, have stood up to London HQ far more than they did. But they wanted the people in London to like them too much to have 'good relationships' with them, when they should really have set their own path far more than they did. The fact they they so efficiently met the request for an invited team could, in another organization, have reflected nothing more than an effective and well-coordinated organization that simply 'got on with it', and, without data to tell me otherwise, that is how I would have interpreted their actions.

But there must have been a reason why the people in that company so ignored the talent that existed in the organization. Doing this was an indication that the organization was failing to meet its control purpose, which by definition is about making effective use of talent and resources. It is too superficial to simply say that the managers in this company were biased. Bias occurs for a reason, so you can use the particular bias

HELPING THE ORGANIZATION MOVE FORWARD

that exists to tell you what the organization is like. Bias will not occur for the same reasons in different organizations.

Needing to sacrifice their comfort zone and 'get on with it'

In this company, apart from any historical or personal reasons, the situation occurred partly because the senior managers wanted to keep their fellow good feeling. They were 'a good team' and wanted to stay together. They 'got on' and they relished the fact that they were praised by London. This was the psychological aim they were meeting at the expense of the business need to 'get on with it'. They felt comfortable with each other. What this company needed to do, therefore, was vastly different from what the South African company needed to do. They needed to sacrifice their comfort zone and run the business in a much sharper and more straightforward way than they were doing at that time. This required that they give their affection needs and feelings a slightly lower priority. The fact that this was their main area of experience, however, meant that the priorities that would make sense to this company were quite different from those that made sense to the South African company. They each had their own, quite different, grain of wood.

Table 8.1 sets out some of the indications that will tell you which of the three areas of experience is the most 'real' or important to that

Table 8.1 Different priorities assumed by different organizations

inclusion agenda has priority	control agenda has priority	affection agenda has priority
talk in terms of 'who owns what', whose territory is where'	talk of 'who is responsible for what', 'who reports where'	talk in terms of 'who works for whom', 'who works with whom'
focus on what markets or niches to be in, what each of these 'say' about them to others	need a strategy to ensure they 'win' so focus on the means to exert influence, e.g. pricing tactics	need to agree how they should conduct themselves with people and focus on the long term
talk in terms of 'including' customers or establishing 'channels' to them	talk in terms of 'target' customers and of 'winning' them or 'influencing' customers	talk in terms of 'genuine relationships' with customers, of 'attracting' them more than selling to them

organization. In subsequent sections I elaborate on one particular aspect or indication, which is the kind of 'language' used.

Detecting the language and voice of the organization

Listen to how they refer to the roles on the organization chart: 'who owns what', 'who is responsible for what', or 'who works for whom'

If it is the inclusion area that is the most important area of experience to an organization, what will matter most to them will be issues of territory. You will hear people in the organization trying to be clear about what is 'theirs', what is 'their' patch and what is someone else's. As a result, when this is the dominant area in an organization, people talk in terms of 'who owns what' because this is how they make sense of things. If it is the control area that is the most dominant area in an organization people say 'who reports to whom' or 'who is responsible for what'. But when it is inclusion that is the key area, talking in terms of 'who is responsible for what' instead of 'who owns what' makes far less sense. When the main area is affection, in contrast, people tend to say 'who works for whom' and 'who works with whom', since that is the area that makes sense of things in terms of relationships. If any other language is used, such as 'who is responsible for what', people in an organization which has affection as its main area will struggle until they have translated those words into their 'own' language and have a picture of 'who is with whom'.

Listen to how they describe their market and customers

When inclusion is the main area of experience, people pay great attention to the image their products give them in the market-place, what it would 'say' about them in their markets. When discussing what kinds of distributors they should use, these too are discussed with great attention being paid to what the different alternatives would 'say' about them in the market-place, if they use x kind of distributors rather than y kind of distribution channels or salespeople. They will talk of customers in terms of which ones they 'own', for example.

When a company has the control area as its main psychological area, people need to work out what competitors are up to and, from there, work out the broad thrust of their own response, or their own way of 'beating' the market or side-stepping it. This, of course, is the very essence of the control purpose. When this is the area that makes most sense to an organization, people have to work out for themselves before anything else, how they, as a company, are going to 'win', how they will exert influence over their environment, which includes other competitors. It includes customers as well, of course, so they will discuss their customers in terms of 'winning' them and of 'influencing' them. Customers will be 'targets', for example. This is the language that tells you that the organization you are dealing with has the control area as their dominant area. Until they are satisfied that they have a way to exert a satisfactory degree of influence over their environment, or some strategy that means they win in their own way, it is a waste of time for them to think of the company's identity, or its image. These things are secondary, a 'waste of time' they will say, until they have 'nailed down' their strategy, by which they mean how they will 'win'. This is their particular organizational reality.

When the affection area is the most meaningful area of experience in an organization the most real things to deal with are those that describe how the business conducts itself. In other words, how people do things rather than what they do. You will detect that the affection area is uppermost when people decide that what is most important is that the company should 'be professional', for example, or that the organization should conduct itself with others in a way that is honest, or efficient, or friendly. When organizations have the affection area as their most meaningful area of experience, customers are described not in terms of 'targets' or in terms of 'winning' them. People talk, instead, of how the organization should deal with, or behave towards, customers. The affection purpose is also about people doing what they believe in and being able to believe in the organization. When this is the main area in an organization, they need to decide and agree the real purpose of that organization and why it exists. Related to this deeper aim, people always talk within a framework of the long term. The way they make sense of anything is from a long-term perspective. They may be discussing a short-term objective, but they make sense of it by understanding it in terms of what it means for the long term. Their priority is what is real and if they can obtain a sense that what is decided is genuine then they can make sense of whatever is being talked about. In contrast to an organization which has the control area as the most important area, an organization with the affection area uppermost will function in a very different way. For the former, the goal determines the purpose of the organization. For the latter, the real underlying purpose will determine the goal.

Helping the organization move forward in its own way

Knowing which is the key area of experience in an organization helps you to understand what is most real to the people within it and also what makes sense to them. If you 'speak the same language' you are far more likely to be able to connect with the organization, in exactly the same way that you do with a person. It is only by knowing what makes an organization tick in this way that you can help it change easily and, if you do not work with this natural grain that it has, then you will be forever pushing against that natural tendency it has. Getting an organization to change and move forward, then, is much easier if you work with the organization on its own terms. In the next chapter we move on to looking at the organization, and the languages it 'speaks' in another entirely new context.

Understanding the perceptual realities of customers and the organization

CHAPTER 9

Setting a new tone

In this chapter we move into the more subtle realms of the organization and our theme is understanding others' perceptual reality. We pay attention to these 'softer' attributes of organizations but within the same overall conceptual approach that we have used throughout. To read the mind of an organization, we need to accept the legitimacy of a perceptual way of looking at it. This has been implicit throughout the book. The entire framework of psychological natures is really a certain kind of perceptual lens that we place over the organization in order to understand the meaning and effects of its various, normal, business activities and aims. Apart from that, the explicit overall stance in every chapter has been that we need to 'see through' the surface appearance, to 'read between the lines'. However, in this chapter, the perceptual realities of the organization is our one and only theme. We make the perceptual filters of each psychological nature visible, and we use our knowledge of these natures to understand what other people pay attention to and what they miss out.

Being able to anticipate how others perceive and receive any communication

One arena where knowing the perceptual realities of others is vital is that of communicating. That is, any situation that involves human beings trying to make contact with each other and be understood. Any communication from an organization, whether to customers or to people within the organization, will be perceived in different ways by different people. One of the key themes of my own work as a consultant revolves around explaining to managers how their messages are received and perceived by others, and how their promotions are received and perceived by different kinds of customers. It is only half the battle to determine a good strategy, policy, PR campaign or advertisement. The real test of how good it is lies with its reception when it is communicated. This is where a perceptual, psychological perspective can add real value, because you can anticipate how people will interpret what you say. Their interpretation will differ depending on the particular perceptual filters they have, so describing, naming and identifying these is what we explore in this chapter. We do so in the context of communicating to customers, which brings in a fresh context for us to apply the ideas to.

Being able to identify what the different perceptual filters are actually like

People have their own perceptual lens, and we can see the impact of this in a wide array of situations. However, very often we are limited in our ability to understand the effects of this, since we are aware only of the general principle that different people notice and are aware of different things compared to others. We can bring some order into the phenomenon of different perceptual filters by using the conceptual framework, since the various psychological natures see, notice and register very different things. We can, therefore, label what those filters are in a more specific way than just knowing that the general principle holds true. While in this chapter we will see and feel those perceptual filters by studying an advertisement to customers, the different realities that unfold will contain the same qualities for any context. We can use the ideas to understand where others are 'coming from' within an organization, or we can use them to figure out how to communicate in a way that makes sense to the widest group of people.

Understanding why some companies have great difficulty reaching certain kinds of customers

We can see the evidence of the effect of perceptual filters when the organization communicates to customers in particular. Some companies have great difficulty reaching certain kinds of customers, for example. Since each of the psychological natures that we have used to characterize organizations applies equally well to different groups of people, customers can be understood in terms of their psychological nature, quite apart from their demographic or market characteristics. Different customers perceive the organization with perceptual filters that see the same organization doing very different things. Knowing what these are can help organizations understand why it is that they reach certain groups of customers but find it exceedingly difficult to reach others. It is this context that I use in order to set out the dramatically different ways in which people see the world, and the organization. In the descriptions that I give of customers, we can see and feel the reality that one psychological nature has, that is entirely different from the reality another nature has.

Seeing what different customers see and what they ignore in an advertisement

Managers can think seriously about perception if you use customers as the context

I use customers as the context to set out the perceptual differences for two reasons. One is that people can see the business rationale for thinking about perception very easily when they can relate it to a context that includes those people that create their sales figures. It is a context that managers know is real and has an impact on the bottom line, so they are less likely to think of these perceptual differences as an added extra.

However, they can resist taking perceptual filters seriously when they are communicating within the organization

The other reason for using the context of communicating with customers is because it reduces any defensiveness that may arise when people start to figure out whether they have perceptual blinkers. It is very simple, for example, to take a company promotion and see whether it reaches certain groups of customers only rather than others. That is, whether it makes contact with, or would be registered by, only certain psychological natures. When managers see this kind of detail, they want to know about it. They actively seek out this information and they are very pragmatic about working out what perceptual biases they may have in this kind of situation. But consider the same purpose within an organizational context. Imagine you are trying to get across the importance of knowing how people in the organization perceive a policy, for example. The reaction from those people trying to communicate in these circumstances, when you point out that their words make sense only to some people but miss other groups entirely, is often that these other groups 'should' know what the policy means. They 'should' be able to interpret it as it stands, as it is meant. The fact that the words by which the policy, or strategy, is set out make sense to certain psychological natures only is seen to be someone else's responsibility. Getting this idea over, that you need to take account of different perceptual natures, is far easier and faster when you put the same phenomenon within the context of being able to reach more customers. So that is what we do in what follows.

Reading an advertisement: we all see the same thing, don't we?

The communication we explore is an advertisement, chosen for particular reasons, as you will see. It is a good example and one that provides a base to illustrate the perceptual filters. Like all other aspects of an organization, we can read between the lines of advertisements. And since the one we will look at is staring us in the face, we can all see the same thing. There can be no dispute about the data. Can there?

An ad from the Union Bank of Switzerland Private Banking

We start by seeing the advertisement as a whole. The ad is from the private banking arm of the Union Bank of Switzerland. We will interpret some things about it just from an immediate impression. Once we have got a general view of it, we then explore which parts of it are seen by each psychological nature. I highlight which words, or parts of the picture, are noticed by customers with one psychological nature, that customers with another psychological nature will be oblivious to. What is important is to ignore whether or not you like the ad. As with reading the mind of an organization, the purpose is to figure it out rather than figure out whether you like it. By the end of the process, you should have been able to perceive in six different ways, and this requires that you empathize with each way of viewing the world, which means leaving aside, for the moment, your own likes and dislikes, as well as your own evaluation of how 'good' the ad is. Judgements like this are the main barrier to being able to understand and accept the perceptual realities of others and understand the organization in their eyes rather than your own. Figure 9.1 sets the ad out in its entirety.[1]

---

[1] *Business Week*, 25 November 1996.

PERCEPTUAL REALITIES OF CUSTOMERS 205

If you admire "Fidelio" and "Otello" let us introduce you to the beauty of a Flag- and Saucer-Formation.

Talking to a regular at "Palais Garnier" or the "Wiener Staatsoper", we'd think twice before entering into an in-depth discussion about opera. However, we'd strike up a conversation about caps and floors any time to show you that investing is an art form and requires a skilled conductor, too. By learning everything about your investment goals and preferences as well as the desired level of risk, we orchestrate a long-term strategy best suited to your needs. It is long-term relationships with our clients, spanning years and even decades, combined with our expertise and global presence, that has made us one of the world's leading asset managers.

UBS Private Banking
Expertise in managing your assets

Union Bank of Switzerland

Zurich, Geneva, Lugano, Luxembourg, London, New York, Hong Kong, Singapore   UBS Private Banking is regulated in the UK by IMRO

Figure 9.1   Union Bank of Switzerland Private Banking

Getting an overview of the advertisement

The first impression is that this company must be sophisticated

Now, what can such an up-market ad tell us about perception, or how to communicate a strategy well? First, let's take the ad at face value. What is its main message? The first impression the organization wants to give us as potential customers, shareholders or members of the public is that it is sophisticated, otherwise they would never show pictures of elegant chairs, or use a reference to opera. They also send a very up-front message that they are a serious business even while they are having interesting conversations about the opera.

They also seem to assume that you have a brain

I know just from a quick glance, without having to really study the ad, what their particular business is, that is that they do private banking, rather than just ordinary banking or selling fund management or foreign exchange transfers to large businesses, for example. It doesn't take long to know what this ad is about, and what their business is. It also doesn't take much attention to register that they really know about their business as well. This is a telling piece of data about the organization just in itself. How many pictures or advertisements of companies have you seen lately where you had to stop and figure out what on earth the company actually does for a living? How many ads from mega-industrial companies or the big consulting groups, have a picture of someone with a baby, or their favourite grandmother, to advertise their products, trying to convince us that this means that the organization has a personal touch and will care for us as customers? This company, however, if you read their ad with an interpretive eye rather than at face value, is assuming that you have a brain, and they are assuming also that you prefer straight talking. In spite of the first impression given by the presence of opera chairs, this company seems quite up-front. What you can interpret from this style is that, while they are involved in an up-market customer niche, they are really much more accessible and easy to make contact with than you may think at first glance if you focus on the fancy chairs. However, it is for other reasons that this ad is effective. There is a much more important appeal to potential customers.

This ad actually 'reaches' all six psychological natures at once

This is one of the few ads I have ever seen that actually speaks in words, and displays its picture, in a way that makes sense to every one of the six different psychological natures. The majority of ads miss out half of the population. What I mean by this is that most companies communicate in a way that is registered by only one psychological nature rather than another. They may aim for the Connoisseur, for example, and miss the Populist completely. They may speak in the words of the Boss, and the Jugglers in the audience, whether customers or employees, are left bemused. If there is nothing in a message, whether an advertisement, policy statement or Annual Report, that speaks in language that is heard by and makes sense to a Juggler, for example, then that is what I mean by saying that 'half the population' has been missed out.

Seeing if the message gives us the emotional information we need as human beings

What we need to bear in mind also is that the different psychological natures are associated with three different areas of experience. So while we can identify the nature of the perceptual filters each nature has, we can also see whether the overall message relates to us in terms of all three of those areas of experience that make sense to us as human beings. As I have mentioned in an earlier chapter, many companies communicate in a way that only 'speaks to' the area of experience we would classify as the control area. The language, style and content of their communications can consist only of meanings that have a connotation of control, such as how successful the company is relative to others, how many resources it has, what it will do for you, how reliable it is, and so on. Yet human beings, whether employees or customers, respond best to a message that reflects all three areas of experience because that is how they make sense of the world. An advertisement needs to convey, in addition to its control stance, some sense of how the organization interacts or positions itself *vis-à-vis* others, and to convey some idea of 'who' it is, its identity, what it is like. These aspects of an advertisement provide the experience and meaning we would associate with the inclusion area. Any part of the message, whether visual or verbal, which carries this kind of meaning gives the person on the receiving end the kind of emotional information they need, and the company will then have communicated in the way people need in order for something to make sense.

People will respond to an organization and remember it if they are given a psychologically 'complete' message

If all that people are given in the message is words and a picture that have only a control meaning and feel to it, and so know how they will be managed and what will be delivered by the organization, they may still do business with it, but they will be far readier to notice and respond to an ad, and remember the organization better if it communicates in a way that conveys a more complete sense of 'who' it is and how it works. Exactly the same principles apply in terms of conveying some sense, feeling or meaning that relates to the affection area of experience. Human beings, whether employees or customers, need some idea of what the organization is like in terms of engaging actively with tasks and people, in order for it to seem 'real'. It will then have provided the emotional information that feels complete to customers.

In the Union Bank ad, we have an example which conveys meaning in relation to all three areas of experience. You can use the exploration that follows as a reference point, therefore, to see if your own messages convey to those on the receiving end what they need in order to notice, make sense of and remember what your message is about rather than just receive 'information'.

Being seen through the eyes of both Connoisseur and Populist customers

We have perceptual filters that 'tell' us about how this company interacts, what its main qualities are

Let's return to our Union Bank of Switzerland ad and see what it means to be able to be noticed by and make sense to all six psychological natures at once. The first exploration is the filters and perceptions of the Connoisseur and Populist. What you will see in the two figures that follow is the same ad that we saw earlier but with the words that each nature would read, rather than ignore, underlined. The perceptual filters we explore are those that relate to understanding the overall identity of the organization, and noticing what its style of interaction would be. Customers will tend to have one of these two natures more dominant than the other, so they will attend to different parts of the same advertisement in order to gather the information they need to make sense of the company behind it. They will be trying to pinpoint whether they want to do business with the company, but also to understand 'who' it is even if they have no immediate call to do business with it. This is what their 'inclusion' filters will tell them.

Figure 9.2 sets out what the Connoisseur would take notice of and Figure 9.3 sets this out for the Populist.

The Connoisseur customer: going to the opera with a company with manners

They are drawn to all the opera house names

Anyone with a Connoisseur nature will read the ad shown in Figure 9.2 and register very different parts of it from someone with a Populist nature. They will pick up, as if lifted out of the script, the different opera house names, for example. They will read of the 'Teatro dell'Opera' and the 'Wiener Staatsoper'. These will appear as if held up for view. What will go on in their heads may be a remembrance of having been to any of these opera houses, or a thought that they wished they could go to this one or that one. They may start to associate these opera house names with particular pieces of music. These are the pieces of the ad they will pick up and register as their way of understanding what this company is about, and 'who' it is. They will go on to read the main text and, here, read of particular opera pieces, the 'Fidelio' and 'Otello'. Note that they may never have heard of either of these, but they will still come to the conclusion, from these references, that this must surely be a Connoisseur-style company. After all, they have now seen several words that 'fit' with their own sense of style and distinctiveness, and there are many words in this advertisement that *feel* right. They have the right quality and tone to them, even if talking of an activity a Connoisseur may have little contact with.

They notice that conversations are polite, a little restrained

They may read on and their perceptual antennae will pick out from the background of detail other words and signals that begin to really register as the Connoisseur nature. They will notice the word 'Private' Banking, for example, whereas a Populist will probably never really make much out of this word. They will read that these people have a discussion that they describe in terms of thinking twice 'before entering into'. The slight pause in this interaction shows consideration and respect for boundaries, and the phrase 'entering into' makes sense to the Connoisseur. This is how they think of conversations themselves, something you 'enter into'. The words say 'introduce you', which also tells the Connoisseur nature

210 READING THE MIND OF THE ORGANIZATION

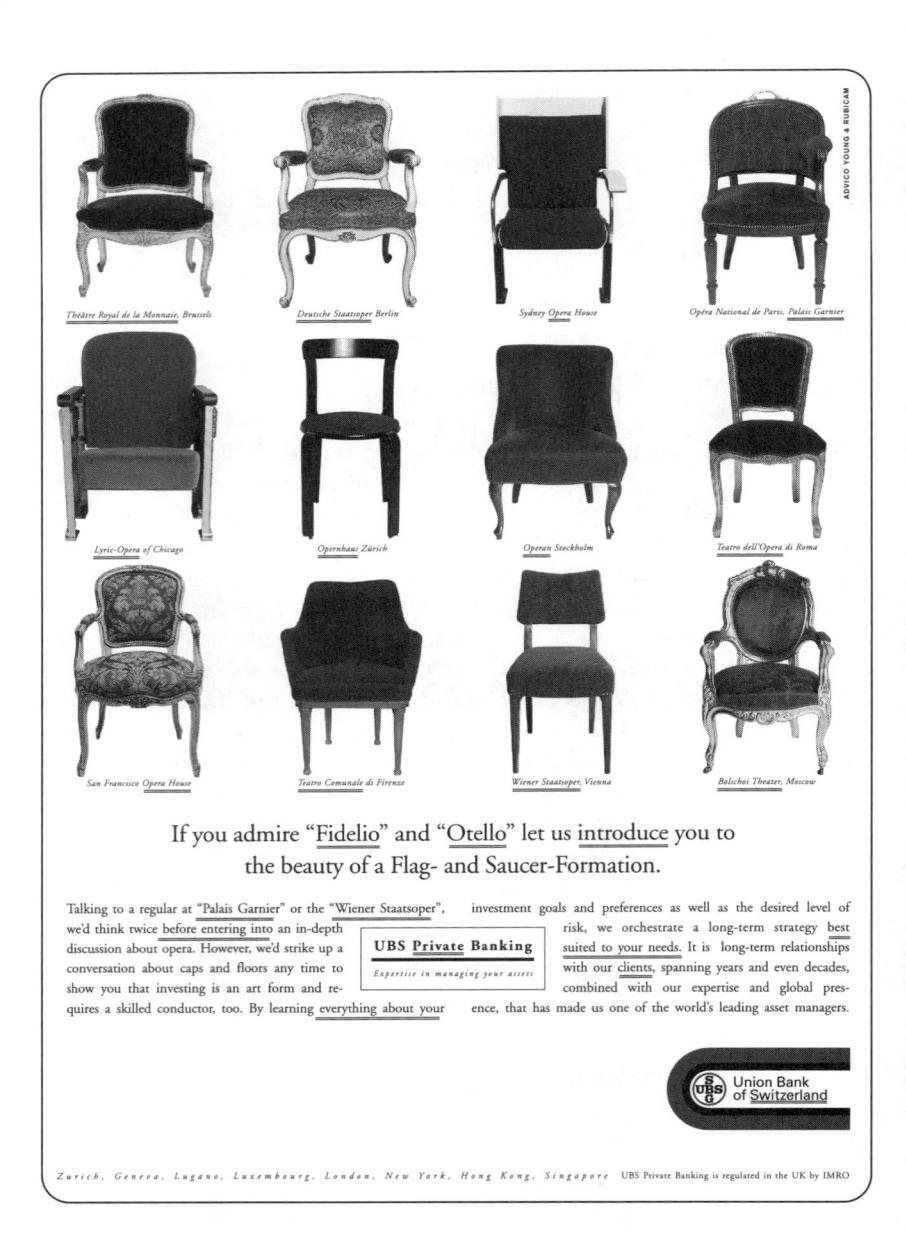

Figure 9.2 Noticing what a Connoisseur customer notices

PERCEPTUAL REALITIES OF CUSTOMERS 211

Théâtre Royal de la Monnaie, Brussels   *Deutsche Staatsoper Berlin*   *Sydney Opera House*   *Opéra National de Paris, Palais Garnier*

Lyric-Opera of Chicago   *Opernhaus Zürich*   *Operan Stockholm*   *Teatro dell'Opera di Roma*

San Francisco Opera House   *Teatro Comunale di Firenze*   *Wiener Staatsoper, Vienna*   *Bolschoi Theater, Moscow*

If you admire "Fidelio" and "Otello" let us introduce you to the beauty of a Flag- and Saucer-Formation.

Talking to a regular at "Palais Garnier" or the "Wiener Staatsoper", we'd think twice before entering into an in-depth discussion about opera. However, we'd strike up a conversation about caps and floors any time to show you that investing is an art form and requires a skilled conductor, too. By learning everything about your investment goals and preferences as well as the desired level of risk, we orchestrate a long-term strategy best suited to your needs. It is long-term relationships with our clients, spanning years and even decades, combined with our expertise and global presence, that has made us one of the world's leading asset managers.

UBS Private Banking
Expertise in managing your assets

Union Bank of Switzerland

Zurich, Geneva, Lugano, Luxembourg, London, New York, Hong Kong, Singapore   UBS Private Banking is regulated in the UK by IMRO

Figure 9.3 Noticing what a Populist customer notices

that here is a company with some manners, some civility. They are going to 'introduce me' to something rather than 'tell' me about it. So, I am beginning to feel that this company will pay respect to my need for boundaries, for space, and will conduct considered and slightly restrained interactions. If I look at the visual picture as well, I cannot fail to notice the elegance, the delicacy of some of those chairs. This company is cultured, I conclude. They would treat me with courtesy. Also, they tell me that they learn 'everything' about my goals and then work something out that is 'best suited to your needs'. This gives me just the sense of focus, of individual attention, that, to me, is the right way to do things. What is more they refer to their 'clients'. This speaks my language. Connoisseurs have clients rather than customers. It signifies a degree of individual attention and discrimination that rings in the ears of Connoisseurs but means nothing in particular to a Populist.

These are the perceptual filters of Connoisseurs, who now have some information to understand the overall style, and kind of interactions, this company believes in. They know what their own inclusion experience would be with this company, so they are satisfied.

The Populist customer: talking a lot with a company that is 'everywhere'

They are drawn to all those places around the world they can visit, and ignore the opera

Meanwhile, the Populists are having a wonderful time exploring 'their' ad (shown in Figure 9.3). By the time they have finished, however, they have concluded exactly the same thing. The company has conveyed a sense of 'who' they are, and what their style of interaction is, that makes sense to the Populist nature. However, they see very different things along the way. For one thing, they are far more likely to spend time looking at all those places that the opera chairs come from. When I show this ad to people with a Populist nature and ask them to tell me what is in it, and what they were thinking of, they tell me about 'Vienna', 'Moscow', 'Berlin', 'Zurich', 'Sydney', 'Chicago'. What about the names of the opera houses? The names of the two opera pieces? They have barely read them or even seen them. They will usually have registered that the names of opera houses are 'there' somewhere, but these will be barely noticed and are not what they used either to make sense of the ad or to draw conclusions about the company. Instead, they reminisce about which of those places like Moscow and Berlin they have been to. They sometimes even go through and count exactly which ones of the place names they have been to and which they have yet to go to, and then they are off in their heads figuring out which one they would most like to go to next. Never mind sitting at home or in an audience listening to one of the opera pieces, which is what the Connoisseurs are doing in their mind's eye by this point. They have created different perceptual realities even before they start reading the text.

They notice that conversations are about anything and this company talks a lot

The Populist nature also thinks that this is a company that would be a good fit, but this is because they are everywhere, with offices all over the world. This is the kind of data they need to take this business seriously. To a Connoisseur nature, it is more important that this company is based in Switzerland, which simply proves what they already know, that this is a Connoisseur-style company. The Populists, for their part, 'know' that this company is operating in a Populist way. And this is confirmed for them by the way the people in this company conduct conversations. What they see as evidence for this conclusion is that, in this company, they interact a great deal, they discuss things, have conversations about a wide range of subjects and explore others' worlds. There are many phrases in the text that refer to talking and interacting. All these parts of the ad are what the Populist reads and they make sense to this nature. To them, this is a Populist company. They have 'global presence' and they talk a lot.

Even the chairs are seen differently: they provide 'space' or they 'fill the space'

Even the visual picture will be interpreted in a different way. While the Connoisseur notices the elegance and delicacy of the chairs, the Populist registers something else about those chairs. What is relevant is that there are so many of them and that they take up all the available space. This is one way in which the Populist aspect of any communication of any sort is revealed. Populists assume that space, territory, is there to be used up, explored, whereas Connoisseurs assume that it is there to provide 'space'. The Populist would feel at ease looking at any ad, or picture, that is spread out in exactly this way.

The ad has given us the emotional information we need about what the company is like to interact with

It is abundantly clear, therefore, that these two psychological natures notice different things. You can see how easily these two natures could have their own perceptual realities, and their own interpretations of the same communication. In this instance, the ad is registered by both. It would feel right to both a Connoisseur and a Populist, and both types of customer would think that this was a company they could take seriously. This need not mean that the company would automatically get these customers. The content of the promotion, as well as whether they even want this kind of business at all, will still affect the ability of this company to attract customers. However, they have a head start since they have, at least, the capacity to make sense and feel real to the maximum number of people if they communicate in this way. Both the Connoisseur style of customer and those who have a Populist emphasis have the information they seek about 'who' the company is, some sense of its style and its way of interacting. The company has provided an indication of what it is like in terms of the inclusion area of experience, which customers of either psychological nature need in order to really register a company's existence.

The visual signs mirror the same principles Connoisseurs and Populists adopt in organizations

What the example brings out more generally are the kind of words, approach and visual display that correspond to the same principles that underlie every other feature of the various psychological natures. The previous chapters have specified a wide range of features of the business that relate to one nature or another. What this exploration of the advertisement's words and pictures does is simply to set out these same natures in a more visual way. The Connoisseur registers or notices anything that tells them that the style of interaction is focused or considered, that it respects territory. They will respond to and see and hear anything that provides those qualities which we have already seen can be associated with the Connoisseur, such as elegance, classicism and refinement. Any communication – whether an ad, policy statement or strategy – that has words that convey this sense will be understood by and feel right to a Connoisseur. And to the Populist, the words and visual signals that make sense and are noticed are those that indicate a style of interaction that is exploratory, seeking and diverse, one that participates with others and is highly interactive. The qualities in any communication – whether an ad, policy statement or strategy – that will feel right to and be understood by this nature will be the same as those we have seen as characterizing the identity and atmosphere of the Populist organization itself, being exploratory and stimulating, for example.

Being seen through the eyes of both Juggler and Boss customers

We can explore exactly the same phenomenon with the two control natures, the Juggler and Boss. Here, we switch our own perceptual filters, because we are looking now for how the organization conveys a sense of control, and how its message provides the information customers seek about what their own control experience is likely to be if they engage with this company. The example tells us what the two control natures, the Juggler and Boss, notice differently, and it tells us in a more general way what kinds of words and style will be picked up on to provide that information which customers seek in order for them to be able to predict how they will be 'managed' by the company.

Many companies assume the voice of the Boss when they communicate with customers

This is one area where organizations commonly speak in only one language, and consequently miss out 'half the population'. In financial services companies, in particular, it is almost always the case that the organization decides to speak only in the voice, and manner, of the Boss. The reason for this is because they try to present themselves as a reliable company. They talk in words that tell you, one way or another, about how controlled they are, in order to convey the impression that they will be in full control of your money. They assume that the recipients want to hear that there will be no risk to doing business with the company. These are the same implicit Boss assumptions that lie behind the various business policies and priorities that we have seen to exist in an organization which is primarily a Boss, in the same way that they will lie behind any communication or advertisement created by such organizations. They are also the implicit principles that explain the perceptual reality of Boss customers, who will, as assumed by the organization, respond to exactly those kinds of words and style of communication.

So they 'miss out' the Jugglers in the audience

However, what most companies fail to take into account is that some people, some customers, are Jugglers. In fact, the more entrepreneurial customers are so, just as their more entrepreneurial employees are Jugglers. When confronted by words, or a visual display, that feels and sounds like a Boss, people with this nature will feel far from reassured and safe. Instead, they will feel that the organization concerned is far too boring and strait-laced to convince them it will ever be able to make much money for them. If the organization is a financial services company, it will be hard for it to speak to or make sense to both Juggler and Boss customers at the same time. So even while the organization may have been successful at conveying some sense of control, it needs to be quite flexible and clever itself in the way it does so.

The Union Bank ad uses words and a visual picture that register with both natures

This is a balancing act that the Union Bank ad manages to pull off, however. Our exploration of the Juggler and Boss response to the ad is a more subtle look at perceptual differences than those we could see so evidently with the Connoisseur and Populist natures. Nevertheless, we can explore what those differences are to see how you can appeal to, and make sense to, both customers at once. We follow the same sequence, of looking first at the ad as it appears to the Juggler and then at the same ad as it appears to the Boss nature. The specific aspects that would be noticed by, and stand out to, each nature are underlined.

We have perceptual filters that 'tell' us about how this company is likely to exert control and 'manage' us

We need to remember that the differences that we are exploring represent the effects of the perceptual filters of each nature. Some of the words in the ad have a significance in terms of the expected style of interaction of the company, and some convey a sense of how the company will exert control. Customers will have both an inclusion nature, whether that of the Connoisseur or Populist, and also a control nature, whether the Juggler or Boss. This is equivalent to an organization having both one primary way of expressing its identity and interacting, as well as one primary way of establishing a sense of effectiveness and control. Customers need to have the experience of both and so have perceptual filters that they use to 'tell' them about the identity and style of interaction that the company is likely to have and another set of filters that 'tell' them about the control style.

Figure 9.4 sets out the ad with the aspects that the Juggler notices underlined and Figure 9.5 does the same for the Boss.

PERCEPTUAL REALITIES OF CUSTOMERS 217

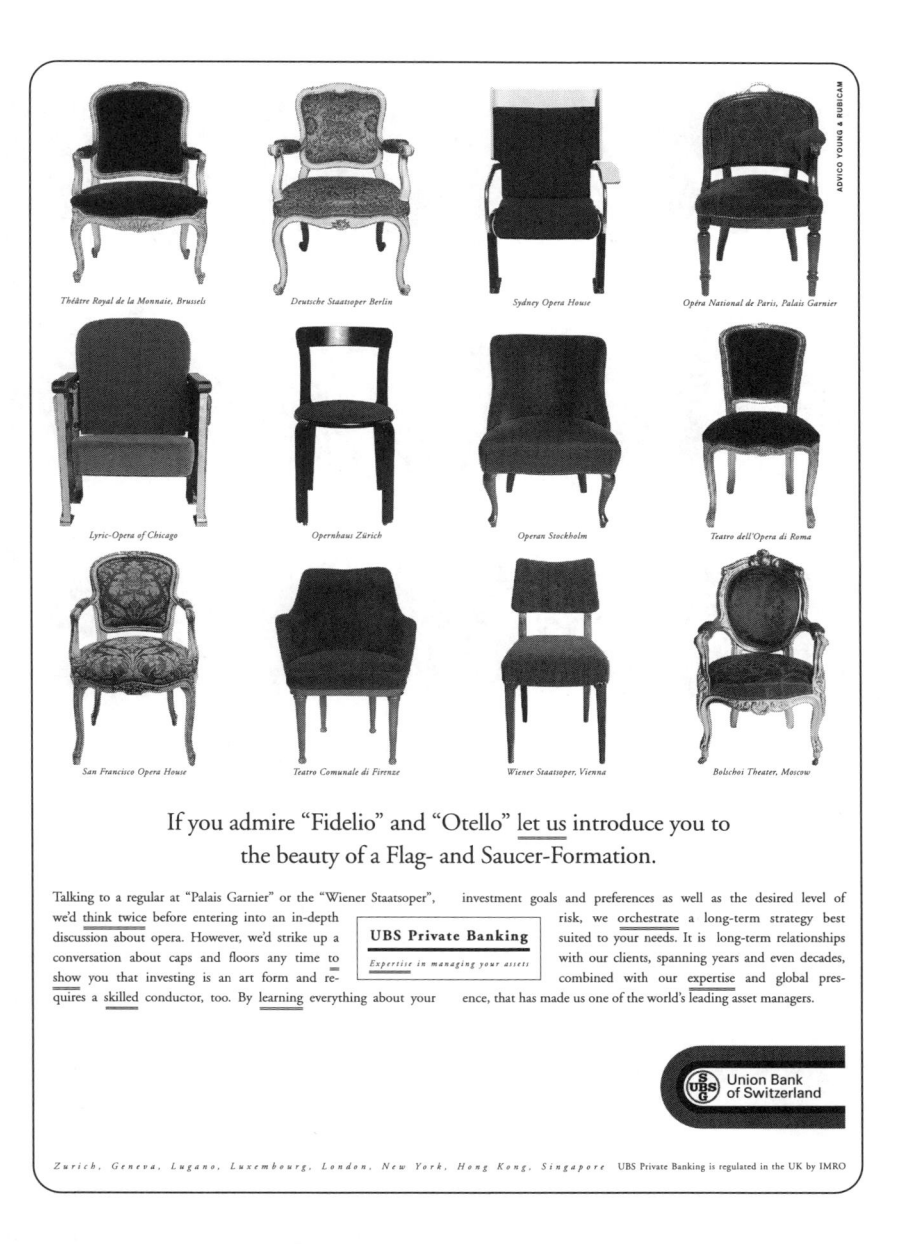

Figure 9.4 Noticing what a Juggler customer notices

218 READING THE MIND OF THE ORGANIZATION

If you admire "Fidelio" and "Otello" let us introduce you to the beauty of a Flag- and Saucer-Formation.

Talking to a regular at "Palais Garnier" or the "Wiener Staatsoper", we'd think twice before entering into an in-depth discussion about opera. However, we'd strike up a conversation about caps and floors any time to show you that investing is an art form and requires a skilled conductor, too. By learning everything about your investment goals and preferences as well as the desired level of risk, we orchestrate a long-term strategy best suited to your needs. It is long-term relationships with our clients, spanning years and even decades, combined with our expertise and global presence, that has made us one of the world's leading asset managers.

UBS Private Banking
Expertise in managing your assets

Union Bank of Switzerland

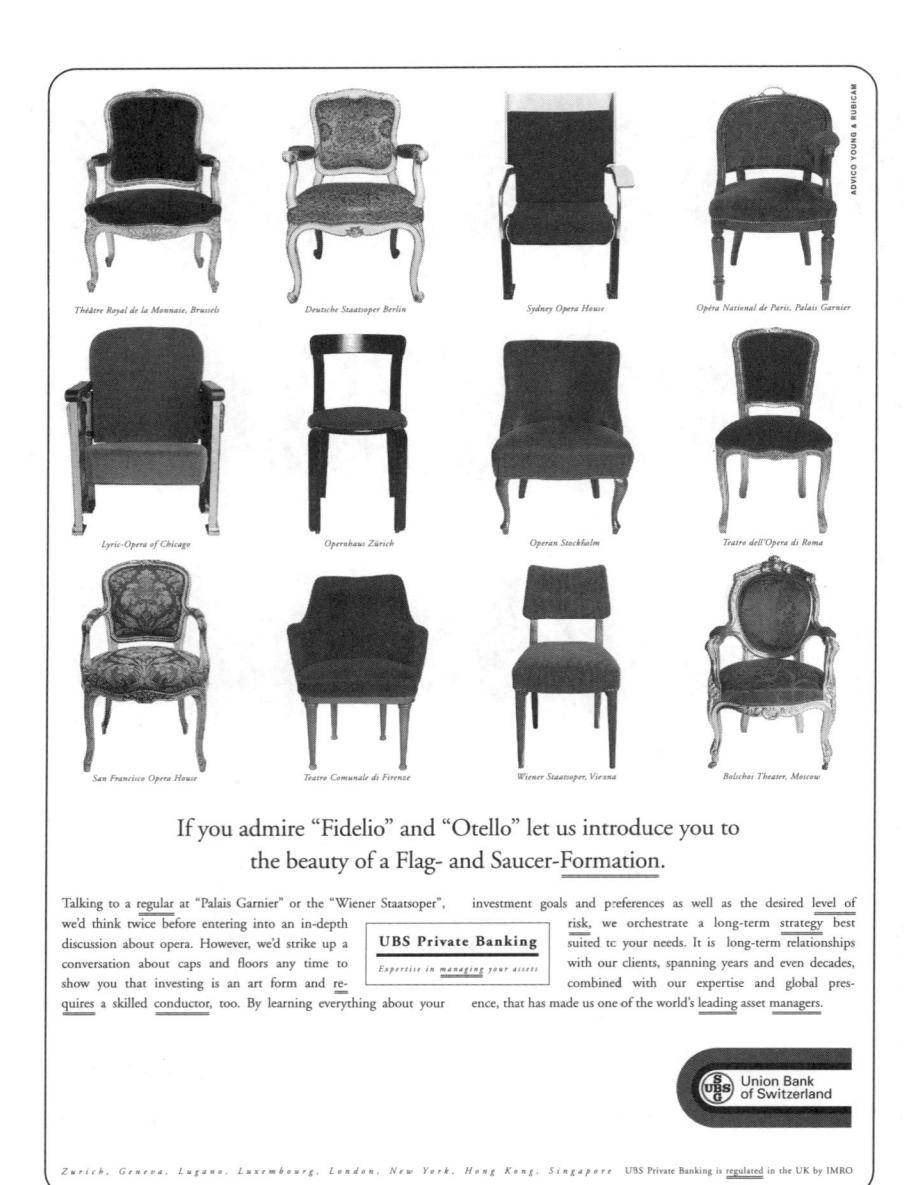

Zurich, Geneva, Lugano, Luxembourg, London, New York, Hong Kong, Singapore   UBS Private Banking is regulated in the UK by IMRO

Figure 9.5   Noticing what a Boss customer notices

The Juggler customer notices that work is like play and they won't be bossed around

They see that this company knows that you need to enjoy your work to be good at it

The Juggler would notice, first, that these people are not 'at work', that is, in a work environment. They are 'at play'. Yet it is clear that they also take their work, their business, very seriously. To a Juggler, this makes sense. To a Juggler, work *is* play. Doing business is playful, enjoyable, isn't it? If it is, then the Juggler takes the company involved seriously. It means, to the Juggler, that they are a good company, rather than that they are a playful company. To a Boss, treating work and business as being fun and 'play' makes much less sense. Play is something you do after work. But a Juggler 'knows' that you do your best work if there is a spiritedness, a sense of adventure, about what you are doing. People need to enjoy what they are doing in order to be good at it. So, far from being an approach that diverts an organization, or the people in it, from achieving the control purpose so dear to both the Juggler and Boss, conveying a sense that their business is intrinsically enjoyable and fun, which the Union Bank ad does, actually tells the Juggler that this company is good. It makes sense. These people are enjoying talking business at the opera and enthused about their caps and floors. There is a lightness of touch about the whole ad which is one thing that Jugglers would notice and be aware of.

And they like this company more as they read on. There is so much focus on expertise and being 'skilled'. This is the Juggler way of being in control and being effective. They are experts, they know what they are talking about. The references to 'expertise' at managing assets (rather than just 'managing assets') would be the parts of the text that would be picked out, the phrases that would pop out from the rest of the detail, because these are the words that make sense to this nature. Jugglers are used to companies saying that they are the 'best' companies to invest in because they have so many resources, because they are big or because they have leverage, and they are singularly unimpressed. They skip over such ads, bored by them. They 'know' that real effectiveness comes not from this show of strength, but from the real leverage that only skill and expertise provide. They can see that this company knows that too. They have been given a clear message about what the control style of this company would be.

They are relieved that the company will 'show' them rather than tell them what to do or boss them around

And there is another aspect that really appeals to the Juggler. They know that this company has no intention of bossing them around. The ad refers to their intention to 'show you', so the Juggler knows that they are unlikely to be 'told'. This is different from the usual approach which tells you that 'you need this' and 'you want that'. The ad even starts by conveying the idea that they don't know something. They say that they would 'think twice' before entering a discussion about opera. Other companies would say how clever they were at talking about opera. The Juggler notices that, while this company values expertise in running their business, they don't feel they have to prove themselves all the time by showing how much they know about everything. They speak, in fact, as an equal. They talk of 'learning' about needs, and then 'orchestrating' a strategy to suit. This is the light control touch that the Juggler knows is the best way to be on top of what you are doing. The company has done better than presume that the customer wants them to 'deliver solutions', which is exactly the pushy control style that turns the Juggler off. By the time they have read through, the Juggler feels quite assured that this company would treat them in a collegial way, in the special control style which they respect and respond to. They have been given the information they need that 'tells' them what their control experience would be like with this company.

The Boss customer notices that they will be provided with a reassuring sense of order and 'management'

They see that this company has a respect for order and structure

So, where are the Bosses in all this? Have they been turned off by the free-wheeling Juggler? No, because they know that the organization is absolutely on top of what they are doing. Customers with a Boss nature have also been gathering the information they need that tells them about the control style of this company. And their emotional experience while reading this ad is rather reassuring. They have such a sense of control. The company has presented the advertisement in such an orderly way, for a start. Each chair placed exactly in line, in perfect formation, just as the reference they make to the flag and saucer 'formation' alludes to. This company respects structure, which is the aspect of the ad that the Boss nature is aware of but which the Juggler nature would have been entirely oblivious to. A Boss customer may only notice these visual details subliminally, but they have been provided with the exact visual setting of control and order that makes sense to them. The ad has also matched the words in the text up exactly, in line, so you know that Boss customers are going to feel very reassured immediately even if they can't put their finger on why this should be so. The entire ad is set out with absolute precision and respect for detail. This will be worth reading, thinks a Boss.

They are reassured that the company takes charge and 'manages' them

They know, once they read the words, that this company puts a priority on taking charge of the assets under their control. They manage them, and they have set out, as clear as day, exactly the words that prove this to the Boss. These people don't just provide expertise or advice, they are going to 'manage' the assets. This is the key word Bosses want to see, and do see. It is placed right in the central box, one of the punch-lines of the ad, and they describe themselves as asset 'managers' right at the end as well, another punch-line. It is one of the words that will always pop out at a Boss in any communication. It implies that this company is going to 'manage' the assets of their customers instead of just providing them with advice, which the Juggler customer has read about. This goes the extra step that the Boss needs. Bosses find it frustrating to be treated exactly as an equal as a customer, since they are paying the company to take control for them, to take responsibility for making the most of their assets, not just to give them advice and assume that they, the Boss customer, knows what is best to do with their money. It is the company's job to do all these things, not the customer's job. And they notice other parts of the ad that 'tell' them exactly the same thing. The ad shows that the company will give a lead because they refer to the 'requires' a 'conductor'. This implies that the company will do the job they should do for the customer. This fact will stand out from the rest of the background detail and information in the ad, and these words convey reassurance to the Boss. The words even say orchestrate a 'strategy', a long-term one. Now, this really is speaking their language. A strategy. Where would a Boss customer be without one?

The ad has given us the emotional information we need about the way we are likely to be controlled or managed

So here too we can enter into two different perceptual realities, those of the two control natures. And as we have seen, the ad has given us the emotional information we need to tell us how we are likely to be controlled or managed by this company. This is one aspect that we need to know about and our control filters actively seek.

The visual signs mirror the same principles Jugglers and Bosses adopt in organizations

With the Juggler and the Boss, the qualities and principles that influence what they pay attention to are exactly the same principles that underlie the different aspects of the control nature of the organization itself and its business stance. For the Juggler, any aspect of a communication – whether an ad, policy statement or strategy – that conveys a sense of expertise, of skill, of work as enjoyable or of a sense of adventure will make sense to them, it will feel right. Any communication that tells them they will be controlled will switch off their antennae. They won't want to know. These are the same qualities that we saw applied to the kinds of organizations that Jugglers create and like. The Boss will respond to any aspect of a communication – whether an ad, policy statement or strategy – that tells them that things will be managed, that some order and precision can be relied on. Any structure, whether visual or in the verbal text, that conveys these qualities, which we have seen reflected in the Boss organization itself, is what they want. If they see or hear nothing that gives them this feeling of reliability and reassurance, they will switch off their antennae. They won't want to hear.

Being seen through the eyes of both Professional and Attractor customers

So, by now, we are doing quite well as customers. We have been given some sense of how we would be interacted with, as well as some sense of how we would be controlled, and the company has done so in a way that has got through to each different nature. What will they do in terms of conveying some sense of the affection area of experience, of engaging actively with tasks and relationships? They convey this in the language and style of both the Professional and the Attractor. We explore exactly the same process with these two natures.

We have perceptual filters that 'tell' us about how this company is likely to engage with us and sustain relationships

In this section we focus on the filters that 'tell' customers what the manner of engagement is of this company. We need to switch our own perceptual filters as well and pay attention to different kinds of things. As we can expect, the two natures read the same words and see the same picture in their own way.

Figure 9.6 sets out the ad with the aspects that the Professional notices underlined and Figure 9.7 does the same for the Attractor.

PERCEPTUAL REALITIES OF CUSTOMERS 223

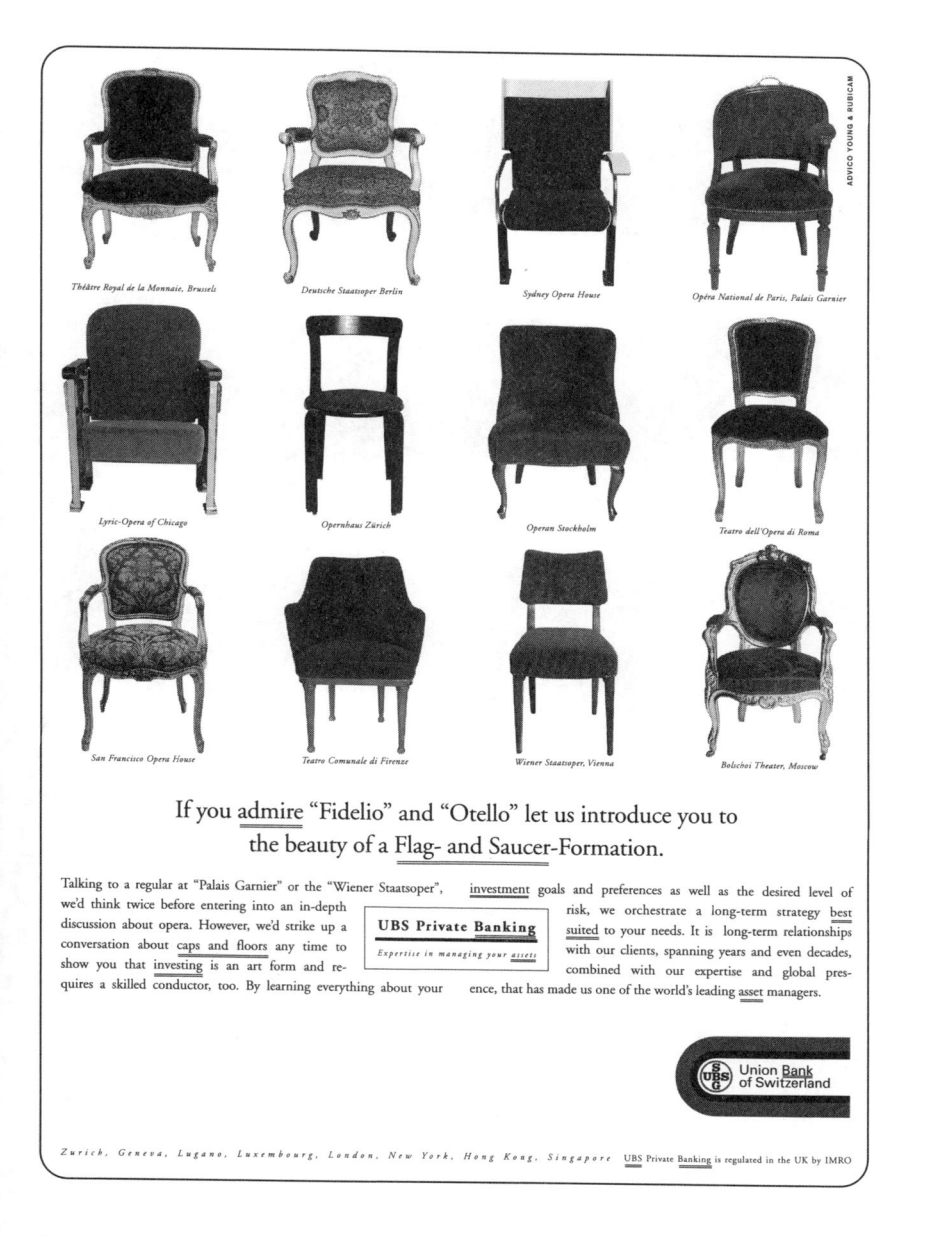

Théâtre Royal de la Monnaie, Brussels — *Deutsche Staatsoper Berlin* — *Sydney Opera House* — *Opéra National de Paris, Palais Garnier*

Lyric-Opera of Chicago — *Opernhaus Zürich* — *Operan Stockholm* — *Teatro dell'Opera di Roma*

San Francisco Opera House — *Teatro Comunale di Firenze* — *Wiener Staatsoper, Vienna* — *Bolschoi Theater, Moscow*

ADVICO YOUNG & RUBICAM

If you admire "Fidelio" and "Otello" let us introduce you to the beauty of a Flag- and Saucer-Formation.

Talking to a regular at "Palais Garnier" or the "Wiener Staatsoper", we'd think twice before entering into an in-depth discussion about opera. However, we'd strike up a conversation about caps and floors any time to show you that investing is an art form and requires a skilled conductor, too. By learning everything about your investment goals and preferences as well as the desired level of risk, we orchestrate a long-term strategy best suited to your needs. It is long-term relationships with our clients, spanning years and even decades, combined with our expertise and global presence, that has made us one of the world's leading asset managers.

UBS Private Banking
Expertise in managing your assets

Union Bank of Switzerland

Zurich, Geneva, Lugano, Luxembourg, London, New York, Hong Kong, Singapore   UBS Private Banking is regulated in the UK by IMRO

Figure 9.6   Noticing what a Professional customer notices

224 READING THE MIND OF THE ORGANIZATION

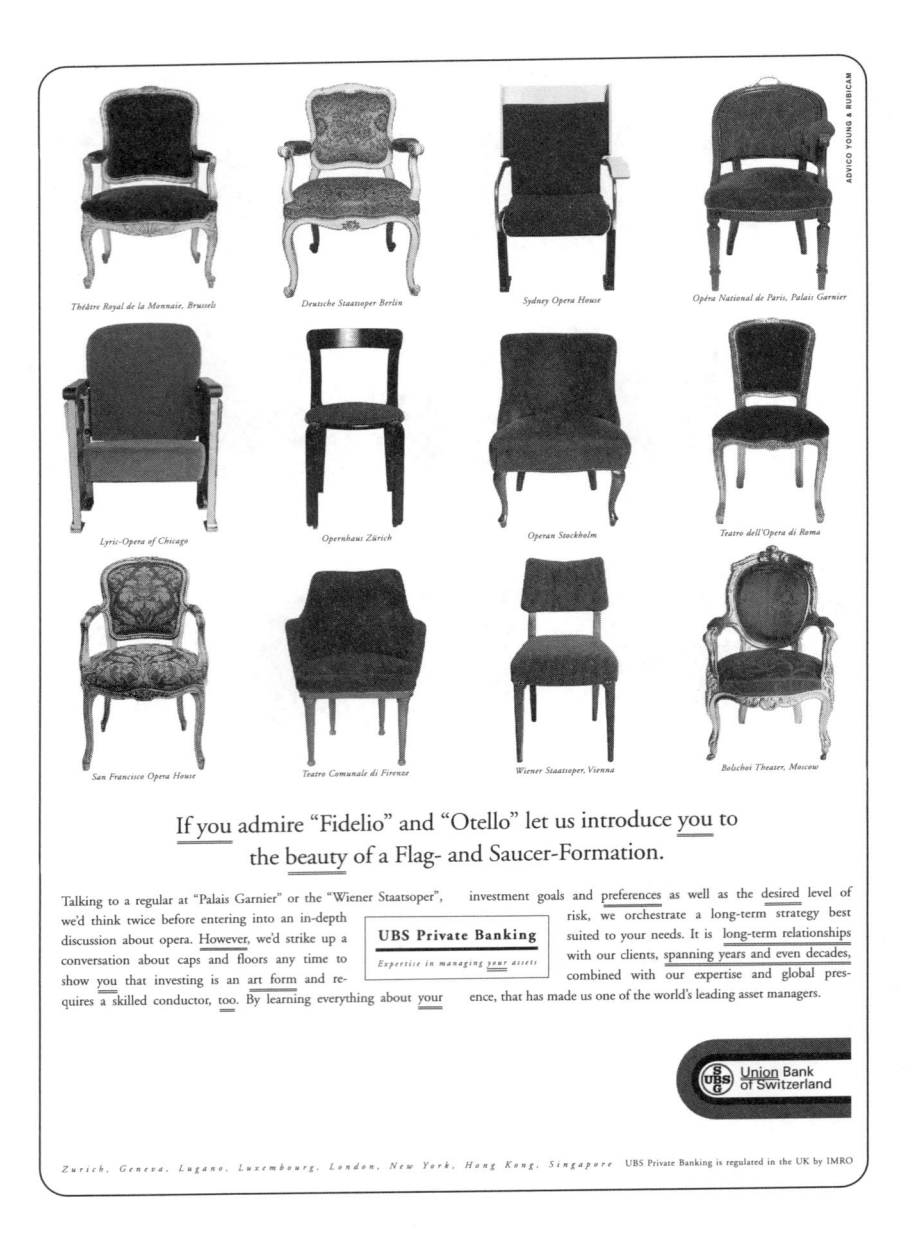

Figure 9.7 Noticing what an Attractor customer notices

We can divide up the chairs to begin with: clear crisp designs or warm and gentle

We start with the visual picture, since that neatly encapsulates the idea that these two affection natures really do have quite unique perceptual filters. The picture shows us twelve neatly arranged chairs. With the Professional and Attractor, we can actually carve up the chairs almost half and half. Some of these 'belong' to the Professional, and the remainder 'belong' to the Attractor. The ad is very clever in this, because both sets of chairs have something that provides exactly the sense of design and colour that both these two natures need. The subtle meaning in this, that life is enriched by such details, conveys the essence of the affection area of experience. But both natures have their own experience when reading this ad. The chairs that the Professional notices are those that look streamlined, clean and crisp in design, with tapered legs. These, indeed, are exactly the same principles by which they think the business itself should be designed. Streamlined, crisp, no waste. So, they take about half the chairs for themselves. The Attractors get the other half, and would not find those streamlined chairs comfortable anyway. The reality is that they barely register their existence. They see an ad that has very soft, relaxing, warm chairs. It is very soothing to an Attractor to get any sense of colour and texture, or of gentleness. 'Their' chairs have a welcoming appeal. They like the ones that have a clear centre to them. These, after all, reflect exactly the same principles that they think should apply in running a business. A sense of life, softness, warmth.

Both natures, therefore, are aware of radically different aspects of the ad simply from a passing glance. The point, though, is that the ability to appeal to both natures simultaneously, even in such a trivial feature, is rather unusual. And while I use the word 'trivial' here, any visual part of a promotion is vital in conveying the sense that the rest of the promotion, or message, is worth bothering about and is worth paying attention to. In this ad, just this visual picture provides both the Professional and Attractor customer with something that draws them into the ad to read it. Which, after all, is the whole point of an ad in the first place.

Our affection filters will be trying to 'tell' us if we would trust this company

The perceptual filters of a customer have already been engaged with picking out those parts of the ad that tell them about the inclusion and control experience with the organization, so now they turn their attention to something a bit deeper. Can they trust this company is a question they are implicitly seeking to answer as they scan this ad, and how will it feel to really sit down alongside them?

The Professional customer: 'getting on with it' seriously, even at the opera

They want to know what this company does for a living so they notice all the business words

The words in the ad that a Professional will notice, in order to answer these questions, are those that convey what the business is about. Anything that suggests to them that this company engages head-on with their work is the cue that the Professional needs to take the company seriously. The Professional is a serious nature and wants the companies they do business with to be so too. They will only really trust a company that 'gets on with it' instead of indulging themselves too much on 'managing the relationship'.

The words that will stand out for Professionals are those that tell them that this is about 'banking', 'investing', 'assets'. They want the formal definition of the nature of the business. The fact that these parts of the message are so up-front is a good sign because it means the company is up-front as well, with no messing around or wasting time trying to be too 'showy' if you deal with them. Professionals like some sign of jargon also, since that means, to them, that the company knows their trade. This company speaks businesslike language – the references to 'flag and saucer' and 'caps and floors' tell the Professional this. Even if they themselves know nothing about caps and floors, this is the kind of matter-of-fact detail they notice in order to take the company seriously. There is little frivolity in this company, that is clear. Also, they don't waste time. Even at the opera they are happy to discuss business. The one thing the Professional wants to see evidence of more than anything else is that time is put to good use.

They notice that this company really gets on with the business without messing around

Another thing a Professional customer likes is a name that is impersonal and straightforward. This is a sign to them that they will be dealing with a company that is professional and businesslike. So far, so good, thinks the Professional in the clipped, no-nonsense way in which they think as well as talk. No fancy name, just initials. Right, what else?

The real cue to the Professional, however, is the main heading of the text. Here, they spell out something that surely only a Professional would understand. They talk of 'admiring' the beauty of something to do with their work. This sounds like a mathematician admiring the beauty in higher numbers. It has the same meaning. The Professional reads this and 'knows' that this is a company that truly engages with their task, with their business. There is no other motivation that would set out words that talk of 'admiring' the beauty of a 'flag and saucer formation'. It says this company knows how to really engage, 'head-on', with what they are doing. This is what the Professional notices. This is music to their ears. They know they could trust such a company to 'get on with it'.

The Attractor customer: living life to the full and having a personal love of something

They want to know that this company knows about life and, therefore, can engage with them properly

The Attractor reads the same ad but it means something very different to them than that the company engages head-on with their work. On the contrary, this ad is showing them that this company focuses on living life. This is quite obvious from many parts of the ad. They notice, for a start, that investing is an 'art form'. Thank heavens, they think, this company isn't too deadly serious. This one has a wider perspective of what business is about. Attractors distrust any company that thinks you should focus only on business all the time, because this tells them that the people there would be inept at dealing with you as a customer.

They too have seen the reference to 'beauty', a strange word for such an ad, yet it is used quite naturally, without seeming out of place or 'stuck in' just for effect. However, to them, it means something other than respect for the craft, or admiration of a task, which is what appealed to the Professional. What it conveys to the Attractor is a love of something, an appreciation of inner worth. It is this that they need to sense in an ad more than any other single thing. Most companies, if they refer to 'beauty', make it sound like the thing they are describing is an object, truly a 'thing'. In this ad, they convey a love of something that is quite idiosyncratic and, therefore, personal. It might be a flag and saucer formation, but to talk like this conveys the information the Attractor is seeking, that people in this company are capable of feeling, and of a personal attachment to something. The evidence they look for is that this company is able to relate to others.

They see the kind of words that only Attractors use and notice the lilt and rhythm to them

The words that an Attractor notices in this ad are different from any others we have touched on so far. This is because they like extra words, the kinds of things that other companies throw out of their ads because they think they make them too wordy. However, an Attractor needs these in order for anything to feel right. This is one of their main clues and most companies get caught out here. So, they read a phrase like 'However, we'd strike up' and notice that this company doesn't set out an ad like a machine, where they would have said 'we'd strike up', and have left out the 'however'. The same pattern occurs throughout the ad. They say 'requires a skilled conductor, too', using the extra word 'too', that brings an uncanny rhythm to the sentence. This is how real people speak face to face, an arena that the Attractor needs. The rhythm creates an 'atmosphere' for the Attractor and they begin to relax. The phrase 'long-term relationships with our clients' appeals to them, but many companies can spin this kind of line out, so an Attractor would notice this but it would mean only a little. But they do register the next line because it refers to these relationships 'spanning years and even decades'. Here is that same sense of cadence and sing-song rhythm. The same seemingly extra word, like 'even' decades. This is music to the ears of the Attractor.

They notice, overall, the way that the text keeps saying 'you', but not as a device that is manipulative. It is written as if the company really is speaking directly to 'you'. That is the verbal structure that is set up. So, while the Professional is busy doing serious business about caps and floors with this company, the Attractor customer is feeling mellowed, made contact with, in a very soothing rhythmical way. This company feels right to them. They know they could trust this company to be able to relate to them, for real.

The ad has given us the emotional information we need about the way we are likely to be engaged with

Notice that it is rare for any ad to speak in a way that gets through to an Attractor. The way companies typically think that they convey the idea of being close to customers, of being personal, is so poorly done that there are very few who get away with it. This is because making yourself believable to an Attractor customer is a far more subtle and indirect process than simply putting words like 'customer relationships' down on the script. I have mentioned already the rather nauseating habit companies have of putting a staged picture of a baby or grandmother into their advertisements. Attractor customers see through this instantly and, in fact, prefer the businesslike ads of an honest Professional to this. This is because, to both the Professional and the Attractor customer, a well-functioning affection area in an organization is always shown by honesty, and a lack of manipulation. The two natures simply go about expressing that honesty and lack of manipulation in very different ways.

The visual signs mirror the same principles Professionals and Attractors adopt in organizations

As we have seen, the fundamental principles that explained the perceptual filters of each of these two natures reflect exactly the same principles that underlie their preferred kind of organizations, such as the business priorities. The qualities that define the perceptual filters of the Professional are being serious, streamlined, formal. Anything that expresses those qualities, whether the words, the overall structure of the ad or some detail like the type of chair, will be noticed by this nature. These are the characteristics of their filters. Those of the Attractor are qualities like warmth, being personal, artistry. And likewise, any aspect of any communication that provides these qualities will pop out to the Attractor more than any others. In this ad, we have been able to see both at once. How can you tell whether the real affection nature is a Professional or Attractor? Here it is almost certainly a bit of both, or the company would never be able to communicate in both languages with the ease it does. However, there is usually a slight emphasis in favour of one or the other nature and here you can tell it is the Attractor. This is primarily because it is only the Attractor that could 'speak' with this lilt, this use of extra words.

Conveying a complete set of emotional meanings to customers simultaneously

What we have seen is an advertisement that has conveyed information, whether explicitly or subtly, that relates to all three areas of experience. While I have set out the process customers go through when reading such advertisements as if they 'see' in a kind of sequence, in reality people take in such details almost instantly and process the different areas of experience simultaneously. The important point is that the ad provides a complete set of meanings, since it communicates in the same way that people make sense of their world all the time. They need some way of registering how the organization includes, and interacts with, others, some sense of how the organization establishes control, and some sense of how the organization would engage in a relationship with them.

You can understand the whole conceptual framework from this visual approach instead

The specification of different perceptual filters helps people because it describes those differences, rather than just saying that they exist. This is the added value, if you like. What we have done in our exploration of the advertisement is to see the psychological natures in a visual way. Some people make most sense of the whole conceptual framework by using their knowledge of these perceptual filters, more than from a knowledge of the different business features that are associated with each nature. They understand the essence of each nature in this way.

You can use the knowledge to help you communicate in other contexts or understand where others are coming from

The ideas can help organizations figure out how to present an ad in a new way. Or how to communicate a strategy in a way that is heard as it is meant. The ideas can be applied in any setting where it is important to understand others' reactions, or why they have the interpretations they have. They can aid you in communicating in a way that is heard by the maximum number of people within the organization, as well as by customers outside the organization. Determining what the different perceptual filters would notice and 'make' out of any situation can help you think through why people are reacting in the way they are. It is often perceptual differences, and interpretations of what you think is self-evident, that explain a situation you want to understand.

The general principles of the different perceptual filters, aided by some music

In order to help you do this, and by way of summarizing the key ideas which we have explored in our look at the advertisement, I have set out in the following table some of the general principles that characterize the different perceptual filters. These are summarized in Table 9.1 and can be used as a reference point to help you with any form of communication in the organization.

With this summary, we end this particular chapter and our focus on perceptual realities and filters. However, we carry over this more subtle and rather delicate look at an organization into the next chapter. In this

Table 9.1 Identifying the perceptual filters with the help of some music

Connoisseur perception

- register words like 'enter into' conversations
- 'see' any visual signs of refinement, elegance
- need space, spaciousness visually
- 'hear' quietness, pauses, even if only implied
- if they feel considered, they will pay attention
- notice any signs of focus in the communication

Music that reflects this world: solo artists, sensitive playing, piano recitals, music from specific traditions

Populist perception

- register words like 'talking', 'discussions'
- impressed by global presence, or activity
- 'see' visual signs of using up or exploring available space
- 'hear' what is spoken but ignore what is unsaid
- if they feel stimulated, they will pay attention
- notice any breadth, diverging in the communication

Music that reflects this world: pop, rock, anything loud, 'world music', whatever is the 'latest' music at the time

Juggler perception

- register words like 'expertise', 'skilled', 'orchestrate'
- 'see' any signs of playful attitude to work, enjoyment of it
- need to 'hear' that they will be uncontrolled
- 'hear' anything different from traditional orthodoxy
- if they feel adventurous, spirited, they will pay attention
- want something unexpected in the communication

Music that reflects this world: anything free-spirited, street music, jamming sessions, music that mixes traditions

Boss perception

- register words like 'manage', 'risk', 'strategy'
- 'see' visual signs that reflect order, precision
- need to 'hear' that things will be managed properly
- 'hear' words that respect regulations, orthodox rules
- if they feel reassured, on top, they will pay attention
- want signs of structure in the communication or ad itself

Music that reflects this world: traditional classical orchestra, band music, music with a script

Professional perception

- register words that reveal the nature of the business
- 'see' any visual signs of being streamlined, no waste
- 'hear' that there is no messing around, wasting words
- notice if the communication is well presented
- if they feel spoken to honestly, they pay attention
- like some formality in the communication

Music that reflects this world: anything they can work to, anything well crafted, delivered 'professionally'

Attractor perception

- register words like 'art form', 'long-term', 'beauty'
- 'see' any visual signs that convey softness, giving
- hear 'extra' words like 'however', as used in conversation
- notice if the communication is personal, direct to 'you'
- if they feel spoken to as if face to face, they pay attention
- like a sense of rhythm in the communication

Music that reflects this world: anything emotional, personal, intimate, opera, soul music, 'nature' music

we will be exploring the special essence of an organization and what it is that makes some organizations stand out. Our exploration of perceptual filters has set the tone as well as given us some specific ideas with which we can uncover this special defining essence.

Taking care of the special essence of the company

CHAPTER

10

Identifying the essence of the organization

In this final chapter, we spend our time on identifying and enhancing the essence of an organization. We home in on two important aspects of this. The first is to identify what is special about a company, what most defines it. With some companies, however, the primary need is to bring out of themselves what is already there but latent or unexpressed. Some companies have, for their own reasons, ways of denying who they are, or they act in ways that contradict their best interests. When this is the case, we need to work in a far more round-about way to uncover what those reasons are, in order to discover what the special essence is in that organization in the first place and enable it to be what it should have been all along. This is the second aspect that we explore in this final chapter.

The common theme is that it is important not only to identify who the organization is, but to do so in a way that tells you what most defines it and gives people in that organization a sense of what is special and unique about it. In each of the aspects we explore, I use a particular company to illustrate the ideas. With both you will see the key values that have been implicit or explicit throughout the book. In that sense, this last chapter acts as a good way of summarizing the philosophy that has provided the book's own essence. We leave behind the conceptual framework, however, and focus on what an organization is all about by using the insights that framework has given us but without needing its vocabulary. Our purpose is to empathize with these two companies and to get close to them. To do that, we need to concentrate primarily on the last of the three components that defined the overall approach in this book. So far, this third component has been implicit but in this chapter it comes into its own. We need to take account of the subtleties in organizations and approach them with far more sensitivity than we often do. This is the key requirement in this third component of my overall approach and it is this that we need to rely on if we are to understand and work with any organization in a way that brings out, or makes the most out of, its true essence and key qualities.

A visual approach and an emotional approach

We have two quite different methods with which to understand the two companies. I start with an unconventional approach, which relies on your intuition and your innate awareness. Some people will find this way fanciful, but it is quite real, quite factual and very informative. This way assesses an organization by 'seeing through' an advertisement and interpreting its meaning. The company we look at is a good example, and we can see its essential nature, what is special about it, quite easily from one of its advertisements. We have looked at an advertisement in the previous chapter, in the context of the perceptual filters of customers. Here, we are curious about the ad because of what it will tell us about the company behind it, rather than what it tells us about the kind of customers it reaches.

The second method looks at an example of changing a company, but in a very different way than we normally think of when we use the term 'change'. It relies, instead, on a slow process of seeing what the company needs at an emotional level. In previous chapters, I have explored the interplay between the strategic or business world, as well as the psychological meaning of events or statements. In this example, we take an even deeper look and we use psychology as it should be used, as a way of understanding human beings. An intellectual or academic understanding of psychology would have got you nowhere with this company. It took, instead, an appreciation of how human beings function or, at times, fail to function. To help this company required not cleverness, but empathy. The attempts to help this company meet its business goals required that we stopped trying to push it to meet those goals. What you will read about is an example of a company that changed faster than any I have ever seen, with a few kind words, some gentleness and letting them discover their own 'way'.

With these two companies, then, we end the book by using our understanding of, and sensitivity towards, human beings. But for now we start with a conceptual context for both approaches that looks at what we mean by 'changing' a company.

THE SPECIAL ESSENCE OF A COMPANY 235

A conceptual context for thinking about changing a company

There are a number of principles for working with organizations in a way that helps to enhance who the organization is, rather than damaging it. One of the consequences of thinking of an organization as merely an aggregate of lines drawn on an organization chart is that we imagine that its make-up, its nature, is something that can be chosen or put together as if from a pic'n'mix store. When we think of an organization in this way, it leads people to change things that make that organization special, that give it its own unique character. As we have seen throughout the book, these intangible aspects of a company are perfectly real, and have a great impact on its ability to function well.

The essence of a company

Some organizations have a clear sense of who they are, and what makes them distinctive as a company, and also successful. A company like Coca Cola is like this, and they cultivate their own unique style quite deliberately. The fact that this company has its own 'essence' in more ways than one, is not an added extra to them, but something they take into account along with their appraisal of the company's business aims. This conscious awareness of who they are, what they stand for, never leaves them and explains some of the extraordinary enthusiasm and dedication in that company.

Other companies, like Apple Computer, also have their own definitive essence, their own nature, but they have had to retrace their steps to recover it. It has only been when Apple has felt some sense of that again, primarily through the presence of Steve Jobs, that that old notion of what they stand for has returned. Any resurgence in Apple's fortunes, if they occur, would have to be partly attributed to reclaiming the company's spirit, their old sense of self, as much as it would be to any new strategies. Steve Jobs referred to this, in the context of the new iMac, in the following way: 'We've brought romance and innovation back into the industry . . . iMac reminds everyone of what Apple stands for' (*Financial Times*, 1 July 1998).

'What Apple stands for'. 'Reminding' people. This is taking people back to their essence, their definable nature. Coca Cola expands its strategy into Eastern Europe, wanting a higher share of whatever people drink, including water, and you cannot fail to notice the extraordinary spirit with which they do so. The complete seriousness and dedication with which they launch into each new strategic impulse. One company remains successful by protecting and enhancing its nature, and another tries to regain some of its edge by going back to that unique sense of who it is. Within our current ways of thinking of 'changing' organizations, this is a contradiction. One company stays the same and another goes back. Aren't organizations supposed to have to change all the time in order to be successful?

What do we mean by 'changing' a company, then?

What, then, do we mean when we talk of 'changing' a company? What are we thinking of when we use that term? Managers' first instinct is often to figure out 'what needs to change'. What is 'wrong' with their organization, they ask me. They are impatient with my suggestion that they work out what they want to build on or keep before they work out what to change. We are not used to thinking like this of the organizations we are in charge of. But there are parts of these organizations that are more delicate than we often realize. The subtle things in organizations certainly are those attributes that make the organization work with ease and grace, rather than with struggle and might.

Using a metaphor of the organization to put it in perspective

One metaphor that I use to understand organizations and which helps managers sort out this apparent contradiction about change is to imagine that the organization is a human being. This metaphor is a way to put the whole organization into perspective. It is not 'real' of course, since an organization is patently not a human being, but the metaphor is useful anyway. You can, then, think of an organization in the following way.

A human being does not ever really 'change', at least not in terms of their deep inner self, their essence, if you like. Trying to change or alter this would not only be hard, but a little stupid. Why would you even want to do so, since it is that part of an individual that sets them out? You would never want to take this away from them. With yourself, for example, you may want to add some skills as you go through life, to bring out of yourself more of what is latent, talents you have not used yet. You may, through experience, add some qualities and certain behaviours that make living with others easier and your work more rewarding. In that sense, then, we become 'different' and 'change'. However, if you look at photographs of someone over a long period, you will usually catch their indefinable unique self, the qualities that are always there, that never leave them. This is what defines them as a person.

There is something equivalent, a special uniqueness, in any organization also. The organization may be absolutely hopeless at many things and perform below the level that it should in terms of business results. Yet, even if this is the case it still has its own uniqueness, its own essence. If a person is underperforming, or is absolutely hopeless at many things, you would not try to improve this person by ripping out their unique sense of who they are, that essence. If you were to do so, they would be worse than before. They might start behaving woodenly and obediently, and something in themselves will have been destroyed. What, then, are we doing in organizations when we keep trying to rip their insides out, and call it change?

On the one hand we do need to change the business systems, update the products, develop new strategies and learn new competitive tactics. These are the equivalent of learning new skills as a human being. Just like human beings, organizations may learn from experience, adopt a new style, add a new approach. This is the equivalent of a person growing and developing. The organization can bring out of itself its own latent talents in the same way that a person does. In other words, an organization can add to its repertoire. However, like a human being, if you rip out its core sense of who it is, its own unique special something, you may well 'change' the organization but it is hardly likely to function better than before. You will create wooden, half-dead organizations. That is not what the game is about.

A critical step, then, is to discern what that special something is in an organization that makes it 'what it is'. You may want to protect and nourish it. Change everything else, but be careful what you do with that part.

We focus on identifying this special something in what follows in order to find out what is most defining of a company. The first of our two approaches to discovering what the essence of an organization is involves looking closely at an advertisement, and it is this that we explore in the next section.

Seeing the essence of a company through an advertisement

With this right-brain approach to figuring out what an organization is like we use our intuition to 'see through' the immediate appearance of a particular company as portrayed in an advertisement of theirs. The aim is to identify the unique spirit of an organization. The company we look at is Merrill Lynch, and we look at one of its advertisements as you would a photograph. One way of tracing who an organization is across time is to look through a series of their advertisements in the same way that I described finding what is unique in a person by looking through a series of photographs across their life. The immediate appearance of a company's advertisements may be quite different from one to the next but if you use your intuition to see through to the symbolic messages it contains, it is a different story. An ad should be able to reveal the company behind it to you if that company knows what it is about and is comfortable with who it is. If you read a series of advertisements with a psychological eye and can see no connection from one to the other, then that company will have a very shaky sense of itself and it would be very hard in such a company to create any sense of meaning or to get other people to believe in it. A series of advertisements should reveal what the essence of a company is because you should be able to see what has remained most constant, what is always there, rather than a company that has simply shifted with the tide. When a company has a more secure sense of who it is, this knowledge is a psychological asset to it. Its advertising agency may change, its chief executive may change many times over, its products may be sold in different industries, the company's strategies may be different, and it may have inverted its organizational structure. And still it 'stays the same'. This is the essence of the company.

Merrill Lynch

Merrill Lynch is a company that has a definite nature, the spirit of which has stayed the same for many years. Some people would love this company and others be rather afraid of it, partly because it has a definite character and partly because it is comfortable with itself. It is 'itself'. Because of this, it is the kind of company that, if it were a person and walked into a room, people would be aware that someone had just walked in, and turn to see who it was. This is the quality of presence in a company. It arises only when a company has a clear sense of who it is and what it stands for. It can be itself, without having to turn itself inside out to become what others want it to be. You can see this presence in the advertisement we look at.

Let's look at what most defines Merrill Lynch.

Figure 10.1 sets out the advertisement for Merrill Lynch.[1]

---

[1] *Business Week*, 25 November 1996.

THE SPECIAL ESSENCE OF A COMPANY 239

Figure 10.1 Merrill Lynch

Looking at the ad to see what makes this company 'who it is'

There is a precision in this ad, as well as an economy with words, that reveal a company that knows what it is about and what it wants to stand for. The clarity in the visual display, as well as in the few words in the ad is reinforced by the strongest visual feature within it. The stare from the eyes of the person on the right-hand side. There is a directness in the gaze here. Few people look so directly, as if they look straight through you in this way. It is a remarkable feature for an ad, as it is using a face at close-up and yet the picture adds to the rather serious message rather than detracting from it. Also, when companies use a close-up, it is also rare for the person to seem intelligent, yet this is the immediate impact this visual has, and it ties in with the verbal message the ad has.

If you let your intuition work for you, you can predict what some of these visual and verbal messages might imply for the company behind the ad. None of these are conclusive, of course, but if you pick up the right signals from the ad itself you are usually on a surer footing. For example, from these small cues I would expect a similar directness and a tendency to look straight through things to exist in the whole dynamic in the company. You could expect a desire to get to the essential point, a need to have things spelt out clearly and directly, and to know things as they stand. This would be quite a straightforward company, wanting to get to the heart of things. This directness is accompanied by a less obvious subtlety, communicated by other visual features of the ad. For example, the spare way in which space is used in the ad conveys a sense of precision. There is a light touch here that becomes apparent only when you look closely, for it is relatively masked by the first impression, which is of such directness in the overall projection of the ad.

Another visual feature that is quite defining of the ad is the containment of it. There are two separate lines of demarcation around the outside. This suggests a tendency to define or contain what they are doing rather than spreading all over the place. You would expect that, within the company, jobs should be finished properly, closed and completed rather than being left floating in thin air. The same idea is revealed in two other ways. The concern for containing things as well as defining them clearly is suggested also because the final words are in the boldest print, and the name is a way of putting a full stop at the end of the whole ad.

The borders of the ad, the beginning and the ending, are marked by the name of the company. It begins and ends with a statement that seems as if they are saying 'this is us, take us seriously, we take you seriously'. There is little frivolity, but a sense of self-containment and self-possession here. All these indications suggest a company that dislikes being messed around, but is quite comfortable with itself. The fact that they have chosen to illustrate such a strong sense of presence in the ad implies that having an innate presence would be an important aspect of this company, perhaps a quality people value highly.

Another key theme contained in the ad is the respect for learning that is conveyed in both the verbal message as well as revealed in a more subtle way in the ad. They admire skill and expertise. The fact that they can 'teach' or impart this perspective is proven by the very exact and clear logic of explanation they use in the main text. It reads like a straight line, with every phrase following in causal sequence. None needs to be reread, they lead you straight through. They sell themselves along the way, but so they should. It helps that they have the innate confidence to do so. Yet, the causal logic of the text is so well done that you barely notice how they have set it out. It seems obvious, but it is remarkable how few companies do this. They either just present 'information' in front of you, or they make leaps in the logic. In this company, the ease with which they have presented the causal steps, as well as the overall messages of the ad itself, tell you that they expect you to have a brain, and that brainpower within the company and in others is just 'assumed' or expected.

There is the same sense of both presence and confidence in the image that they use to represent the company, which is in small detail at the base. The bull has its tail up, flaring. The eyes of the bull seem to look straight at you as well and it seems to be pawing at the ground, bursting with energy. It is the image of the bull which gives the energy to the ad, as does the face in the visual, but there needs to be some direction to this. Such power must have some expression, so the requirement in the company would be to channel the energy and activities in very deliberate directions. And in the ad, they tell us what some of those are. The intention is to 'open eyes', and this creates the link with the gaze in the right-hand side of the ad. The key words that relate to this are 'knowledge', a 'development tool', putting 'developing economies into perspective' and 'opening the eyes of the world to a country's potential'. There is a respect for learning here, allied with the energy and 'fire' indicated by the symbol of the bull along with the simple directness in the gaze.

The key words in this message are 'potential' and 'perspective'. This is a company comfortable in a position as leader or catalyst. This is what most defines this company, one that is supremely comfortable with learning, power, influence and seeing what is possible, opening eyes. The implications of an ad like this is that the company it is describing is accustomed to being a catalyst or leader, not just that they are so, because the ad has such a natural style without having to grab our attention, or to do something dramatic in the ad to 'prove themselves' as a company.

In any company, these factors would suggest that it had an influence. In the case of Merrill Lynch, it is clearly financially successful, but even if it wasn't people would ask this company what their opinion was. People in the media would want a comment about trends in the industry, for example, because it is so apparent that this company knows what it is about. They project an innate authority and you can identify in the ad the exact parallel visual and verbal clues that tell you that this is so.

The ad also implies that they want to do more than simply actively run around. They stand back and take a view and this is implied by the gaze as well as the words which speak of 'perspective'. When a company focuses on showing us how busy and hard-working it is, it conveys that they feel a lack of ease with themselves and with using their own skills. It suggests that a natural use of talent and energy is lacking in some way and that they are trying to prove themselves, which is quite different from actually achieving. A sign of health is shown, instead, by a company that is intent on being effective instead of simply trying hard or working hard. A key aspect of being truly effective is being able to see ahead and strategize. It requires the ability to think clearly as well as to act. This idea is reflected in the verbal message of the ad with words like 'perspective' and 'seeing', and is reinforced by the economy of words used and the spareness of the spacing. This is a company that would appreciate really achieving things rather than just appearing to do so. You can see the implicit value placed on such factors in almost every feature of the ad.

Another key implication of the points I have drawn out is that the ad reveals a purpose. It tells us why they do what they do. The gaze is an indication of feeling at ease with contact and direct engagement. We have seen also that there is a sense of fineness and delicacy in the visual spacing of the ad. All these particular aspects bring in a touch of lightness and soften the ad a little, since it is quite serious overall.

Some people may even be intimidated by this company, because of the fact that it reveals a lot of presence, self-possession as well as confidence. There is a comfort with influencing implied by the face, the image and the words. Power is probably perfectly acceptable in this company. What we need to bear in mind is that a company like this is off-putting only to those people or organizations who are uncomfortable with themselves or with power generally. To others, a company like this should be energizing, exciting and interesting. Companies like this help you think that you can do more than you thought you could. It is all a matter of potential, perspective and seeing what is possible. That is the essence we were looking for.

Taking a short cut using your intuition

Exploring an advertisement in the way we have just done can be quite fun, but it is, like the company we have just looked at, also perfectly serious. You can often use it as a short cut to see many aspects about an organization that tell you what is most important to it and about it. The focus here has been on deciphering the ad in order to discern what the company's essential qualities are. However, once you have identified these, you need to ensure that this part of the organization, its essence, is thought about in a very deliberate way. You need to make sure that any changes you are thinking of making within the organization add to this part of it, nourish and cultivate it rather than detract from it, damage it or conflict with it. These are the kind of things you can think about once you know what that special essence is.

Thinking about what you are doing with the company

Too often, we neglect to ask such questions until certain parts of the organization start squealing and resisting what we are trying to do to it. If this happens with any change or reorientation process you are embarked on, before you decide to push harder, or to sell your ideas more or to get more people behind the process of change, you need to ask yourself whether those areas of resistance are voicing the real spirit in the organization, and trying to protect its nature and what most defines it, that you have forgotten about. Sometimes, but not always, it is those voices which represent the organization's true interests more than those voices trying to push through a change programme. Sometimes, of course, you do need changes for the good of the organization. Whichever is the case, it is a fundamental component of creating organizations that function successfully as well as smoothly that you have understood the implications of what you are doing to it from this more subtle and psychological perspective.

Table 10.1 Some questions to remind you why you are doing what you are doing

> what most defines this organization, what is **special** about it, its essence?
>
> what qualities or features of the organization would you want to **enhance** or bring to the fore?
>
> what aspects or features would you want to **change**?

In Table 10.1 I have set out some questions you can ask yourself about the implications of any change you are involved with in the organization. You can use these as a reminder of what it is all about and why you are doing what you are doing with it.

Bringing out the essence of the company rather than just identifying it

While we can look at an advertisement using our intuition to guide us to the essence of an organization, sometimes we need more than our intuition to help a company become who it should be. One way or another, we need to find out what that special something is that most defines an organization because every organization needs a reference point. It needs to know who it is and where it starts from because knowing this gives people in the organization a sense of meaning and identity. We need to know where the organization 'starts from' before we make extensive changes. However, sometimes we need to find and uncover for the organization what its essence is, when it is not at all obvious. While it was relatively obvious with Merrill Lynch, in the company we explore in the last part of this chapter, finding out who they were was not at all easy. This is the process we explore next.

Aiming for some emotional stability for the chemical company

I end the book with a tale of a company which needed to be understood in some depth. One of the basic precepts of my approach is that an organization should function successfully, but in an easy way, smoothly. Doing so almost always implies that the organization is 'itself'. Some companies find this easy. And others find it extremely hard. Helping such organizations be the success they can be requires bringing out of them who they are meant to be in the first place. Doing so gives them an emotional stability and poise which is otherwise lacking. However, the process involved is not one that can be easily met with our usual approaches to organizations. It requires an emotional approach because, typically, the lack of emotional stability in the company will create a certain dynamic that not only affects the business but also the everyday behaviour.

In the company I describe in the following sections, I never referred to the fact that I was using an approach that was based on psychology and nor did I ever use the words 'emotion' or 'psychology' with the people there. The agenda the company had was a purely business one. However, under the surface it was necessary, as a consultant to know what the intangible implications were of everything that was done. When you are trying to help an organization improve the way it functions, even if that is for the apparent purpose of meeting its financial or strategic objectives, you often need to use an awareness of emotion and psychology. However, rather than being alarmed by this statement, remember that all that this involves is applying your ordinary, everyday understanding of human beings, which we often forget to use in business. It does not require a degree in psychology to understand human beings and, in fact, such degrees often get in the way of doing so and feeling empathy towards people or a company in general. Using our innate understanding of human beings is, however, often ignored while we try to 'get on with it'. In this company, the whole problem in the first place was that they had, for years, kept 'getting on with it' instead of tackling the real problem. Let me tell you what happened.

Discovering the company

I was asked to work with this company, along with a colleague, to help it implement its strategy more effectively. One key mechanism for change was a series of four-day workshops for their top 300 people, a massive commitment of time for an extremely busy company. The format involved two to four teams working together for those four days, with the purpose of determining for themselves some goals for their business areas. This kind of target-setting and strategy deliberation was something they were used to. However, what they were less used to, or good at, was implementing their strategy well.

One of the first things we noticed, as the consulting team, related to our own ability to work productively with this company. I remember describing my first week with them in terms of 'being run over by a juggernaut', and my colleague had rather more colourful ways of describing the events, and the client. The groups operated as if they were heavy-duty lorries that ran all night and day without stopping. Our own reaction to the dynamic in the organization was something we had to pay attention to in order to decipher what the company was like, and how to change it. The heavy-duty style and atmosphere in the teams mirrored the strategic bottlenecks they were describing to us. This company was trying to move the emphasis, and the source of their revenue, away from large, heavy items and processes to smaller, more technologically based items and more flexible processes. Often, helping a company meet its strategic objectives is aided by seeing the connection between the reasons why they cannot easily meet those objectives and the ordinary everyday behaviour unfolding in front of your eyes. The latter will always tell you how to help the company meet the former, if you decipher it.

Some of the things we noticed when working with the groups started to tell us what was really driving this company. The heavy atmosphere continued even over lunch, as they would relentlessly charge on. I never once heard a discussion or reference to anything outside their immediate line of business, whether about a social or a political issue for example. In the workshop discussions themselves, what was noticeable was the emphasis on framing a goal in terms of being the 'best', or of being 'number one' or 'number two', or, occasionally, 'number three', in a particular market segment. They would have been embarrassed to express a goal in any other fashion, yet their actual positions in their respective markets or niches often fell short of this. Their ambitions to be number one and so on were often so unrealistic that it was almost childish to listen to, except that you knew that they must be really seeking something underneath this kind of ambitious claim. It is not that I dislike managers stretching themselves. So as I watched these managers I was puzzled as I tried to decipher what need in them was so strong. Why did they need to set such goals? Some of them would be met but others would never be and, by the time the next year came around, would have been replaced by a new set. In order to work with this company, and get the juggernaut to be more flexible and lighter, we needed to find out what this need was, and work out another way for it to be met. If we did not, we might be able to help the company temporarily but we would not have truly helped it unless we found a way of getting it to function, and people to behave, in a quite different way than they were.

One key aspect of helping them in this more fundamental way was to discover who they were in the first place. Because, until they had some sense of who they were, they would never be able to release the dynamic that drove them and got in the way of meeting their own business goals. The dynamic that existed was so dominant that it characterized everything else about the company. In order to add to, bring to the fore or protect any special essence in this organization, we needed to find it first.

Helping the juggernaut ease up

One of the clues that explained the dynamic that we had identified, seen and felt became clear when I realized that they never talked of which markets they should get out of. They never talked of which goals and activities they should stop, and they never had a product line that should finish. This, in spite of the overall strategic stance expressed in terms of moving away from the heavier end of their industry to a lighter end, which implied that certain things should stop. They never made those specific decisions. The dynamic that was driving this behaviour, as well as the over-stretching that meant they had little time to make the goals they did set actually work, was that they found it hard to finish, to complete, to stop things. They needed to focus and to be able to say no, rather than to set ambitious goals and new ones of the same nature the following year.

These managers worked themselves to the bone, and they drove themselves like no other company I had ever been in. Why did they drive themselves so hard that it almost hurt to be with them? If people never feel they have finished things and they never have a sense of completion, they will never be able to feel any satisfaction over their achievements. One of the reasons why these managers kept repeating the same pattern was quite simply because they never experienced the completion of their own goals. They never allowed themselves the satisfaction of saying 'that's over', 'we have done that, completed that piece of work', or of saying 'we really did it', 'we made that goal'. These are the kinds of words or phrases that people need to hear or think or feel in order to register that a cycle has ended, and that they can let go of the last goal–work–completion cycle. If this cycle is never completed psychologically, people will just keep on going round and round in the same pattern. What you will see is very different goals and objectives on the surface, but they are simply the external manifestation of exactly the same underlying, incomplete emotional pattern.

In this company, the fact that these managers never experienced fully that they *had* achieved something was the reason they kept driving themselves on, even though they should have learned to be lighter on their feet, more nimble, instead of working so hard. It was the underlying cause of the problem the company had themselves identified, which was that they set good goals and devised clear and good strategies, but didn't achieve or implement the strategy as effectively as they should have or could have.

What was needed was for a way that allowed these managers to realize and to experience the satisfaction of their own achievements. It sounds small, trivial, but it is often quite a small thing in the psyche of the organization that can lead to wide-ranging effects and seriously impact the business. It was clearly doing so in this company, and we needed to help them get rid of it.

Drawing the sting of a past event

One factor I wanted to understand was what had set off this dynamic in the first place. We found the answer to that in the fact that about eighteen years earlier the company had had to be rescued with a financial package from a then-parent company. They had since become independent, but there was in the company history an event that had scarred them, and which still meant a great deal to them. Many of them remembered it and it had clearly left its mark. As a result, they were still trying to prove themselves. Who to, is anybody's guess, but they had never had the kind of experience that was necessary to stop this process or to draw the sting of that past event. They just kept going and going, instead.

What we had to do as consultants was behave and act in a way that demonstrated to these people that they *had* achieved things, and that they could be satisfied with whatever those achievements were. In their immediately previous experience with consultants, they had become used to being told that everything they were doing as a company was 'wrong'. What this company needed, instead, was some proof that they had got it right, were getting it right, were perfectly capable of getting it right and, in fact, were pretty good at what they did. That was the process we needed to engage in, as well as helping them to improve themselves in a way that they chose, once they had stopped striving.

Since it was actually true of them that they were good at many things, it was not difficult to start to get across to them that the company was genuinely capable and effective. We didn't need to dream this up, only to make sure that we focused as much time on what they did right as it occurred in front of our eyes and to make sure that we meant any comments we made so that they seemed real rather than fake. We had to make a point of doing this, and to know ourselves why we were doing it, and what effect we were after by doing it. In that way, they would be able to let go of a dynamic that had become unnecessary and which was impeding them from running their business well and smoothly. What we were 'teaching' them was how to register and experience that they had achieved something, so that they had less need to strive and more capacity to achieve and function well. We were 'teaching' them how to experience and feel satisfied with a work–goal sequence, so that it was 'complete'. Remember that we had no need to talk directly, or work explicitly, in a psychological way. As I have mentioned, we had no need to use such a term with them. It is often unnecessary to do so, but what is necessary is that you can work out the meaning and effects of whatever you do so that it is consistent with what is required psychologically not just in terms of the business.

Letting them be

The client started to blossom, mainly due to the style we adopted with them rather than because of any of our ideas. The style was to deliberately foster a sense of 'letting them be' and not driving them too hard. We wanted to open them out, give them the working environment that meant they could stretch wide rather than rush headlong. So the way we structured sessions, the way we orchestrated discussions and the rather relaxed way we facilitated were designed with that clear psychological objective in mind. It was different from the natural style of both of us when working as consultants, and it taught us something about how productive it was to create space to explore, without pushing. That, and a few kind words.

Doesn't sound very hard, does it? But it worked. The people and the company changed faster than any client I have ever seen change. The shift in emphasis in the business seemed to happen in a few months, although it was certainly longer. The company started to open out like a flower. The old organizational structure was jettisoned and the company as a whole became quite malleable and flexible. They slowed down but achieved more of their goals. They became interesting as a company, and were talked about by other companies because they did so many unusual, innovative things. They started to become 'their own company'. It was not as simple as I have just portrayed it, of course, but what that company taught me was how easy it was to simply say a few kind, genuinely meant words about how good they were at their business. This very tough, hard-bitten juggernaut simply needed a few kind words, not more toughness. They had had enough of that already. They needed to lighten up so that they could become who they were, as well as achieve the success for the company that they wanted. We needed to let them be and we needed to be gentle with them.

They turned out to be quite rebellious underneath all that striving. They had an irreverent spark that was quite hilarious, and it was this aspect of themselves that was 'released' more than anything else. They used it, for example, to experiment in quite radical ways in how they organized as well as in some of the ways in which they claimed space and promoted themselves in new market areas. They were quite an adventurous company, in fact. This hint of rebellion often surfaced in the workshops we had with them, as well as in the company itself. What was surprising was how easily the most senior people in the organization took this. It was perfectly natural to them, or so it seemed. In many other companies some of this spirit would have been suppressed, but here it was always greeted with a kind of humour and pride by the top echelons. They used to tell me about it, amused. This was one sign that told you that this was a key aspect of the company's character, that it was natural for them to be like that, even though it had rarely been glimpsed before. It 'told' you also, if you were looking, that this company was on its way to recovering their special essence and a sure emotional foundation. They started to develop some stability and poise.

Sometimes it isn't so hard to find some small way that changes the psyche of a company. In this one, it involved 'letting them be' and a few kind words. In other companies there may also be a magic key that can turn everything around quite easily and fast. You just have to find that key.

Taking the right overall stance: you can help organizations live inside or die inside

The overall stance you take matters too. I encapsulate it for myself now in the form of a decision. The basis of this stays the same whether the decision is a major long-term one or an everyday decision we have to make to keep everything going. It is the same for how you live as a human being as well as for how you manage an organization. The basis of the decision is this. You can die inside. Or you can live inside. That is the essence, and the implication, of many of the decisions we make, only we often fail to realize that that was the basis of many of them. If we are aware that that is the basis of a decision, the choice is not hard to make. The basis of the decisions we make when we run organizations is often the same. Only, we also fail to realize that that is the effect, or implication, of many of the decisions we make. The organization can die inside. Or it can live inside. That's the basis of the decision. That's not hard to make either, is it?

Index

achievements, satisfaction in 247–8
advertisements 204–29, 237–42
'affection' area of experience 29–30, 32–4, 49–55, 64–5, 70–71, 103, 178–9
  addressed by advertisements 207, 222, 225, 229
  as the most real area for the organization 192, 198–9
  assessment of organizations with regard to 109, 118
  deep roots and long fuse of 143, 149
  different ways of addressing 55
  effect of atmosphere on people within 148–9
  feelings associated with 127–30
  illustrations of 137–42, 196–7
  in Daimler-Benz business statement 92–102 *passim*
  priorities assumed within 197
  reactions to investigators in 195
  sensitivity in relation to 131–3
  signs of a need for attention to 145–6
  signs of well-being within 150
'affection' purposes of individuals 165, 172
Aids 61–2
aims
  genuine achievement of 113
  of the individual 165
  see also goals
alliances with other organizations 40–41, 54
American Airlines 49
anticipation 91, 172
Apple Computer 235
appraisal of people 47, 176–7

appreciation of people's effort 140–41, 144–5
areas of experience 29–34
  advertisements relating specifically to 207, 229
  atmosphere corresponding to 148
  evaluating achievement of aims within 111
  illustration of 57
  in relation to business aims 84–6
  reading between the lines in respect of 87–8
  specific feelings associated with 125
  the most real 183, 191–3, 197–9
  ways of functioning within 112
atmosphere 125, 134–41 *passim*, 147–8, 167–75 *passim*
  effect on people of 148–50
  in relation to business aims and activities 151
attention, demands for 138, 146
'Attractor' consumers, advertisements appealing to 222–9 *passim*
'Attractor' organizations 49–55, 72
  changes implying greater emphasis on 75
  examples of 55
  in Daimler-Benz business statement 92–5, 97–8
  questionnaire for identification of 121
atypical companies 141
automatic inclination to be efficient 156, 164
away-days 135–6, 145

belief in the organization 33, 51, 102, 174, 199

belief in the product 150
betrayal, feelings of 129
bias 196–7
blaming others 138
'Boss' consumers, advertisements appealing to 215–22 *passim*
'Boss' organizations 42–8, 71, 155–6
  changes implying greater emphasis on 74
  examples of 47, 49, 65, 70
  in Daimler-Benz business statement 96–8
  questionnaire for identification of 120
brain functions, left and right 35, 237
British Petroleum (BP) 49
bureaucracy 158–9, 162
business strategy statements *see* reading between the lines

cadence, sense of 228
Calvin Klein (company) 55
can-do spirit 149, 170
capability and self-capability 169–70
change
  for a company 235–7
  how much is necessary 108
  in the external situation 59–62, 68–72, 170
  learning from incidents occurring at times of 184–90
  starting-point for 244
  treated as a challenge 170
Chase (company) 49
choice for customers 48
Chrysler 42
Citibank 42
Coca Cola 55, 235
'collusion with the aggressor' 12
colours used for branding 72
comfort zone 197
commitment of and to the organization 33, 102, 132, 173
communication
  'complete' messages 208
  with customers 202
  see also advertisements; interaction
company names 226
company symbols 241
Compaq 42
competence
  in Schutz's theory 126
  sense of 170, 177–8
completion, sense of 247–8

computer companies 42, 49
conceptual framework 27–30, 55–8, 83, 102
  benefits of using 151, 191
confidence, air of 149
connections within an organization 6–8, 16–21, 56
'Connoisseur' consumers, advertisements appealing to 208–10, 213–14
'Connoisseur' organizations 36–41, 61–2
  changes implying greater emphasis on 73
  examples of 41–2, 65, 67–71
  in Daimler-Benz business statement 88–90, 98, 100–101
  questionnaire for identification of 119
consultants
  damage which can be done by 18–20
  power which can be exercised by 10–11, 107
'control' area of experience 29–30, 32, 42–7, 64–5, 70–71, 74–5, 156, 170, 177–80, 196
  advertisements relating to 207, 216, 219–21
  as the most real area for the organization 192, 198–9
  assessment of organizations with regard to 109, 114
  different ways of addressing 48
  effect of atmosphere on people within 148–9
  feelings associated with 127–30
  illustrations of 138–41
  in Daimler-Benz business statement 91, 95–6, 98, 100, 102
  priorities assumed within 197
  reactions to investigators within 195
  sensitivity in relation to 131, 133
  signs of a need for attention to 146
  signs of well-being within 150
'control' purposes of individuals 165, 169
corporate citizenship 95
corporate culture 13–14, 93–4
cult-like behaviour 12
customer relations 33, 41, 48, 51, 53–5, 71; *see also* interaction with customers

INDEX 253

customer service companies 49

Daimler-Benz 42
    statement of business priorities 85–102
data *see* information-gathering
deciphering
    of advertisements 243
    of companies 245–6
    of feelings and emotions 138, 144, 148
    of incidents 186, 189, 191–2, 194
    of statements of business priorities 85–6; *see also* Daimler-Benz statement
dedication to the organization 141–5
delayered organizations 162; *see also* flattening of management structures
Dell (company) 42
Digital (company) 42
direction, sense of 42
discrimination in adoption of solutions 113
Disneyland 41
distinctiveness of organizations 41, 243; *see also* uniqueness
doors kept shut 136–7
duplication of work 157, 163
'dying inside' 250

Easy Jet 49
EDS (company) 52
effectiveness of an organization 32
efficacy, concept of 169
efficiency, automatic inclination towards 156, 164
emotional analysis 142
emotional explanations 71, 76, 80
emotional factors entwined with the strategic 60, 72
emotional 'food' 131–2
emotional orientation 162–3
emotional sense and reality 67, 69, 84–5, 98
emotional world of the organization 125, 130
    illustration of 133–45
    related to business aims 153
    signs indicative of 146–7
empathy 234
energy in an organization 146, 167
engagement of an organization with tasks, with people and with itself 33, 50–55, 103, 141, 160, 162, 172
enjoyment of business activity 219, 222
esprit de corps 125, 128, 132, 134, 141, 147, 180
essence of the organization 233–8, 243–6, 250
evaluation of people 176, 180
exclusion, feelings of 129
expertise, attitudes to 219–20, 241
external changes 59–62, 68–72, 170

feelings
    applying equally to everyone 126
    associated with different talents, qualities and performance 179
    associated with particular areas of experience 125–8
    framework of 128
    in relation to business aims and activities 151
    signs which help understanding of 146
    taking account of 124–5, 176
    taking care of 147
    triggering of 130
    'what' and 'why' of 139–40
    'what is' and 'what should be' 143, 203
    which ones to address 144–5
finance companies 49, 215–16
Financial Times 85, 87
finesse 113
fine-tuning
    of actions 113
    of understanding 130, 177
flattening of management structures 44, 162
flexibility of approach 112
flying boats 123–8
forward thinking 160, 164, 172–3

Gap (company) 55
Gestalt theory 28
globalization 87
goals
    establishment of 42
    specified but not fulfilled 64, 140, 246
    see also aims
'golden rules' 111–13
government departments 155

helplessness, feelings of 129
Hewlett-Packard 42
hierarchical management 43–5
human assets 54
humiliation, feelings of 129
hype 146

identity
  of individuals 165
  projection of 41, 62, 70, 103; see also inclusion
iMac 235
image of the organization 23, 100
immediacy of responsibility 157–8, 164, 168–71
implicit meanings 98, 103
imposition of a new 'way' on another (part of the) organization 107–8
inadequacy, feelings of 129
'inclusion' area of experience 29–31, 37–8, 61–5, 70–73, 103, 177–82 *passim*
  advertisements relating to 207, 209, 212, 216
  as the most real area for the organization 192, 198
  assessment of organizations with regard to 108, 116
  different ways of addressing 41, 68
  effect of atmosphere on people within 148–9
  feelings associated with 127–8, 130
  illustrations of 138, 141, 192–6
  in Daimler-Benz business statement 91–2, 95, 98, 102
  priorities assumed within 197
  sensitivity in relation to 130–33
  signs of a need for attention to 146
  signs of well-being within 150
'inclusion' purposes of individuals 165–7
information-gathering 24–7, 136–9
innovation 90–91, 141, 167, 177, 180, 182
instinctive behaviour ('can't help themselves') 148–50
intactness 165–7, 194
intangible assets 112
interaction
  between people 40, 79
  with customers 208, 212, 216, 222
interpersonal behaviour, theory of 28, 125

interpretation
  of advertisements 234
  of business statements 87–8; see also statements of business priorities
invasion of boundaries 166
irrelevant feelings 128–9

J P Morgan (company) 49
jargon 226
job design see work design
jobs, creation of 92–3
Jobs, Steve 235
'Juggler' consumers, advertisements appealing to 215–22 *passim*
'Juggler' organizations 42–7 *passim*, 71
  changes implying greater emphasis on 74
  examples of 47, 49, 155–6, 158–9
  in Daimler-Benz business statement 91, 95–6, 98
  questionnaire for identification of 120
Jung, Carl 28

kind words 249–50
knock-on effects 173–4

language of the organization 198
liking (in Schutz's theory) 126
long-term perspective 199
long-term relationships 54

markets
  adapting to or influencing 47
  primary focus on 40, 88
Massachusetts Institute of Technology xix–xx
MBA students xix–xx, 188, 196
media, the 62–3, 141
mental structures 162–3
Merrill Lynch 238–42, 244
metaphor of the organization as a human being 76–80, 236
Microsoft 40, 49
mundane details 24–7, 72
music 230–31

needs of the individual and of the organization 174, 176
negative feelings
  denial of 126–7
  removal of 128

INDEX 255

networking 62–3
New Zealand Treasury 154–63 *passim*
Nigeria 186–9, 195–7
Nike 41
numerical scores 117

Omega watches 42
opera house names 209
organizational structure 161–3
ownership, sense of 157

passion for what a company does 50
pep talks 124
Pepsi 41, 55
perception 4, 8, 13
  purpose of 80
perceptual filters 201–4, 208, 212–16, 222, 225, 229–30
  principles characterizing 230–31
performance criteria 176–82
pictures in advertisements, interpretation of 213, 225
place names in advertisements 212–13
plans, making changes to 42–4
'Populist' consumers, advertisements appealing to 208–14 *passim*
'Populist' organizations 36–41
  changes implying greater emphasis on 73
  examples of 41–2, 67–9, 71
  in Daimler-Benz business statement 88–90, 93, 98, 100–101
  questionnaire for identification of 119
power of organizations 32
presence, sense of 238, 241
products, primary focus on 40, 88–9, 198
'Professional' consumers, advertisements appealing to 222–9
'Professional' organizations 49–55 *passim*, 72
  changes implying greater emphasis on 64, 75
  examples of 55
  in Daimler-Benz business statement 92–4, 97–8
  questionnaire for identification of 121
professional service firms 55
promotion

of people 2–3, 176–7, 180
of the company and its products 61–4
psychological meaning 61, 88, 98, 108
psychological natures 13–17, 25–8, 38, 67, 72, 85, 105–6, 109
  advertisements appealing to 207, 213–14
  appropriateness for particular organizations 110
  continuum of 110
  determined for each organization 113–14
  images of 35–6, 42, 49
  mixing of 89, 91, 100, 110, 112
  perceptual filters applied to 202–4
  radical changes in 68–70
  revealed in business statements 88, 99
  seen in a visual way 230
psychological perspective xxi, 4–6, 8, 13–14, 20, 59, 80–81, 84
  benefits of 29, 37, 100, 102
psychological purposes of individuals 153, 165, 172
psychological rules of the game 77–8
psychological sense 153, 168, 171, 175
psychological significance and meaning 85, 92, 103
  of business strategies 83–5
psychological stock-taking 105–6, 109
public relations (PR) 55
purpose
  assessing achievement of 109
  atmosphere of 173
  of the individual 181; *see also* psychological purposes
  sense of 33, 50, 53

qualitative information 43, 91

reading between the lines
  example of 85–103
  of advertisements 204
  of business strategy statements 83–5
'reading the mind' of an organization xx–xxi, 1, 23, 201
  applied to competitors and customers 2
  components of 3–8

illustration of 8–20
reassurance, feeling of 96
rebranding 72
recognition 149, 166, 177; *see also* appreciation
redundancy 12, 15
Reebok (company) 41
reference points 66, 69, 72
responsibility
   for end-effects 160, 164
   formal and real 157–8, 162–3
   see also immediacy
reward criteria 176–82 *passim*
rules, attitudes to 45, 47–8

satisfaction in achievements 247–8
Schrempp, Jurgen 85
Schutz, Will 28–9, 125–6
'seeing-through' skills 3–4, 20, 81, 86, 237
self-awareness of organizations 112
sensitive area of the organization 130–32, 140–43, 148, 192
   characteristics of 133
significance (in Schutz's theory) 126
sophistication in communication 205
South Africa 184–97 *passim*
space
   as distinct from a job 163–4, 167
   for an organization 30–31, 36–41 *passim*, 62, 103
   in advertisements 213
spin doctoring 55
spirit of an organization 237
statements of business priorities, deciphering of 85–6; *see also* Daimler-Benz statement
strengths/weaknesses/opportunities/threats analysis 67
subliminal messages 220–21
Sun Microsystems 47, 49
Swatch watches 42
Swiss banks 42

taking people for granted 142–4
talent
   feelings associated with 179
   use of 156, 188–9, 196
territory, psychological 156–7, 163–8, 193–4, 198
timelessness, feeling of 149, 173
tone of an organization 147–50
translation of business words 103
transparency 97
Treasury *see* New Zealand Treasury; UK Treasury
trust and trustworthiness 33, 50, 52, 102, 140
turf wars 166, 178

UK Treasury 155–63 *passim*
Union Bank of Switzerland
   advertisement 204–29
uniqueness
   in ways of creating esprit de corps 147
   of individuals 236–7
   of organizations 16, 36–7, 40–41, 56, 111, 233–7 *passim*
usefulness, feelings of 172

Virgin Group 47, 49
virtuous cycles
   in evaluation criteria 180, 182
   in work structures 153–4, 164–73 *passim*
vocabulary 6, 55–6, 103
'voice' of the organization 198

wandering about xx–xxi, 2, 136
well-being, signs of 150
who an organization is *see* psychological natures
whole-organization perspective 5, 178
wider agenda 172–4
wordsmithing 101
work design 153–7, 168–9, 174–5

Awesome Purpose

Nigel MacLennan

Only the best businesses achieve the level of success that comes from aligning every member of their team behind some worthwhile goal. Few achieve such success, few become world class. Creating that alignment is not simply a matter of drafting a mission statement, but of understanding and placing each of the elements of the culture behind a single awesome purpose. Nigel MacLennan presents a definitive 'how to guide' to changing and aligning organizational structures.

For the first time a clear framework which incorporates all the elements of organizational culture, and how they relate to each other, is presented. The relationship between purpose, values, vision, mission, strategy, objectives, tactics and so on is presented in the Corporate Alignment Model (CAM).

Taken as a whole, this book provides a step-by-step guide to achieving culture change and alignment through the application of three innovative models - the CAM, the 9R Model and the 6P Model.

Business leaders and organization development specialists alike will find clear and innovative material in this book to stimulate and inspire them. They will find that they are provided with the tools to align their organization and inspire their staff to performance levels not possible without an awesome purpose.

Gower

Benchmarking

Sylvia Codling

Benchmarking is designed for the reader who wants to know what benchmarking is, and what the real benefits are to them and to their company - in a nutshell.

Benchmarking is simply about being proactively aware: understanding what we have to be best at, then comparing ourselves openly and honestly with others who excel in those areas, recognizing the standards that we have to achieve in whatever market we're in. And once we've recognized them, setting out to meet - and exceed - them by managing that knowledge in order to achieve, or secure greater, competitive advantage.

Benchmarking equips you to use the techniques to good effect in your own organization. Tables and figures provide a ready reference and quick answers to common questions.

Gower

The Empowerment Manual

Terry Wilson

Most thinking managers would probably claim some knowledge of empowerment - the underlying philosophy, the potential benefits, perhaps some of the techniques involved. But how do you turn that knowledge into action that will match the specific needs of your own organization and the people who work in it? How do you measure their readiness to embark on an empowerment programme? How do you choose the best starting point and the most appropriate policies?

Terry Wilson's manual is based on his experience helping many organizations to empower their staff - and it can help you to do the same. Part I will enable you to decide on the most suitable type of programme and the best way to introduce it into your company or unit. Part II contains a series of activities through which you can assess your existing level of empowerment and then develop a detailed scheme for increasing it. The final Part tells the true story of how a successful company adopted empowerment to help it achieve its business goals. Throughout the text you will find questionnaires, checklists, exercises and action plans designed to help you map out the best way forward.

If you're serious about empowerment, but need a guiding hand to support planning and implementation in your organization, this manual is for you.

Gower

Ethics at Work

Bob Kelley

Do you buy your raw materials where they're cheapest – even when they are produced by Third-World workers in conditions that would be illegal in your own country?

You're negotiating with a government department in a developing country: to secure the contract that will safeguard your company and your workforce, do you pay the customary 'commission' to the minister responsible?

When recruiting staff in Britain it isn't unlawful to discriminate on the grounds of religion – but is it right?

It's hardly possible to operate in the business world without encountering ethical dilemmas. Yet few companies pause to work out a set of policies and a way to apply them in its day-to-day dealings. In this timely book Bob Kelley identifies some of the underlying questions, explores possible answers and describes recent attempts to control corporate conduct.

Part I discusses ethical behaviour, including the attitudes found in various different cultures, and explains why the subject has risen so high up the current business agenda. Part II looks at the issues from the point of view of each of the five 'stakeholders' involved - owners, employees, customers, suppliers, and the community. Part III examines some of the methods used to regulate business, indicates some of the practical implications and speculates briefly about the future. The book concludes with a set of appendices containing the Nolan recommendations, the Institute of Management's guidelines, and details of relevant organizations.

Bob Kelley's book will be invaluable to every manager seeking guidance in this important and sensitive area.

Gower

Gower Handbook of Internal Communication

Edited by Eileen Scholes, The ITEM Group

Employee commitment can mean the difference between success and disaster. So internal communication is now a key issue for senior management. This new *Gower Handbook* recognises IC's emergence as a new management discipline. It is aimed both at the generalist manager who needs to come to terms with the theoretical and technical aspects of internal communication, and the media specialist now seeking wider management skills and perspectives.

Early chapters examine changes in IC's strategic context. These include organizations' increasing need for innovation and flexibility; the disappearance of 'loyalty' among employees; growing recognition of the importance of corporate 'brand' and how to sustain it; and the effects on traditional work and management patterns of new computer networks. Step-by-step guides introduce the reader to creating IC strategies and to carrying out research and measurement. Over 45 communication techniques, from team meetings to web sites, are evaluated for use in differing circumstances. The *Handbook* also looks at how to set about developing good communicators; and finally presents 16 practical case studies in key application areas. Organizations featured are all leaders in their field, among them Andersen Consulting, The Body Shop, BP Chemicals, IBM, The Boots Company, Glaxo Operations, Rover, SmithKline Beecham, WH Smith and Unigate Dairies.

Eileen Scholes and her team have compiled what is probably the most comprehensive - and is certainly the most authoritative - guide available to the principles and practice of internal communication.

Gower

Living Tomorrow's Company

Mark Goyder

Living Tomorrow's Company is written for all those who care about the success of business - be they entrepreneurs, managers, investors, policymakers, educators or citizens. It describes an inclusive approach which defines success in relation to all the stakeholders involved with a company, including the local community, employees, investors, suppliers, customers and society generally. It puts people and their relationships at the heart of the successful business. This sounds deceptively obvious: in practice it is the recipe for a never-ending search for improvement.

Mark Goyder, who worked in manufacturing industry for 14 years before creating the Tomorrow's Company inquiry, describes the battle between two views of business: one of which reduces it to a narrow concept of contracts and transactions; the other an inclusive approach which is about inspiring people to produce extraordinary results by concentrating on the human beings whose needs lie behind every business relationship.

The book offers action agendas for managers, educators and investors. Its compelling logic and direct style makes it a stimulating and entertaining answer to the questions 'What is a company for?' and 'What will a business need to do differently if it is to succeed today and tomorrow?'

Gower

The Merlin Factor

Keys to the Corporate Kingdom

Charles E Smith

For over 25 years, Charles Smith has been using the Merlin process to help organizations in America and Europe to determine and achieve their long term goals. In this remarkable book, he uses the legend of King Arthur and the Knights of the Round Table to illustrate his ideas.

The Merlin Factor is about finding new ways for leaders to operate within their organizations whilst staying true to themselves and their personal life goals. The balancing of business and relationship energies offers real opportunities for creativity and innovation. Good ideas and quality products and services are not enough in today's world: over time, the organizations and the people with the most energy will prevail.

The corporate King Arthur addresses concerns too often avoided in real life, drawing on the wisdom of Merlin as his mentor. The ancient cities of Glastonbury and Avalon become metaphors for tangible performance on the one hand, and for the invisible but vital world of people's relationships and spirit on the other. Finding the balance between these two is the key to making a success of organizational change, or, to continue the metaphor, merges them into the perfection of Camelot.

The Merlin Factor is an inspirational book, that gracefully conveys timeless principles through the Arthurian legend, but which is also illustrated in practice with examples from organizations that have made them their reality.

Gower

The New Guide to Identity

How to Create and Sustain Change Through Managing Identity

Wolff Olins

A Design Council Title

It is, of course, commonplace for corporations to operate sophisticated identity programmes. But identity has now moved way beyond the commercial area. We live in a world in which cities, charities, universities, clubs - in fact any activity that involves more than two or three people - all seem to have identities too. However, very few of these organisations have released the full potential that effective management of identity can achieve.

In this book, the world's leading authority on corporate identity shows how managing identity can create and sustain behavioural change in an organisation as well as achieving the more traditional outcome of influencing its external audiences.

The New Guide to Identity provides a simple clear guide to identity, including what it is and how it can be used to full effect. If a change of identity is required, the whole process is described from start-up (including investigation and analysis of the current identity), through developing the new identity structure, to implementation and launch. For anyone responsible for the identity of an organisation, or for designing it for someone else, or attempting to achieve change in their organisation, or studying the subject, this straightforward guide is essential reading.

Gower

Qualitative Market Research

A Practitioner's and Buyer's Guide

Wendy Gordon and Roy Langmaid

This book opens the black box of qualitative market research and reveals the inner workings of the qualitative process. The influence of group dynamics on the data itself, the significance of body language in the interaction between researcher and respondent and the application of techniques to discover the private world of the individual are all exposed for the first time. So too, is the least visible part of all research projects - the interpretation of content given the fact that people often 'don't say what they mean' and 'don't mean what they say'.

This book brings together a detailed overview of procedures and techniques in contemporary qualitative market research. These evolving techniques are making qualitative research increasingly influential. A clear understanding of their strengths and weaknesses is therefore vital to anyone involved in research - whether market, industrial, social, governmental or medical.

Gower